The Debo Family History

By Darrell Debo

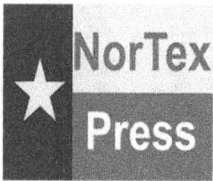

NorTex
★ Press

Copyright © 2016
By Darrell Debo
Published By NorTex Press
An Imprint of Wild Horse Media Group
P.O. Box 331779
Fort Worth, Texas 76163
1-817-344-7036
www.WildHorseMedia.com
ALL RIGHTS RESERVED
1 2 3 4 5 6 7 8 9
ISBN-10: 1-68179-056-4
ISBN-13: 978-1-68179-056-5

DEBO HISTORY

Foreword 1
Introduction: The Name 9
Chapter I - Background 13
Chapter II - Coming to the New World 22
Chapter III - Leaving Pennsylvania 30
Chapter IV _ Michael Debo, Sr. and Bedford County 38
  A. Henry Debo 50
  B. John Debo 60
    1. Reed Perry Debo 65
    2. Allen Burton Debo 74
    3. Dabney Claiborne Debo 76
    4. Thomas Benton Debo 79
    5. Cornelius Patrick Debo 85
      a. Jennie Prudence Debo Fisher 105
      b. Mary Thomas (Mollie) Debo McFarland 110
      c. Lilbon (Lib) Debo 113
      d. Eppa Debo 122
      e. Frank Debo 124
      f. Sam Hardy Debo 127
      g. Sallie Esterline Debo Simpson 131
      h. Cornelia Ruth (Nell) Debo Johnston 133
      i. Julia Southerland (Jubie) Debo Landtroop Wolf 138
      j. William Clay Debo; John Henry Debo; Cora Lee Debo 139
    6. Sarah James (Sallie) Debo Bowmer 142
    7. Marie Eliza (Mollie) Debo McClure 145
    8. Martha Prudence; Bettie Jane; John Bruce Debo 146
  C. Elizabeth Debo Blankenship 147
  D. Sally Debo Blankenship 150
  E. Margaret (Peggy) Debo Saunders 151
  F. Valentine Debo 155
  G. Daniel Perry Debo 155
  H. Mary Debo Hubbard 157
  I. Michael Debo, Jr. 170
    1. Harriet Tompkins Debo Stevens 173
    2. Annie K. Debo Craghead 174
    3. Sarah Katharine (Cassie) Debo 174
    4. William L. Debo 176
    5. John Franklin Price deBoe 177
      a. Michael Price deBoe 182
      b. Wilmoth Flora (Willie) deBoe Leterman 183
    6. Monterey W., McHenry F., Michael S. C. deBoe 184
    7. Ellen Rose, Wilmoth E., Ella R., Joel D. deBoe 184
  J. Samuel Debo 184

Chapter V - Other Virginia Debos 186
  A. Betsy Debo Rohrer (Rorer) 187
  B. Christina Debo Crider 189
  C. Abraham Debo 191
  D. Benjamin Debo 192
  E. Joseph Deboe 193
  F. Catherine Debo Hedrick 195
Chapter VI - The Kentucky Deboes 197
  A. Philip Deboe (3) 197
    1. Nancy Deboe Crayne 197
    2. Philip Deboe 199
    3. Ellender Deboe Woodall 205
    4. Mary (Polly) Deboe Crayne 207
    5. John Deboe 208
    6. Abram C. Deboe 208
    7. Eliza Deboe Hill 212
  B. Mary (Polly) Deboe Crider 214
  C. Sarah (Sally) Deboe Hughey 220
Chapter VII - "Other" Kentucky and Missouri Debo(e)s 223
Appendices
  A. Snakebite Recipe 231
  B. Letters
    1. From unknown Confederate soldier to Sarah James (Sallie) Debo (1863) . 231
    2. From Cornelius Debo to his brother Reed in Missouri (1872) 232
    3. From Cornelius Debo to Reed after he had had a sunstroke (1891) . 233
    4. From Reed Debo to Cornelius in Texas (1894) 236
    5. From Grover Evans Debo, son of Reed, to a Texas cousin (1896) . 237
    6. From Reed Debo to Cornelius in Texas (1896) 238
    7. From Newt Simpson to Clay Debo, son of Cornelius (1896) 240
    8. From Newt Simpson to Clay Debo (1896) 241
    9. From Will Rountree, a friend, to Eppa Debo;
         and one to Clay Debo, sons of Cornelius Debo 242
    10. From Fannie Wilson Debo, wife of Thomas, to
         Martha (Mattie) Debo in MO (1913) 243
    11. From Mrs. Sallie Debo Bowmer to niece, Martha (Mattie) Debo (1916) . 244
    12. From Mrs. Lilbon (Hattie) Debo to the
         Lewis C. Debo family in Iowa (1954) 246
    13. From Lilbon Debo to his cousin, Luther Debo, in Missouri (1958) . . 247
    From Mizpah Otto deBoe, wife of M. P. deBoe,
         to Lewis C. Debo (1958) 247
  C. Rohrer (Rorer) Genealogy 248

Foreword

Why would one attempt to write a family history? Perhaps to carefully preserve gathered genealogical data for posterity; or, maybe because of curiosity about one's forebears, when they lived, how they lived, and what guided their pathway of life in their migrations and settlements. Whatever the reason and motivation, I have decided to do as God told the prophet Isaiah: "Now go, write it before them in a table, and note it in a book, that it may be for the time to come for ever and ever." Isaiah 30:8

Personally, my decision to take on the task of detailing the story of the Debo (Deboe, DeBoe) family came about in a rather strange and unique way. More than sixty years ago this year I graduated from Burnet High School as the valedictorian of my class, and in September of that year (1948) I enrolled as a 16-year-old freshman at Texas Christian University in Fort Worth, Texas. The teacher of my freshman course in social studies was Professor Marguerite Potter, who was a native of Missouri. One day after the class was over she called me up to her desk and told me she had noticed that my name was Debo. She asked me if I had any relatives in the state of Missouri, particularly in Cooper County and around Boonville, and said she was well acquainted with some Debos there.

As a young freshman, I knew very little about my relatives except for the close ones with whom I had grown up around my hometown of Burnet, Texas. I told Miss Potter I didn't know whether I had Missouri kinfolk or not, but I was going home for the holidays and would ask my Grandfather Debo. When I asked him, he said that we had cousins in Missouri and that many years ago one of them had come to Burnet County to visit his Texas kin. All of this piqued my curiosity and interest and I began to collect genealogical data and stories of the olden days from the older relatives while they were still alive. I was also able to contact the Missouri relatives, who sent me genealogical material on their branch of the family.

My grandfather's oldest sister, Aunt Jennie Debo Fisher, didn't

1

much want me to dig into the family's past for fear that I might uncover a horse thief or some scoundrel who would bring reproach on the good name of the family. I told her, however, that should I uncover such a one or ones that that would be a part of our history, and that I had never heard of any family who had reached the pinnacle of perfection and were without flaws of various and sundry kinds. Thus, I was not deterred from the task I set out to pursue. Sixty years of research, diggings, and gathering material have produced this volume.

In addition to the data gathered locally and from relatives in Texas I have traveled to Virginia many times throughout the years, once to Franklin and Marshall College library in Lancaster, Pennsylvania, once to Kentucky and several trips to Missouri, researching the family and interviewing various parties. I would be most unappreciative were I not to give recognition to the many who have aided in the gathering of family data and research. Those who have contributed records, research, time, and effort in much of the contents of this volume, many who have closed their earthly sojourn, include: Mrs. Sallie Debo Simpson of Winters, TX; Fay Carol Crider of Marion, KY, who contributed so much of the western Kentucky Deboe data and checked its accuracy; Mrs. R. M. Anderson of Gretna, VA, who contributed the Rorer (Rohrer) records in the appendix; Lewis Debo of Ottumwa, IA, who helped gather the Cooper County, MO, records; Bruce Debo of Devil's Elbow, MO, who contributed data on the "other Missouri" branch of the family; Mrs. Harry (Lena H.) Debo of Roanoke, VA, who contributed the western Bedford County records of the Lodowick C. Debo family; Mrs. Weldon (Virginia P.) Simpson of Nicholasville, KY, who helped research some of the Thomas Deboe family of Jessamine County, KY; Mrs. Alex Bower of Nicholasville, KY, who also helped supply information on the Jessamine County, KY, group; John Alex Rorer of Charlottesville, VA, who contributed much of the western KY material gathered by his father; Sherrie Stidham of Sadieville, KY, and her mother Geneva Woodall, of Stamping Ground, KY, who contributed much of the western KY material; and J.O. Deboe of Paducah, KY, who sent me copies of Miss Era Deboe's material, which she had compiled throughout the years, including some traditional stories of the early days of the family.

Biography

Clyde Debo and his bride, Lucille Atchison, were united in the bonds of holy matrimony on June 7, 1930, at the First Christian Church of Llano, Texas, and left on a weekend honeymoon trip to San Angelo (mind you, this was in the midst of the Great Depression). After returning to Llano so Clyde could go back to work on Monday morning at the Orr wholesale business, the newlyweds rented an apartment west of the Llano square from Mrs. Rabb and there set up housekeeping. It was there that I, Darrell Debo,

Darrell Debo

first saw the light of day at 3:48 a.m. on September 15, 1931, having been brought into the world by Dr. G. L. Gray and his faithful nurse, Mrs. L. T. Schrank.

After living awhile in Llano, my parents and I moved to Fort Worth where my father had found employment at the federal courthouse. We lived there till 1936 when we moved back to Central Texas to Burnet where my father and his brother, Bert Debo, had purchased the restaurant that my grandfather, Lilbon Debo, had operated since 1919 as the Cowboy Café. The new owners moved the café from just off the west side of the townsquare to the east side of the Burnet square and changed the name to Debo's Coffee Shop. A new house was being constructed for us on south U.S. Highway 281, and while it was being finished, my mother and I were staying with her parents, Mr. and Mrs. W. T. Atchison, in Llano. It was here that my brother, Jack Debo, was born October 29, 1936, before we moved into our new home in Burnet in December.

I began school in the second grade and graduated from Burnet High School May 1948 as valedictorian of my class. In September of that year I enrolled as a 16-year-old (soon to be 17) freshman at Texas Christian University in Fort Worth with the aim of pursuing a degree in applied music with a major in piano. (I became the first of my family to both attend and earn degrees from an institution of higher learning.) Music had been an important part of my life almost from the beginning. I had played various instruments (whatever was needed at the time) in the Burnet High School Bulldog band, but the piano had always been the prime interest almost from the time I could sit on a piano stool. My mother was my first piano teacher, followed by her sister and my aunt, Faybelle Atchison Boxell Martin, Mrs. Ella Opp in Llano, and Mrs. A.B. Griffith in Burnet.

I studied with Miriam Gordon Landrum at the Texas School of Fine Arts in Austin before entering TCU, traveling to Austin by bus on Saturdays. Upon entering TCU I was under the tutelage of Jeannette Tillett for the four years spent there. While at TCU I played double bass in the TCU Symphony Orchestra, and as a senior performed the Tchaikowsky Concerto No. 1 in B-flat minor for piano with the orchestra prior to receiving a Bachelor of Music degree, summa cum laude, in 1952. Through the years I had performed in recitals in Llano, Burnet, Austin, and Fort Worth, and at an early age had performed over radio stations KNOW in Austin and KCYL in Lampasas.

Upon graduating from high school in 1948 my grandmother, Mrs. Jessie Atchison, gave me a Bible for a graduation present. Although I had on occasion attended various denominational Sunday schools, I did not own a Bible and knew very little about one. The gift by my grandmother whetted my appetite and with a neophyte's curiosity I began an earnest reading and studying of the Word of God. After considerable Bible study privately on my own I concluded that I needed to become a Christian in order to possess an abundant life here and eternal life in the world to come. I was buried with my Lord in baptism for the remission of sins on October 16, 1949, just like believers did on that first Pentecost after the resurrection of Christ from the dead (Act 2:38), and began worshiping with the Christian church. I was completely convinced that if I did what those Pentecostians did that I would be what they were, Christians, no more or no less, and be added to the same church they belonged to. After receiving my degree in piano performance in 1952, I become convinced that I needed to become prepared to preach the gospel of Christ. I entered the seminary at TCU and after three years of study earned the Bachelor of Divinity degree in August 1955 with a major in church history. During the time I was working toward this degree I preached for the Christian church

4

in Ringgold, Texas, driving to that small community in Montague County each weekend. After receiving my degree, I moved to Hooks, Texas, where I preached for the Antioch Christian church, a conservative Christian church in Bowie County. The more I studied my Bible and the more elements of liberalism and unscriptural errors I denoted in the religious body with which I was affiliated, I determined to take my stand with the churches of Christ (who were standing on the original grounds of the Restoration movement), which I did on January 13, 1957, in Hooks, Texas, at the church of Christ there.

After preaching during the spring of 1957 on an ad-interim basis for the church of Christ in Nocona, Texas, I returned to my hometown of Burnet, Texas. Since that time I have served as the local preacher for the congregations of Fredonia, Bertram, Kingsland, and Burnet, all in Texas, and directed the singing for gospel meetings in many of the congregations in the Central Texas area. I helped to establish a new congregation in the Buchanan Dam community during this time, and beginning in 1995 helped to establish a new congregation in my hometown, the Burnet church of Christ. After preaching for this group until 1998, I have retired but continue to be engaged in the work of the church preaching on a fill-in basis, teaching Bible classes, directing singing, visiting residents of the local nursing home, the sick and bereaved, and conducting funeral services. For more than thirty years I have regularly played music to entertain residents of the local nursing home every two weeks. While preaching for the Kingsland congregation I was privileged to baptize a longtime friend, Burnet County Sheriff Wallace Riddell, and in later years helped to conduct his funeral service. It's not many times that a preacher has the opportunity or privilege of baptizing a sheriff of the county in which he lives!

In addition to wearing the religious hat during my life, I also have been engaged in writing and in journalism, having engaged in work for local newspapers as a typesetter, reporter, and sportswriter, along with historical features, and local news. I served as editor for Eakin Press 1981-83 while it was located in Burnet. From 1983-95 I was employed as a home typesetter by G&S Typesetters, Inc. of Austin. Beginning in October 1976 I was employed by the county commissioners of Burnet County to write the county history, as mandated by the state of Texas. The Burnet County History, Vol. 1, was published in October 1979; and Vol. 2 (containing the history of pioneer families of the county) was published the following year. The county history was awarded state and national recognition and awards. I also did much of the work on the companion volume, Burnet County Cemeteries, with its Supplement. I have been a member of the Burnet County Historical Commission since 1977, serving as chairman and vice-chairman, and at present am the longest serving member of that organization.

From early in childhood history has been a venue of great interest to me. Historical fields of interest have included the War for Southern Independence (sometimes known as the "Civil War") in history; the history of Poland and the Polish people; the history of music and classical musicians; and the history of the Restoration movement and churches of Christ. I was awarded the Jefferson Davis Medal by the Daughters of the Confederacy in July 1984 for county history work and helping to locate Burnet County graves of Confederate veterans.

Civic activities have included employment by Burnet County in the tax-assessor and collector's office during the tenure of Brownlee Field in 1980. I worked as a clerk for election precinct 2, beginning in 1971, and was named election judge of that precinct in 1983 for school, primary, and general elections.

I was honored by my home community by being named "Honor Citizen of Burnet" in 1989. Also, on September 13, 2011, the Burnet County Commissioners Court honored me by naming that week "Darrell Debo Week" in Burnet County, Texas, at my encroaching 80th birthday, which occurred on September 15th. On the afternoon of the 13th the Burnet County Historical Commission sponsored a reception for me at a café on the Burnet public square, largely attended by relatives, friends, and acquaintances from over the county and state.

Organizational interest and personal support throughout the years have included membership in the TCU Frog Club, the Civil War Preservation Trust, the Museum of the Confederacy in Richmond, VA, and the Kosciuszko Foundation.

Hobbies that have been of interest include stamp collecting; collecting and maintaining historical records of Burnet High School football and basketball games; reading; playing the piano and fiddle; visiting historical places of interest throughout the United States. During vacation trips I have always enjoyed visiting and touring the battlefields of the War for Southern Independence back in the East, and on one occasion to stand at the "stone wall" where a great-uncle was last seen in 1863 standing on the breastworks waving the blood-stained banner of the Old South.

What a life it has been thus far! And I look forward with anticipation to whatever remainder may be granted me in the future, not only to what may occur in this world but still with greater interest to what I await in the world to come by reason of my faith in the unadulterated and pure gospel of Christ and the promises contained therein by my Lord and Savior.

Burnet, Texas
May 2015

Introduction

To forget one's ancestors is to be a brook without a source, a tree without a root.

— Chinese proverb

The Name

In compiling the history and tracing the lineage of a family, one must of necessity begin with the name of the family itself – its origination, derivation, changes in form and spelling throughout the years and ages, etc. The name DEBO (DEBOE) is one that is not common, nor is it frequently found throughout the country when compared to such names as Smith, Jones, Davis, Johnson, Williams, and the like. The difficulties encountered in over sixty years of researching the Debo name and family at times have been almost insurmountable because of the numerous spellings and changes of the name due to the name being recorded according to how it sounded, or else was written in old German script [the "e" being written n as in Dnbo or Dnbon].

In the course of this history I am going to use the spelling I am most accustomed to. I am aware and realize that most of the members of the family in Kentucky and in Pittsylvania County, Virginia, add the final "e" – DEBOE – but the Bedford County, Virginia, Missouri, and Texas family members have never used a final "e." Most of the time the "b" has not been capitalized, but occasionally it has been. I have found the name recorded or spelled the following ways: Debo, Deboe, DeBoe, deBoe, Diebo, Dubo, Depo, Debow, DeBow, DeBoise, etc. There are also some similarly spelled names such as Debon, Deboy, Debooy, Dubois, but I am convinced that these have no connection with our family unless it be in the long ago antiquities of ancient France.

The prefixes *de, de la,* or *du* (a contraction of *de le*) are said to be badges indicative of noble French extraction. The origin of the name duBois seems to be de le bois – of the wood or forest or one who lived in or near a wood – according to *Colonial Families of America* by Smith. The same source reveals that the name Dubosc means of the thicket,

9

while variations of the name are said to be de la Boe, Dubos, Dubose, and Dubost. This is the only reference I have ever found where Debo or Deboe might have been a derivation of or have any connection with Dubois.

In Stapleton's *Memorial of the Huguenots in America* it is stated that the Debos (DeBus, DeBow) name was originally DeBeau[1] in France and it is so listed in families of noble rank described in de Maigney's *Science*,[2] as a name among the Huguenot immigrants to America. In another list of French nobility as a family of patrician rank, the name is listed as duBos.[3] The word "beau" in French means beautiful, handsome, fine or good.

I know of at least three other families in the United States who are not in any way connected with our family and who have gone by the name Debow, DeBow, or even Debo. In 1941 the late William Henry Hoyt of Greenwich, Connecticut, was gathering material for genealogies of these families, and wrote the late Mrs. Michael P. deBoe of Coral Gables, Florida, seeking information on our particular line of Debos (or Deboes).[4] In that letter he stated, "There are two distinct and unrelated families now called DeBow or Debow. One was founded by Hendrik deBoogh of Amsterdam, Holland, whose children migrated to New Amsterdam (now New York) about 1649. The other was founded by Jan Tibout of Flanders, who came to America as early as 1656. (A branch of Tibout's family adopted the name Debow, and in 1824, in Genesee County, New York, was called "Tebow, alias Debow.")" We of the Debo (Deboe) family are of an entirely different line and have a different immigrant as our progenitor, as we shall see shortly.

I have in my possession the military records of a John Debow (Debough), who served as a private in the 5th (and 9th) Virginia Regiment; a Philip Tiboe (Tieboe, Teebow, Teboe, Tebow, Teebo, Tebo, Teaboe), who served as a private in the Continental Army, all of these during the Revolutionary War. Since most of the battles in which they fought were in New York and New Jersey. I feel confident these were some of that group. After all, people in those days most often spelled a name like it sounded and not by any rigid or fast rule or standard.

A Solomon DeBow from Bucks County, Pennsylvania, was a resident of Orange County, North Carolina, in 1755.[5] A John DeBow was sent as a missionary by the Presbytery of New Brunswick, New Jersey, to a Huguenot settlement in Duplin County, North Carolina, at an early day, and died there about 1778.[6] Another Solomon DeBow (possibly a son or descendant of the other Solomon) was married March 22, 1804, to Nancy Murphy in Caswell County, North Carolina,[7] which adjoins Orange County, North Carolina, as well as Pittsylvania County, Virginia. Also, on June 15, 1812, Solomon DeBow of Caswell County purchased from John Barnett of Danville, Virginia (Pittsylvania County), some tracts of land on Dan River as well as lots in the city of Danville.[8] We believe these have no relationship to our family but are a part of the Debow connection in New York and New Jersey.

The other family I am aware of who went by the name Debo came to this country too late to be connected with our line. This Debo family began with the immigration of two brothers, Jacob and Peter Debo.[9] Jacob landed in New Orleans in 1853 and had moved up the Mississippi River to Peru, Illinois, by the time his brother Peter, his widowed mother, and sister Anna Marie came to New Orleans. The mother and sister died there of cholera, and Peter went on up to Illinois where his brother Jacob had settled. Peter Debo often said that there were many Debos "in the old Country." The late Miss Angie Debo, noted author and authority on Indian life and lore, who lived in Marshall, Oklahoma, until her death, was the granddaughter of Peter (Pierre) Debo, being the only daughter of Peter's oldest son, Edward Peter Debo. Miss Angie told of seeing a linen shop in Houston in 1935 with "Debo" on the front. The owner, Ed Debo, a Syrian and French in name only, was a descendant of one of Napoleon's soldiers, who had been abandoned by the emperor in Syria in 1799 after his fleet had been destroyed in the Battle of the Nile.

One never knows where, when or in whom the name might pop up. A cousin, the late Lewis Debo of Ottuma, Iowa, learned of an Iroquois Indian named Debo living on a reservation near Quebec, Canada. Lewis found another Debo named Albert (Abdullah in Arabic) in Altoona, Pennsylvania, who had immigrated to this county in 1921 from Raskefa, Lebanon. The man told Lewis, "The Debo family in Lebanon is very large. The only other Debo family I know of came from Tripoli, Syria, and settled in Pittsburgh, Pennsylvania, in 1900."[10] These are only a few of the examples one runs into in trying to trace the lineage of a particular family – especially one whose name is as different and unique as ours!

After all of this, then just who are the immigrants from whom our family is descended? Two brothers, Philip and Abraham Debo, along with a sister Anna landed on October 17, 1732, in Philadelphia with other refugees from the Palatinate on the ship *Pink John and William of*

Sunderland, of whom Constable Tymperton was master. The vessel had initially sailed from Rotterdam, The Netherlands, and had last sailed from Dover, England.[11] These immigrants settled in Lancaster County, Pennsylvania, one of the three original counties in that state. After the division of this county into other counties, Debos lived in Lebanon and Berks counties also. Our family is descended from that first Philip Debo, and I have never been able to learn what happened to Abraham and Anna. One record spells Philip's name Diebo or Dubo; another Depo (More about him later.)

We thus far have established the difficulties encountered in our research; those with whom (as far as we have been able to ascertain) we have no connection; and the immigrant from which we are descended. Now we shall enter into a study of the background of our family.

I. Background

'Tis a great thing to search the store houses of memory and wipe the dust of forgotten deeds, done by those pioneers gone before in the years past.

— *Author unknown*

Where Did We Come From?

The fascinating story of surnames dates back thousands of years into antiquity. As late as the Middle Ages, people were still being called by a single given name. With the passing of time the addition of another name to distinguish people who had the same given name from each other was adopted. This practice had become fairly widespread by the twelfth century. These second names, however, were not hereditary and did not apply to families. By the late fourteenth century the term "surname" appeared in documents, and by the middle of the fifteenth century the fixed, hereditary surname had more or less become a common reality.

The origination of the Debo family is lost in antiquity. The beginning of modern knowledge of our family is credited to oral tradition handed down through the ages and preserved by some of the family members in Kentucky. The late Miss Era Deboe of Paducah, Kentucky, wrote down some of the family traditions that she had been told by older members of the family through the years, and I am indebted to her material for data used in this regard.

The Debo family in ancient France was of noble lineage and their location of residence was in the northeastern province of Alsace. The provinces of Alsace and Lorraine border Germany and have been fought over between France and Germany throughout the years, being exchanged in possession time and again between those two countries. They are now once again a part of France. The place of residence of the Debos can more or less be verified by the fact that the late Mrs. Michael P. (Mizpah) deBoe had in her possession five dinner plates that the family brought with them when they came to the New World.

13

The plates had been passed down to her late husband, Dr. Michael P. deBoe, from a cousin, Mrs. Annis P. Hubbard Rorer, whose mother was Mary Debo, daughter of Michael Debo, original settler and progenitor of the Bedford County, Virginia, Debos as well as some of those in Missouri and those in Texas. Mizpah deBoe said the plates came from Alsace (as well as a desk she also had in her possession), and before her death in 1979 she gave the plates to Lewis Debo, of Ottumwa, Iowa, because she wanted them to stay in the family and she had no descendants.

The Debos in France were Huguenots. Were that statement made to most of the Debos that I have known during my lifetime, they probably would reply, "What in the world is a Huguenot?" To give a simplistic answer to the question I would reply that a Huguenot was a French Protestant, who lived in the midst of a majority Catholic population. Because of the great effect this fact had on the family and the very personality and character of its members, I deem it only proper and right to present some pertinent information on the Huguenots that it may be understood how and why the Debos had to leave their native land and why they became the kind of people they are with distinct personality traits that are present among us even today.

As a "protest" against the abuses of the Roman church, Martin Luther in 1517 had nailed his ninety-five theses or articles on the doors of the Wittenberg church in Germany, and this set in motion what would later be termed the Reformation.[1] Luther was not the only reformer to challenge the authority of the pope and the introduction of practices into the church foreign to apostolic and biblical teaching. In Switzerland, Zwingli had advanced many of the same ideas. The Anabaptists, so-called because of their belief in the immersion of adult believers, were also gaining numbers of followers in Switzerland and Holland.[2]

A young Frenchman named John Calvin, born at Noyon in Picardy,[3] a studious young man whose education in disputation, logic, the acquisition of good Latin style as well as more than ordinary knowledge of Greek and Hebrew, along with the study of civil and canon law and a comprehensive understanding of the Roman Catholic religion, had bred a keen mind, orderly and acute. He became convinced by cold reason that the teachings of the Roman church were wrong, and to save his life he fled France, going to Basel in Switzerland.[4] Although Jacques Lefevre, also born in Picardy, is generally credited with being the one who initiated Protestantism in France,[5] it was Calvin who later gave the greatest impetus of the movement.

Some of the doctrines espoused by Calvin were that it was the duty of Christians to spread the teachings of God's Word, established for all time in the canon of the scriptures. Like Zwingli, Calvin rejected the traditions of men and would accept no doctrine not found in, or clearly deducted from the Bible. The sacrifice of the mass, the mediation of the so-called saints or the virgin Mary, the cult of images and relics, monastic vows, auricular confession and much else of Roman trappings were decisively rejected by the Frenchman, as by the German also. There was no need for bishop or priest, for a minister or servant of God's Word chosen by his hearers could lead them in prayer and expound the duties and obligations of the Christian. Baptism and the Lord's Supper were the only ordinances authored by the authority of heaven to be observed.[6] The emphasis on the translation of the Word of God into the tongues of the common people, and the distribution of it among the people brought severe conflict with Catholic authorities, resulting in the beginnings of persecution which would last for many years.

The Bible had at the beginning of the sixteenth century continued to be a comparatively scarce book, little known to the "clergy" and still less by the people. By many priests it was regarded with suspicion and even downright hostility. The fears of the priests increased as they saw their flocks becoming more intent on reading (or hearing read) the scriptures than attending mass; they were especially concerned at the growing feeling among the people to question the infallibility of the Roman church and its priesthood.[7] The effects were the same wherever the Bible appeared and was freely read by the people. There developed an anxious desire for a purer faith without the admixture of human traditions and the inventions and corruptions of men which had impaired and obscured the simple beauty of primitive Christianity.

The Sorbonne with its Faculty of Theology in Paris proceeded to make war against religious books and their printers. Bibles and New Testaments were seized wherever they could be found and were burned.[8] The *Bourgeois de Paris*, a publication of a zealous Catholic, gives a detailed account of human sacrifices offered up to ignorance and intolerance during the six months ending in June 1534, from which it was reported that twenty men and one woman were burned alive for printing and/or selling books.[9]

The same scene became common all over France wherever the Bible had penetrated and found followers. The massacre of the Vaudois of the province of Provence in 1545 is only one of the horrible examples.[10] "The Vaudois peasantry knew the Bible almost by heart. Raids were from time to time made into their district by the agents of the Romish church for the purpose of seizing and burning all such copies of the Bible as they could lay hands on. Knowing this, the peasants formed societies of young persons, each of whom was appointed to preserve in memory a certain number of chapters; and thus, though their Bibles were seized and burnt, the Vaudois were still enabled to refer to their Bibles through the memories of the young minds in which the chapters were preserved."[11] Three thousand of the Vaudois people were slain; 600-700 were enslaved and sent to the galleys of ships; many children were sold as slaves; and the slayers left ordinances forbidding anyone on pain of death who would dare give "asylum, aid, or succor, or furnish ,money or victuals to any Vaudian or 'heretic'."[12]

The persecutions only accelerated the spread of the reformed religion. Centers of strength developed in the area of Lyons, in Normandy, Languedoc, the valley of the Rhone, and in southern France generally.[13] By 1550s the reformers had become almost one quarter of the population of France.[14] "There was not a corner of the Kingdom where the Protestant churches were not considerable." Adherents attached to the cause included the cream of society, with philosophers, jurists, surgeons, printers and scholars, sculptors, musicians, agriculturists, and a large number of the naval forces and military, as well as many of the nobles.[15]

It was about 1560 that the Protestants acquired the name of Huguenots. The origin of the term is obscure. Several explanations have been given, the most generally accepted being that it was "derived from a French and a faulty pronunciation of the German word *Eidgenossen* or confederates, the name given to those citizens of Geneva who entered into an alliance with the Swiss cantons to resist the attempts of Charles III, duke of Savoy, against their liberties. The confederates were called *Eignots*, and hence, probably the derivation of the word Huguenots. "It was first applied as a nickname and later borne with pride."[16] Some suppose the term to be derived from *Huguon*, a word used in Touraine to signify persons who walk at night in the streets – the early reformers, like the early Christians, choosing that time for their assemblies.[17] A third idea concerning the name is that the people used to assemble at night near the gate of King Hugo in Tours. A monk in a sermon declared that they "ought to be called Huguenots as Kinsmen of King Hugo inasmuch as they would only go out at night the same as he did."[18] A fourth surmise is that the word was derived from one *Hugues*, the name of a Genevese Calvinist.[19]

The Religious Wars between Catholics and Protestants, which began in 1562, continued until 1595. Admiral Gaspard de Coligny and Prince de Condé gave leadership to the Huguenots. Conde was shot dead in battle in 1569, and Admiral Coligny was murdered in 1572.[20] Then followed the St. Bartholomew Day massacre August 24, 1572, when thousands of Huguenots were slaughtered in Paris and many more in the provinces. Rome was thrown into a delirium at the news, and Pope Gregory XIII and his cardinals went in procession from sanctuary to sanctuary giving thanks to God for the massacre.[21]

King Henry IV of France, a Protestant, came to the throne in 1589 and in order to bring the civil war to a close, abjured Protestantism in 1592 in preparation for his coronation in 1594. He said "Paris is well worth a mass." The Protestants bitterly resented their ruler's abjuration. In 1598 Henry came to terms with them by the Edict of Nantes, which gave them the right to hold their synods, political assemblies, to open schools, and to occupy a hundred strong places for eight years at the king's expense. Thus, the religious war, which had lasted off and on for forty years, ended.[22] Although, granted freedom of worship by the Edict, the results for the Huguenots were only nominal. They were feared, hated, and persecuted by the Catholic authorities.

By the time of the reign of King Louis XIV, the king was persuaded to act with finality against the Protestants, and on October 18, 1685, he signed the Revocation of the Edict of Nantes and ordered all Huguenot forms of worship to cease and all Protestant chapels and temples to be immediately destroyed. Protestants could not practice as doctors, surgeons, lawyers, or teachers, or be employed by the government even as grocers. All Protestant books, including Bibles and Testaments were collected and burned. Even Protestant washerwomen were excluded from their washing places at the rivers. All Huguenot ministers were given a fortnight to leave the country; but others were forbidden to follow them under the pain of the galleys and confiscation of their property.[23]

The consequences were terrible for the Huguenots. They no longer had any civil rights, their marriages were regarded as null and void, and their children were considered bastards. The property of many was confiscated upon proof of their Protestantism, and a great number of ministers were executed.[24] By the stroke of his pen, Louis XIV literally drove out of his country some 500,000 to 1,000,000 of its citizens,[25] including most of her skilled artisans. An enormous amount of wealth went out of the country with the emigrants, and French commerce was prostrated. About nine thousand of the king's best sailors, twelve thousand soldiers, and over five hundred of his best trained officers left the country.[26] Many of the nobility found refuge in Geneva in Switzerland; many tradesmen and artisans went to Holland; and many others found peace in the German Palatinate (which adjoined the eastern border of France) where they could worship without persecution. Huguenot refugee settlements in Germany included Todenhausen (Kur-Hessen), Hesse-Nassau; Neureut bei Karlsruhe; Waldensberg (Kur-Hessen-Waldeck); Schonenberg bei Muhlacker; Gottstreu; and Gewissenruch (Lipperland).

Who were these Huguenots and what kind of people were they? During the sixteenth century, there were at least two essentials if one became a Protestant: an inquiring mind and exceptional courage. The person had to be desirous of living by new ideas and brave enough to sacrifice friends, position, and even life itself in order to maintain them. When they weighed something carefully and determined the correct course to pursue, it was not likely that they would change their minds. Thus, in some respects they might be charged with stubbornness and not be far wrong. Having made up their minds about a certain thing or course of action, they tenaciously held to it as being that right and correct position or practice to follow. The Huguenot desired personal salvation which could not be obtained through humanism, though that sharpened his desire for it; nor could it be found in the Roman church because of the evils and departures from biblical teachings. Driven then to the Bible, he found peace of mind through direct contact with his Maker.

Years ago after the death of Miss Era Deboe and after obtaining copies of her material on the family, I was avidly reading through it and suddenly came to an amazing statements in which she declared that a notable characteristic of the Debo(e) was independence and stubbornness. I had to laugh, and then considered how well she knew "us." There was no doubt in my mind, then, that we were all from the same roots, for I never have known a Debo who didn't have a right ample streak of stubbornness. Could it not be some of our old Huguenot stock showing itself?

It is thought that the Debos, along with many of their friends and acquaintances, left France some time after the Revocation of the Edict of Nantes in 1685. Although Huguenots were immigrating during the days of persecution prior to the Revocation, the loss of civil rights and freedoms following that act resulted in a wholesale departure in many areas. In Miss Era Deboe's account of the oral tradition handed down through the year in that branch of the family, she reported: "The French Huguenots, of which our family were members, objected to the ways of the land and spoke out loudly against them. They left France and went to Germany [the Palatinate] in search of a place where they could be free... In Germany they intermarried with Germans and still expressed themselves freely in spite of the trouble which this brought upon themselves. Next, they moved to Holland. When some father died, the mother, with a bit of thrifty German in her, took the family to a sister in England." If the Debo family left France around 1685 or shortly thereafter and arrived in America in 1732, that leaves about forty-five years to spend in Germany and Holland.

The Palatinate and Emigration

The Palatinate (called *Pfalz* in German) was divided between two small territorial clusters, the Rhenish or Lower Palatinate, and the Upper Palatinate. The Rhenish Palatinate included lands on both sides of the Middle Rhine river between the tributaries Main and Neckar. Its capital until the eighteenth century was at Heidleberg. The Upper Palatinate was located in northern Barvaria, on both sides of the Naab River as it flows south toward the Danube and extended eastward to the Bohemian Forest. The boundaries of the Palatinate began in the north on the Moselle River about 35 miles southwest of Coblenz to Bingen and east to Mainz, ran down the Rhine River to Oppenheim, Guntersblum, and Worms, then continued eastward above the Neckar River about 25 miles east of Heidelburg to Speyer, south down the Rhine River to Alsace, then northwesterly back up to its beginning on the Moselle River.

During the Thirty Years War, the Palatine country, as well as other parts of Germany, was ravaged from pillage and plunder by the French armies. The war was based upon politics and religious hatred as Roman Catholic armies from France sought to crush the religious freedom of a politically-divided Protestantism. Many unpaid armies and bands of mercenaries, both of friends and foe, devoured the substance of the people and by 1633 even the Catholic French supported the Elector of the Palatinate for a time for political reasons. By the end of the Thirty Years War the people and the country lay prostrate.

In 1688-89, partly to vent his malice against the Protestants, the Grand Monarch Louis XIV had the Palatinate laid waste again. During the War of the Spanish Succession, Marshal Villars, crossed the Rhine in May, 1707, and terrorized southwestern Germany, plundering and requisitioning freely on the Palatinate citizens. In September of that year, the French once again retired across the Rhine. The incursions by the French was a political blunder for it united Germany against King Louis. But for the people living in the war zone, these invasions wiped out the fruits of many labors and discouraged further struggles for better living conditions.

To the curse of devastation was added an unkind prank of nature. At the end of 1708 a winter, cruel beyond the precedent of a century, set in to blight the entire region. As early as the beginning of October the cold became intense and by November 1st, it was said, firewood would not burn in the open air! In January 1709 wine and spirits froze into solid blocks of ice; birds on the wing fell dead; and, it is said, saliva congealed in its fall from the mouth to the ground.[27] Most of Western Europe was frozen tight. The Seine River in France and all other rivers of the area were icebound, and on the 8th of January the Rhone, one of the most rapid rivers of Europe, was covered with ice. What had never been seen before occurred when the sea froze sufficiently all along the coasts to bear up carts, even heavily laden. Several men were frozen to death in many countries, and the Arctic weather lasted well into the fourth month of 1709. The period of heaviest frost was from the 6th to the 25th of January, whereupon snow then fell until February 6th and the fruit trees were killed and vines destroyed. The calamity of this unusually bitter winter fell heavily on the farmers and vine-dressers, who made up more than half of the emigrants of 1709.

The year 1709 became a year of emigration and between May and November of that year variously estimated totals of two to thirty-two thousand arrived in London, most of them from the Rhenish or Lower Palatinate. The devastation from wars and the severity of the past winter were not the only reasons for the exodus. Other influences, almost as malign, were harassing the inhabitants of the Rhine Valley. The petty German rulers in an attempt to emulate the lavish court life of Louis XIV of France were levying heavy taxes on their subjects, often so exhausting to the inhabitants that the peasants themselves were left without bread. This naturally aroused bitter feelings against the ruling class. Also, the need for additional money to carry on the various wars made the taxes mount higher day by day. Conditions did not improve during the next twenty-five years apparently, for an unbiased report from the Palatines waiting in Holland for transportation to England stated they came flying "to shake off the burdens they lay under by the hardships of their Princes governments and the contributions they must pay to the Enemy."[28]

The passage down the Rhine River to Rotterdam took from four to six weeks, and tolls and fees were demanded by authorities of the territories through which they passed. By June 1709, the number of Palatine entering Rotterdam reached 1,000 per week. Later that year, the British government issued a royal proclamation in German that all arriving after October 1709 would be sent back to Germany, for the British could not effectively handle the number of Palatines in London and there were said to have been as many as 32,000 by November of that year. The hunger for more and better land, the advertising of the English colonies in America, and the favorable attitude of the British government toward settlement in the North American colonies gave impetus to the desire of many emigrants to come to the New World for a new and better beginning. Pennsylvania, New York, and South Carolina became eventual destinations for many of these hard-working and freedom- loving folk.

Whether the Debos were included in this migration or came later has not been ascertained. We know that after leaving France and remaining in Germany for awhile, they came down the Rhine River to Holland (The Netherlands), and from there came to England before sailing for America. It is interesting to note that the vessel on which our family immigrants came to the New World sailed from Rotterdam, initially, and last touched land at Dover, England, prior to its arrival in Philadelphia, Pennsylvania, in October 1732. It is my judgment that the Debos did not stay very long in England. I had the membership lists of the Huguenot churches that were established in England searched, and no names that even approximate the name of our family were found. In the New World work could be had for those old enough to toil, and the opportunity for a new start in a land of freedom was a great attraction, drawing many refugees from religious oppression and persecution to its shores. And thus came the Debos – in a vessel containing 169 Palatines with common desire, purposes, and goals.

II. Coming to the New World

We owe it to our ancestors to preserve those rights which they have delivered to our care; we owe it to our posterity not to suffer their dearest inheritance to be destroyed.

— Unknown

A New Start and a New Country

In the *Pennsylvania Gazette*, begun by Benjamin Franklin in 1728, there appeared the following on October 19, 1732:

"Sunday last [Oct. 11] arrived here Captain Tymperton 17 weeks from Rotterdam, with 220 Palatine – 44 died in their passage. About three weeks ago, the passengers dissatisfied with the length of the voyage, were so imprudent as to make a mutiny, and being the stronger party, have ever since had the government of the vessel, giving orders from among themselves to the captain and the sailors, who were threatened with death in case of disobedience. Thus, having sight of land, they carried the vessel twice backwards and forwards between our capes and Virginia, looking for a place to go ashore, they knew not where. At length they compelled the sailors to cast the anchor near Cape May, and eight of them took the boat by force and went ashore; from whence they have been five days coming up by land to this place, where they found the ship arrived. Those concerned in taking the boat are committed to prison.

* * * * * *

"Ordinarily 10 to 12 weeks were quite sufficient to make the passage. But these people saw no land after 12, 13, yea 14 weeks of patient sailing. Then they became frightened – horror stricken. They felt they were lost – lost on the great Atlantic Ocean, with no land in sight anywhere. They threaten the master and seamen and take charge of the ship. This they did at the end of 14 weeks or as the account states about 3 weeks before landing.

"Think of the scene on that ship from another point. According to the record there were 98 women and children on the vessel when it landed in addition to about the same number of men. What terror they must have experienced and how the children must have cried in tears. How desperately in despair were the mothers. How helpless all of them! Think too of the deaths – 44 deaths that voyage. That is one each 3rd day dies and is sunk in the sea.

"It took brave souls indeed in those days to cross the ocean and found a new land. This was, no doubt, one of many similar fated ships. And according to the preceding item, that vessel had a much more terrifying experience. These people were surely persons of grim determination; and it is not a great wonder that they succeeded in establishing themselves comfortably in a little while after they reached their new home here on the Conestoga."[1]

While doing research a number of years ago, I became excited and considered myself most fortunate to have come across the above quoted vivid account of the voyage of the vessel on which our immigrant forebears first came to this country. One can only wonder at the thoughts welling up in the minds of those pioneers as they despaired of ever seeing land again and considered themselves for a time lost in the vast expanses of a great ocean. No wonder our forefathers developed such courage and moral stamina as they faced the unknown in a foreign land. I fear these qualities are sadly lacking among those of us today who are privileged to have lived among the niceties and conveniences of a pleasure-filled twentieth and twenty-first century.

The *Colonial Records* also revealed that eleven ships had landed in Philadelphia in 1732 with Palatines: 762 heads of families and around 1,950 persons. There were not many old people, and the men averaged 28 years of age and women 27. (One ship landed in May; two in August; seven in September; and one in October.)

The landing of the vessel was recorded in *Colonial Records*, as follows: "At the Courthouse of Philadelphia, October 17th, 1732, Sixty-one Palatines, who with their families, making in all 169 persons, were imported in the *Pink John & William of Sunderland*, Constable Tymperton, Master, from Rotterdam, but last from Dover [England], as by Clearance thence." Another (Qualified Oct.17th, 1732, Sixty-one Palatines, who with their families, making in all 169 persons, were imported in the *Pink John & William of Sunderland*, Constable Tymperton, Master, from Rotterdam, but last from Dover, [England], as by Clearance thence."[2] Another record stated: "Palatine Passengers on

Ship *John & William*, Constable Tymperton, Master from Rotterdam (Qualified Oct. 17, 1732)." On board the vessel were Abraham Dubo [Dnbo?], Philip Dubo [Dnbo], sick; their sister, Anna. (Abraham could not sign his name.)[3] Also aboard the *Pink John and William of Sunderland*, was Jacob Bieber [later changed to Beaver], who possibly could have been a brother of Magdalena Biber, one who later became the wife of Philip Debo. For that matter, Magdalena could have come over on the ship also, for the women were not listed by name on the passenger lists, only men over 16. It is also possible that the mother of Philip and Abraham Debo could have been aboard, and this would bear out Miss Era Deboe's story that the mother and older sons came to America. This has never been verified, however, and I just mention the possibility.

In an article titled "Passengers from the Rhineland to Pennsylvania," the *Pennsylvania Gazette* of March 22, 1733, called attention to the fifteen derelict passengers to the "stern rule of life and the sea," in German as well as English: "Those Palatines who came Passengers from Rotterdam, in the Ship John and William, Constable Tymperton, Commander, and have not yet paid their Passages, nor given Security, are hereby required to make speedy Payment, or to give good Security, to Mr. George McCall, Merchant in Philadelphia; otherwise they may expect to be prosecuted as the law directs. Their names are as follows: Hans Peter Brechbill, Philip Melchoir, Nicholas Pashon, George Adam Stees, **Abraham Diebo**, Matthias Manser, Hans Emich, Stephen Matts, Frederich Kooler, Michael Bloemhower, Hans Riel, Caspar Willaar, Philip Melchoir Meyer, John George Wahnzodel."[4] As to why Abraham Diebo had not paid his passage money, judge ye. Did the family have just enough money for the rest of the family, or was there some other reason?

The Huguenots who settled in Pennsylvania seldom settled in a group. Many of the nobility had fled to Geneva upon leaving France; tradesmen and artisans travelled to the Netherlands to settle either in Leiden or Amsterdam; and vinters from Champagne and Burgundy along with many others escaped the persecution by fleeing to the Palatinate or other German States.[5] Most of the Huguenot emigrants coming to Pennsylvania came with the German-speaking Swiss and Palatines with whom they or their fathers had sojourned after their flight from France. Many had already Germanized their French names and had also adopted the language of their German friends.[6] More than a thousand Huguenot families who came to the Quaker State, however, preserved the original integrity of their surnames in the emigration previous to 1755, and many more after that date.

One of the interesting stories about the journey to America by the Debos, handed down from generation to generation in the family and preserved by Miss Era Deboe as told to her by her father, Jesse Watkins Deboe, concerned a stowaway most often referred to as the "apple barrel boy."[7] After one of the family fathers died while the family was in Holland, the mother took her family to a sister in England. In the New World work was plentiful for those who were old enough to labor at various jobs available. The mother made a no doubt heart-rending decision: she would leave her youngest child with her sister until he grew older (he was just too small to go to the "wild" country!), and she and the older boys would go ahead.

When it came time for the ship to sail, the "baby," who was reportedly about five years old, keenly observed all the separation and departure without tears. The child began playing down at the docks from which he had seen the ship depart. Sometime later when he observed a ship was about to sail for the same destination to which the family had gone the boy disappeared. He came out of hiding only at night, and no one ever saw him – or if they did, they did not report him.

As the ship reached its destination [Philadelphia], at night, he ran ashore. In the storage area of the vessel an empty apple barrel was found – and that was all he had eaten on the journey over! Since the lad was already here in this country, he was permitted to remain. The older brothers would work enough to support him along with the rest of the family, but the lad was so independent he worked from the very first to support himself and let his brothers know in no uncertain terms that he was fully capable of supporting himself!

In her account of this episode in our family's history, Miss Era added most succinctly: "Independence or stubbornness is a strong family trait. It is quite pronounced in all DeBoe descendants." Miss Era, who was a teacher for many years, was attending college, she, along with two or three others, was chosen to be the guides for the governor of North Carolina, who was to speak at some function at the college. At lunch when he found out her name was DeBoe, he said, "We have a lot of Deboes in our state. You might be kin to me." Then he added, "You wouldn't be related to the apple barrel boy, would you?"

Information from "Pennsylvania Church Records from Adams, Berks and Lancaster Counties, 1729-1881" reveals more than any other source that I found about Philip Debo (1), the forebear from which we are descended. In the records of the First Reformed Church of Lancaster, Pennsylvania, the following was gleaned: "Philip Dibbo of the Kestenberg, age 51 years, died April 26, 1750, in Lancaster County. He was married for 16 years, had 8 children: 4 sons and 4 daughters, of which 3 sons and 4 daughters survived him. He was sick for 4 weeks." This would indicate that he was born in 1699, but the location is not given. It could have been France, Holland, or England. It also shows he was 33 years old when he came to America.

On November 12, 1734, Philipp Diebo was married to Magdalena Biber at Coventry in Chester County Pennsylvania[8] (adjoining Philadelphia County), a little more than two years after landing in this country. The ceremony was performed by a Lutheran minister, John Caspar Stoever, who had come to the New World on the ship *John Goodwill* September 11, 1728. He was a native of Frankenberg in Hesse, Germany, and first had located in Virginia. Stoever went back to Europe in 1737 and died on board the vessel on his attempted return to America. His son, John Caspar Stoever, Jr., a native of Luerdorff, in Solinger Amt, Duchy Berg, in the Palatinate, was born December 21, 1707, and came to America on the *James Goodwill* with his father in 1728. He died at Lebanon, Pennsylvania, May 13, 1779.[9]

Philip Debo only lived 19 years after arriving in this country – 16 after his marriage to Mary Magdalena. One record noted upon his arrival at Philadelphia that he was "sick."[10] Whether the illness was due to the stress of the journey here on the vessel or whether it might have been some chronic ailment is unknown and it would simply be a matter of conjecture either way. It is known that Philip and Magdalena had four sons that the following three survived him: Philip, John Conrad, and Abraham. The record also states four daughters. A Catherine Dibo was married to Andrew Thess August 9, 1760. No more is known about her. If she were born circa 1742, she would have been 18 at the time of her marriage.[11] Anna Christina Dubo is listed in the "Southeastern Pennsylvania Birth Index, 1680-1800" and she was born and christened February 22, 1745 at the Reformed church, Bern Township, Berks County. Johan Philip Dubo is named the father and Madlena Dubo the mother. Nothing further is known of the other daughters.

It is my judgment that Philip (2) was the firstborn and was born in about 1736 (I have no authentic proof, but it was common practice for the firstborn son to be named after his father). John Conrad was born June 25, 1738,[12] and Abraham possibly was born circa 1740. Philip (1) died intestate April 26, 1750, at which time his wife Magadalena, along with Jacob End and John Unger, was placed under a 200-pound bond for the purpose of inventorying his estate. An account of this bond follows, to wit:

"KNOW all Men by these presents that We Mary Magdalena Depo, Jacob End and John Unger all of the County of Lancaster, and Province of Pennsylvania, are held and firmly bound unto William Plumsted Esqr, Register General for the Probate of Wills and granting Letters of Administration in the Province of Pennsylvania in the Sum of two hundred Pounds lawfull Money of the said Province to be pay'd unto the said William Plumsted or to his certain Attorney, Executor, Administrators or Assigns To the which payment well and truly to be made. We do bind ourselves Jointly and severally, our Heirs, Executors and Administrators, each and every of them firmly by these Presents. Sealed with our Seals and Dated this fourth day of September in the Year of our Lord one Thousand seven Hundred and fifty one.

"The condition of the above Obligation is such, that if the above bounden Mary Magdalen Depo Administratrix of all and singular the goods and Chattles, Rights and Credits which were of Philip Depo Deceased, Do make or cause to be made, a true and perfect Inventory of all and singular the Goods and Chattles, Rights and Credits, which were of the said Decendent at the time of his Death, or which at any other time his, or shall come to the Hands, Possession or Knowledge of the said Mary Magadalen Depo or unto the Hands or Possession of any other person or persons for her and the same so made, do exhibit into the Registers Office at Lancaster at or before the fourth Day of October next ensuing, and the same Goods Chattles and Credits, Do well and truly administer according to Law: and further Do make or cause to be made true and just Account, Calculation or Reckoning of the said Administration on or before the fourth day of September next which will be in the Year of our Lord one Thousand seven Hundred and fifty two and all the Rest and Residue of the said Goods, Chattles and Credits which shall be found remaining upon the said Administrators Account the (same being first examined and approved of by the Orphans Court of the County aforesaid) Do deliver and pay such Person or Persons respectively as the Orphans Court by their Decree or Sentence pursuant to the true intent and Meaning of an Act intitled and Act for the better settling Interstate Estates, shall limit and appoint. And if it shall hereafter appear that any last Will and Testament was made by the Decedent and the Executor or Executors therein named, do exhibit the same into the registers Office at Lancaster making Request to have it allowed and approved, accordingly if the said Mary Magdalen Depo above bounden being thereunto required. Do render and deliver up the said Letters of Administration (Approbation of such Testament being first had and made in the Registers Office) then the above Obligation to be Void & of none Effect else to remain in full Force & Virtue.

Sealed and Delivered in the presence of us.[13]

		her		
Emmanuel Carpenter	M. Magdalen	X	Depo
		mark	

Tho. Cookson

Jacob End

His mark X

John Unger"

Following is a list of the possessions of Philip, the immigrant, as her inventory:[14]

"Inventory of the Estate of Phillip Dippo Deaseased Praised by Phillip Lenherr John Utzman & Michael Hubly the 8th day of May 1750

	*	**	+
First to the Mans Cloth	£	S	d
to a Gunn at	1	10	0
to 2 axes 2 Hadched & one atch at	0	9	6
to a gruben hoo at	0	4	0
to a cross Cut Saw at	0	10	0
to Two hand Saws at	0	2	0
to Pewter Whears at	0	19	0
to Iron Ketchen Whearspots, pans & Lettels at	1	7	0
to a Waggon and Plow at	6	10	0
to Chains at	1	1	0
to aagers and gimlet at	0	7	0
to 3 feilles, Throw Knife Geessels & a little anvell	11	7	6
to 3 Happels at	0	2	6
to 4 Hamers at	0	1	6

	*	**	+
to 5 Coom & 2 Saifs at	0	8	0
to a Sattle at	0	3	0
to 4 Keattles at	0	4	0
to 4 Cocks at	0	5	0
to a Spinnin Wheell at	0	4	0
to 3 Iron Weatches at	0	2	0
to 4 Hogsed at	0	7	6
to 2 Cocks at	0	2	6
to a halfe bushel & a baske at	0	2	6
to Dups at	0	3	0
to Two Cowes at	4	10	0
to one Horse at	3	0	0
to 2 Sickles at	0	2	6
to Hows & one Iron Racke at	0	4	0
to forcks at	0	3	0
to a Pewter Tancker at	0	3	0
to 2 Bridles & one Halter at	0	3	0
to 2 Jacks at	0	1	6
to Loder at	0	2	0
to oult Iron	0	7	6
to 4 Hocke of bees at	1	0	0
to 3 bonds of	40	0	0
the Improvement	80	0	0
	146	14	0
and the Estate is Debted to Sundry Persons	37	14	6

(*= English pounds; **=shillings; +=pence)

III. Leaving Pennsylvania

It is indeed a desirable thing to be well descended, but the glory belongs to our ancestors.

-Plutarch

The data from the 37-year span of time between the death of Philip Debo (the immigrant) in 1751 and the move of the Debos to Virginia around 1788 is rather sketchy, and much of what I am including here is based on my study of certain proven and authentic facts that are known, and then making a judgment on those facts. Most of the authentic facts are based on material obtained on a single research trip made to Lancaster, Pennsylvania, in 1973. Perhaps additional data could be obtained in Lancaster, Lebanon, and Berks counties, but I have never had the time or opportunity to return to that area for further research efforts. Since I have not been able to obtain any information regarding the immigrants Abraham and Anna (brother and sister of Philip), both of whom came over on the vessel with him, Philip and his descendants are the ones with whom we shall deal in this story. After all, he is the one from whom this family descends. [To distinguish the various Philips in our saga, we will begin by numbering the immigrant Philip (1) and continue in the order successively by generations. The names Abraham (Abram), Michael, Joseph, and John are all quite common in the family, occurring generation after generation.]

Since we have practically no information on Philip's son Abraham except that he went to Virginia with his brother Philip(2) and settled in Pittsylvania County, we will proceed with what has been obtained on Philip's(1) son, John Conrad. Then we shall conclude this chapter with Philip(2) for whom we have the most data and from whom we are descended.

John Conrad Deboe was born June 25, 1738 (as has already been proven), and his christening followed on August 23, 1738, with Conrad Scharff and his wife as sponsors. The event took place at the Little Tulpehoken church (also known as Christ Church), located one and a half mile south of Bernville in Jefferson Township, Berks County, Pennsylvania, and was performed by John Caspar Stoever, son of the one who performed the wedding ceremony of Philip (1) and Magdalena. By 1775 John Conrad at age 37 was living in Dunmore County (after 1778 called Shenandoah County), Virginia. In Capt. John Denton's census list of 1775, he was enumerated as having 5 white males and 3 white females in his family. On a list of men in the lower district of Dunmore County he is named in a military unit under the command of Capt. Joseph Bowman.[1] In the Virginia Census of 1790 John Conrad Deboe is reported living in Shenandoah County, Virginia, in 1785 with a family of 8 white souls and possessing 1 dwelling and 2 other buildings. John C. Deboe and wife Esther (her maiden name is unknown) purchased 200 acres from Christian Miller in Berkford Parish, Shenandoah County, September 24, 1782,[2] but sold that same acreage to Christian Stover March 24, 1789.[3] No other information has been found on John Conrad as to whether he left the county, or whether he died and was buried there.

Although I have no documented proof and therefore cannot prove it, I would not be at all surprised if some of the Deboes who settled in Jessamine, Mercer, and Jefferson counties in Kentucky were descendants of John Conrad or some of his children, who migrated west from Virginia – though I have never been able to make the tie-in for sure. An Anne Deboe married a British soldier, Capt. William Jameson around 1780. He had been quartered in a Deboe home during the Revolutionary War, and supposedly fell in love with young Anne. They settled in Jessamine County, Kentucky, where he died at Nicholasville in 1814. They had 5 sons and 2 daughters [I have their names and years of birth].[4] Anne supposedly was a sister of Joseph Deboe.

Martin Deboe (born in 1786) and Joseph Deboe (born in 1792), both of whom supposedly were born in Virginia, lived in Jessamine County also. The Deboes first purchased land in that county in 1816, and both married there: Martin to Lydia Walls, daughter of Eliza W. Walls, September 19, 1835; and Joseph to Milly Hudson, daughter of Joshua Hudson, June 29, 1824.[5]

Henry Debo of Jefferson County (Louisville), Kentucky, was born between 1780 and 1785 in Virginia, as was his son, Horatio, who was born in 1807. Henry is listed in the U.S. Census of 1840 for Kentucky but not in 1850, which would indicate that he had possibly died between 1840 and 1850 or moved to some other state. Their descendants not only were in Jefferson County, but some of them established Debo lines in Missouri.

Ransom Debo was born September 5, 1810, in Madison County, Virginia, which is in the same area as Shenandoah County. He was married January 7, 1834, in Boyle County, Kentucky, to Rhoda Henderson, born December 25, 1814 in Mercer County, Kentucky. Their first child, Susan Elizabeth, was born October 14, 1838, before they moved over into Indiana. This family eventually migrated to Kansas where Ransom and wife both died and were buried in Elk City.

Here is another puzzling possibility. Abraham and Joseph Debon (familiar family given names!) were taxpayers in Berkeley County, Virginia (now West Virginia), in 1782.[6] By 1810 they were listed along with George and Samuel as residents of Mercer County, Kentucky, which adjoins Jessamine County on the west.[7] Could the name Debon have been a transcription of Deboe in German script (Dnbon)?

On October 7, 1743, the ship *St Andrew*, Capt. Robert Frown, Master, landed at Philadelphia from Rotterdam, last from Cowes, England. Listed as passengers are Lodwick Debus, 36; Daniel Debus, 28; Jacob Debus, 26.[8] Another source states, "In 1743 arrived Ludwig De-Bos, aged 36, Daniel, aged 28, and Jacob, aged 26 years. They came in the same vessel and were doubtless brothers. In 1745 Daniel died at Lititz, in Lancaster County."[9] Daniel must have died shortly after his marriage, for he was married April 16, 1745 to Barbara Stingler in the Moravian Church at Lititz.[10] Whether these brothers were any kin to Philip, Abraham, and Anna is anyone's guess.

Philip Debo (2)

If Philip Debo(2) was the firstborn of the immigrant Philip(1), he was born around 1736. No records have been found of his birth or marriage. In a register (journal) kept by Winston Dalton, a school teacher in northern Pittsylvania and southern Bedford counties, Virginia, after the Debos were living in Virginia, he mentions that "Old Miss Debboe died 24 September 1822"; also, "Sena Debboe died 18 January 1826."[11] Either one of these could have been Philip's(2) wife; or could "Sena Debboe" actually have been Lena (Magdalena) Deboe, Philip's(2) mother and wife of Philip(1), the immigrant? Who knows?

This much is known about Philip (2): he was a physician and served in the Revolutionary War, being with Gen. George Washington at Valley Forge during the terrible winter of 1777-78. Though I have only one documented reference in which he received 50 pounds June 30, 1779,

Lewis C. Debo assembling the medical scales of Dr. Philip Debo(2).

for guard duty in the Pennsylvania militia in Lancaster County,[12] Philip(2) is referred to as a revolutionary soldier in the obituary of Senator Joseph Deboe of Kentucky, who was a great-grandson. I know he was a physician for his medical scales on which he measured out his dosages and his brass candle holder have been handed down through the years to various branches of the Michael Debo family. Evidently Michael, Philip's(2) eldest son, received these heirlooms at Philip's death because his granddaughter, Annis P. Rorer (daughter of Michael's daughter Mary), gave them to Dr. Michael P. deBoe, her first cousin, who was a noted opthamologist of Miami, Florida. After his death and before the death of his widow, Mizpah Otto deBoe, she gave them to Lewis C. Debo of Ottuma, Iowa (now deceased), because she wanted them to remain in the family.

Mizpah deBoe said old Dr. Philip Deboe practiced medicine all of his life. She also related how that the family remembered him as an old man around his Virginia fireside telling about that winter at Valley Forge and how that he never could keep the tears from streaming down his cheeks as he told about the ragged, barefoot soldiers coming to abandoned camps where the horses had died and would take their hooves and roast them over the campfires to keep from starving to death.[13]

Valley Forge

No battle was fought at Valley Forge, Pennsylvania, during the Revolutionary War. The British were content to spend that frigid winter of 1777-78 in the warmth of Philadelphia, some 18 miles away, while Gen. George Washington's soldiers were enduring the ravages of weather and disease as well as a pitiful lack of food, clothing, and fuel. The real "battle" of Valley Forge, among the most significant of the seven-year long American Revolution, was in a fight to the death of man against the elements rather than an army against army. It was here that Washington's ragtag band of poorly trained soldiers were to become a cohesive fighting force, and it was here that the seeds of victory were planted in their struggle against the British.

A Prussian officer, Baron Friedrich von Steuben, taught the Continentals how to march, to drill, and to function as a unified, motivated army. If one place could be said to be the turning point of the Revolution, Valley Forge, Pennsylvania, was that place. With snow on the ground and a howling wind chilling the bones, it is easy to image the hardships that Washington and his men endured during that frightful winter and there were many.

The Continental Army had moved into its winter encampment on December 19, 1777, shortly after losing Philadelphia to a British force under Sir William Howe. The site, named for an iron forge on Valley Creek, was selected by Washington because its high ground made it readily defensible and it was also close enough to Philadelphia to keep a wary eye on the British. The first order of business was to prepare defensive works and build log huts for the 12,000 troops of the Continental Army. These crude huts would sleep up to twelve men, and Gen. Peter Muhlenberg's brigade would man the outer line of defense. One of the army's major problems was keeping the force up to strength, for the men signed up for a few months or a year and once their enlistment was up they simply went home.

Washington's army left Valley Forge exactly six months after its arrival – on June 19,1778 – but not before more that 2,000 men had died due to exposure, disease, and other privations of winter. But it was a vastly different army than that one which had encamped there the preceding December. It was now a disciplined fighting force, one fashioned under the iron hand of von Steuben, who had arrived from France February 23, 1778. There was a new spirit in the air too, thanks in large part to the decision of France to enter the war on the American side. A great parade and artillery salute was staged by von Steuben on May 6, 1778, to mark that momentous occasion.

The American Revolution ended with the surrender of Cornwallis at Yorktown, Virginia, October 19, 1781, and the United States was recognized as a nation with the signing of the Treaty of Paris in 1783. It is shortly thereafter that the Debos pull up stock and leave Pennsylvania for a new home in southern Virginia. It would be interesting for us today to know the reason for this move. There were the Debos in

Frederick County, Maryland, prior to 1780.[14] Palatines had migrated to western Maryland on their way down the Shenandoah Valley of Virginia and a considerable number of early settlers of Huguenot ancestry were among them.[15]

There were three well marked trails over which early settlers traveled into southern Virginia. One of these trails led down the Valley of Virginia and across the gaps of the Blue Ridge Mountains into the southern Piedmont area, following the line of the Great War Trail of the Iroquois. Harmon Cook was a colonizer who had purchased large tracts of land on Tomahawk Creek and the Pigg River in northwestern Pittsylvania County. He brought in many families from Pennsylvania in the latter part of the eighteenth century, among whom were Quakers, Germans, Welsh, Scotch-Irish, and Palatines.[16] Sometime around 1786 or 1787 Cook led a large migration of interrelated families from Lancaster County, Pennsylvania, down the Shenandoah Valley into Pittsylvania County, Virginia. In the group were the Debos (Deboes), Rohrers (Rorers), Daltons, Saunders, Criders, Sheltons, Bennetts, Vances, Nolins (Nowlins), Wilchers, Robertsons, Reithers, and Swanes. These families settled in the northwest part of the county near Frying Pan Creek, which flowed into Pigg River, a tributary of the Staunton (Roanoke). On December 8, 1788, Philip Debo (2) purchased from Harmon Cook the first parcel of land in the county by one of the Debo family. It was located on Potters Creek.[17]

William Smith and wife Lucy, parents of Sarah (Sally) Smith Debo, sold a 50-acre tract of land on Potter's Creek in Pittsylvania County to their son-in-law, Abraham Debo, September 19,1803, for "twenty pounds current money of Virginia."[18] On the same day Smith sold the same amount of acreage on Frying Pan Creek for the same price to Abraham's brother Philip (2).[19] Thus the Debos expanded their holdings in the northwest section of Pittsylvania County.

It is unknown just when Philip Debo (2) died or where he was buried in Pittsylvania County. It seems reasonable to assume that his death occurred sometime between 1810 and 1820 because he does not appear in the U.S. Census of 1820. If he was born in 1736 and died even in 1810, he would have been 74 years of age – quite an old man for that day and time when few lived that length of time.

* * * *

The children of Philip Debo (2), all of whom were born in Lancaster(Lebanon) County, Pennsylvania, except Sarah (Sally) are:

1. BETSY (possibly named Elizabeth, but always listed as Betsy), probably born either in January or February 1769.[20] She was married to David Rohrer Jan. 21, 1793, in Pittsylvania County, Virginia. John White is listed on the marriage bond as bondsman and Philip Debo is named as her father.[21] Betsy died circa 1850 and was buried in the John D. Rohrer (Rorer) graveyard in the same county near Brights, Virginia, and Somerset church.[23] David Rorer was born circa 1766 in Lancaster (Lebanon) County, Pennsylvania, and was the son of John and Barbara Weidman Rohrer. His death date is unknown but he presumably was buried in the Rorer graveyard where Betsy was buried. They had three children.

2. MICHAEL, born Dec. 17, 1769.[24] He was married Jan. 3, 1795, in Pittsylvania County, Virginia to Katherine Saunders, and Jacob Saunders, her brother, was bondsman.[25] Michael died in 1843,[26] in Bedford County, Virginia, with burial in the family graveyard on his plantation there. Katherine Saunders was born July 27, 1772,[27] in Lancaster County, Pennsylvania (names of her parents are unknown), and died May 14, 1852,[28] in Bedford County, with burial beside her husband. Michael and Katherine had ten children.

3. CHRISTINA, born circa born 1773-74. She was married Jan. 1, 1796,[29] to Andrew Crider in Pittsylvania County, Virginia, and on the bond her father is listed as Philip Debo with Abraham Debo as bondsman. Christina died and was buried in Pittsylvania County (date and place are unknown). Andrew was born in 1775 in Philadelphia County, Pennsylvania, and was the son of Daniel and Catherine Berger Crider.[30] He died in 1856[31] and was also buried in Pittsylvania County. Christina and Andrew were the parents of seven children.

4. ABRAHAM, born in 1775.[32] He was married Nov. 14, 1797,[33] in Pittsylvania County to Sarah (Sally) Smith with Hezekiah Barber named as bondsman on the marriage bond. He died in May 1850[34] in the same county and was buried there. Sarah (Sally) Smith was the daughter of William and Lucy Smith,[35] but her birth and death dates are unknown. Abraham and Sally had four or five children (the exact number is uncertain).

5. PHILIP (3), born circa 1777-80. He was married Jan. 17, 1799,[36] in Pittsylvania County to Eleanor (Nellie) Smith, also the daugh-

ter of William Smith and wife Lucy, and James Nowlin was listed as bondsman on the bond. Philip died Oct., 19, 1835,[37] in Caldwell County, Kentucky. Nellie died sometime before 1830 and was presumably buried in Pittsylvania County, Virginia. They had nine children.

6. POLLY, born 1786.[38] She was married June 15, 1807,[39] in Pittsylvania County by Joseph Hatchett to Samuel Crider; the marriage bond listed Philip Debo as her father and William Dalton as bondsman. She died in Nov. 1869[40] in Caldwell County, Kentucky. Samuel was the son of Daniel Crider and Catherine Berger Crider. He was born April 21, 1783,[41] in Lancaster County, Pennsylvania, and died in Livingston County, Kentucky, and was buried in Piney Fork Cemetery, Crittenden County, Kentucky. Polly and Samuel had nine children.

7. SARAH (Sally), born 1791 in Maryland,[42] was married in Pittsylvania County Dec. 26, 1811[43] by Joseph Hatchett to Coleman Hughey. Philip Debo, Sr. is named as her father on the bond and Abraham is listed as bondsman. The Hugheys migrated to western Kentucky possibly circa 1810 and died there. They had five children.

IV. Michael Debo and Bedford County, Virgina

Like leaves on trees the life of man is found
Now green in youth, now withering on the ground
Another race the following spring supplies,
They fall successive, and successive rise
So generations in their course decay
So flourish these, when those have passed away.
                                        --Unknown

[Since Michael Debo, Sr., is the line through which I am descended from the immigrant, Philip Debo (Diebo, Dubo), and because it is this line of the family of which I have the most material, it will be the greater emphasis in the telling of the story of the grandsons and granddaughters of the immigrant Philip. Despite the preponderance of the data on the Michael Debo line, I am including all the material I have on the other lines. It must also be stated that in every reference to Michael and his children that I have seen the surname is spelled "D-e-b-o" without the final "e," with the exception of Michael Debo, Jr.'s son, Dr. Michael Price deBoe, and Lauriston Deboe, son of William Henry Debo.]

Michael Debo, Sr., was the oldest son of Philip Debo (2), who migrated from Pennsylvania via the Shenandoah Valley to Pittsylvania County, Virginia, about 1788 in the large group of settlers led by Harmon Cook. He was born December 17, 1769,[1] in that part of Lancaster County, Pennsylvania, that in 1813 was formed into Lebanon County. [His sister Betsy was also born in 1769,[2] and was either a twin or was born in the first month or two of the same year.] Michael was 19 years old and just entering manhood at the time of the migration of his family to Pittsylvania County, Virginia.

The marriage bond for Michael Debo and Katharine Saunders (born July 27, 1772, in Lancaster County, Pennsylvania; died May 14, 1852 in Bedford County, Virginia is dated January 3, 1795.[3] Saunders families were also a part of the migratory caravan who came from Lancaster County, Pennsylvania, to Pittsylvania County, and Jacob Saunders, her brother, was surety for the marriage bond. It has never been ascertained from which of the Saunders families Katharine came nor who her parents were; however, we know she had brothers named George and Henry.

While living in Pittsylvania County, Michael and Katharine's firstborn, a son Henry, was born in 1796 or 1797. On April 11, 1799,[4] a second son, John, was born to Mike and Katie, and the young family moved across the Staunton or Roanoke) River into adjoining Bedford County where Michael purchased the first tract of land on the headwaters of Rockcastle Creek from Robert Harper and wife Margery for 65 pounds on October 28, 1799.[5]

Beginning in 1806, Michael Debo began purchasing adjoining lands and by the time of his death in November 1843 he had amassed around 700 acres of land in the Rockcastle-Goose Creek area of southside Bedford County. His holdings were described in the common parlance of that day as his "Virginia plantation." He evidently had evolved into a right prosperous gentleman farmer and landowner during his lifetime.

Additions to his initial tract of land include the following:

1. Dec. 22, 1806 – 78 acres on Wagon Road from Thomas Stump and wife Polly for $160.[6]
2. October 26, 1807 – 100 acres on the South side of Goose Creek, adjoining Leftwich and Fealdser on Wagon road from James Williams and wife Sarah for $300.[7]
3. July 9, 1817 – 154 acres on Goose Creek below Fish Trap Falls, adjoin Harris from William Headon and wife Polly for $770.[8]
4. Sept. 29, 1821 – 34 ½ acres on waters of Rock Castle Creek from Daniel Saunders and wife Francis (Fanny) for $100.[9]
5. Sept. 29, 1821 – 55 ½ acres on the waters of Rock Castle Creek from Daniel Saunders and wife Francis (Fanny) for $130.[10]
6. Nov. 6, 1824 - - 95 acres on the south side of Goose Creek, adjoin Hadon (Headon?) from William Oliver and wife Winifred for $150.[11]
7. October 5, 1829 – 106 acres on the southwest side of Goose Creek, and on Mill Creek, adjoining Tinsley, Hurt, McGhee, Ashwell and Martin from Joseph Krantz and wife Lucy for $600.[12]

After the death of Michael Debo on November 1, 1843,[13] his estate was divided, with various transactions taking place throughout the years. For example, shortly after Michael's death Abraham and Elizabeth Debo Blankenship (daughter of Michael) sold to their son, John Blankenship, their "portion of the estate of Michael Debo, Sr. for $300" in lands, money, and so forth.[14] Later, on May 10, 1847, John Blankenship and wife Christine would sell to Preston & Leftwich for $150 the interest in Michael's estate.[15]

On January 20 and 24, 1844, Katharine Debo, widow of Michael, was allotted by the court a widow's dower of 78 and 147 acres respectively.[16] The next year, on February 24, 1845, the many heirs of Michael sold to Wesley Hackworth 50 acres on Goose Creek, adjoining Hackworth and E. Turner on the north side of Blackwater Road.[17]

Daniel Perry Debo, a bachelor son of Michael, had purchased from his older brother John his interest in their father's estate. As Daniel came to the end of his life (he died January 3, 1850), he willed on December 11, 1849,[18] the 50-acre tract of land on which the John Debo family was living to John's wife Jane.

In order to set forth what happened to the last 147 acres [a part of Katharine's dower] of the Michael Debo, Sr., estate, the final few sale transactions will be given. Sarah Catherine (known as "Cassie"), the last member of the family to live in the old log house on the Debo land, on July 26, 1906,[19] deeded her half-interest in the acreage to her brother, John Franklin Debo (Cassie and John Franklin were children of Michael Debo, Jr., who had inherited their father's portion of the Michael Debo, Sr., estate). John F. Debo and wife Ruby sold the 147-acre parcel on June 20, 1921,[20] to Romie J. Ayres after the death of Cassie in 1918. Ayres and wife on January 20, 1932,[21] sold to R. W. Craghead; but on October 17, 1934,[22] the acreage returned to ownership by a member of the Debo family as Craghead sold the land to Dr. Michael Price deBoe [his spelling of the family name is unique] of Miami, Florida, the son of John F. and Ruby Price Debo.

The last acreage of the Michael Debo, Sr., estate continued in family hands until after the death of Dr. deBoe in 1955.[23] Finally, on September 27, 1967,[24] the widow of Dr. deBoe, Mizpah Otto deBoe, sold the land to Warren L. Burnette and Leonard J. Bays, reserving ten acres that included the family cemetery and home with ingress and egress to the cemetery. Two days after the sale Burnette sold his half-interest to Bays, who on November 21, 1968, sold to the West Virginia Pulp and

Paper Co. (now known as Westvaco Corp.), "a corporation created and existing under the laws of the State of Delaware, and having an office at Covington, Virginia.[25] On June 5, 1978, Mrs. Mizpah deBoe sold to Burnette and Bays the last ten acres she had previously reserved and the land passed out of Debo possession forever. It was said by Bedford County residents that once a pulp and paper company obtains possession of land they never relinquish it.

In June 1967, I had the good fortune of going to Bedford County, Virginia, on a vacation trip – the first of a number of journeys made from Texas to the Old Dominion State. After some investigation and inquiries with various Bedford County residents, I made my first journey out to the location of the old Debo estate, being guided by Odie S. Overstreet, who was kind enough to stop cutting wood long enough to accompany me there. Since the place was overgrown with timber, undergrowth, and weeds I did not try to enter the premises as it was also muddy due to recent rains.

In June 1970 I returned to Bedford County and went back out to the old home place location off Virginia Rte. 737. I went down to the Clark Meador home across the road from the old former Providence Methodist Church building [the Debo family had attended services there in former days] that Meador now used for a feed barn. The Cassidy brothers, who worked for Meador, offered to go back up to the home place and show me the old log house, which must have been erected around 1800. It had no nails in the log part but was entirely put together with mortar and pegs. The homemade staircase was of steep vintage and went up to the upper half-story. A shed room – supposedly a kitchen – had been added in later years on the north side of the house, and I was fortunate to be able to make some pictures both within and without the structure. The trees and brush had grown up so close to the house that it was very difficult to obtain decent shots of the outside.

I had always been told that a family cemetery was located north of the house. After further investigation I located it. The fence was down and the brush and timber around it made it difficult to see. There were no gravestones with the exception of one rather large upright stone with no inscription, but several slightly sunken places indicated the presence of a number of graves. To the best of my reckoning, I would surmise that the following are interred in this cemetery: (1) Michael Debo, Sr.; (2) his wife, Katharine Saunders Debo; (3) Sarah Katharine

41

Old plantation home of Michael Debo, Sr. (Bedford County, Virgina), built CA. 1800 of logs and square wooden pegs; and handmade stairs.

(Cassie) Debo; (4) Michael Debo, Jr., and wife Wilmoth Leftwich Debo; (5) Michael and Wilmoth's children, (6) Monterey W., (7) McHenry, (8) Michael S. C., (9) Joel D., (10) Ellen Rose, (11) Wilmoth E., (12) Ella R.; (13) Jane Nichols Debo, wife of John; John and Jane's children, (14) Martha Prudence, (15) Bettie Jane, and (16) John Bruce, all of whom died of typhus or typhoid fever. It was at one time thought that Michael and Katharine Debo's son, Daniel Perry Debo, was also buried there, but later research revealed that he was buried in the Old Hubbard Cemetery on Body Camp Creek along with his brother-in-law, Taliaferro G. Hubbard, and probably his wife and Daniel's sister, Mary Debo Hubbard. The tombstones have simply T.G.H. died May 7, 1850 and D.P.D. January 3, 1850.[26]

On subsequent trips to Virginia and numerous visits to the old home place I was never able to locate the cemetery again. In August 1976 when my parents and I made a trip there, my father and I spent some time searching for the burial spot but timber cutting and vegetation growth prevented any location of the site since nothing at all looked familiar. Mizpah deBoe, last owner of the property, was quite upset when she learned that the demolition of the house had occurred. She had always wanted to fence the cemetery and erect one large marker there as a memorial to the entire family, but it was never accomplished due to her delicate health and advanced age. In later years I have been told that the cemetery is still there but I haven't been back to Virginia to verify it.

Once when I was visiting the Debo home place I was astonished to hear the sound of a train not too far away passing through the countryside. It was only later that I learned that the Norfolk Southern Railroad bisected the Debo land. Bedford County historian and a personal acquaintance, the late Kenneth E. Crouch, sent me information concerning the railroad's construction and Debo's Bluff.[27]

With the development of coal interests in West Virginia, Henry Huttleston Rogers of New York, who had built a fortune with Standard Oil, became interested in a rail line from the coal fields of West Virginia to the Virginia seacoast, and from this came the old Virginian Railroad Co. The Deepwater Railway Co. of West Virginia and the Tidewater Railroad Co. of Virginia were merged on March 8, 1907, to form the Virginian Railway Co. Rogers' dream of a rail line of 443 miles from Deep Water, West Virginia, through southside Virginia to Sewell's Point at Norfolk became a reality. Crews of Germans, Italians, and some Russians began construction on the line from each direction, and the final spike joining the line was driven in 1909 just upstream from Headen's bridge over Goose Creek west of Huddleston, Virginia, near Debo's Bluff (on the old home place). The Virginian Railroad was later merged in 1959 with the Norfolk Western Railway system, and is now the Norfolk Southern Railway.[28]

Michael Debo, Sr., must have been a respected and prominent citizen in the area where he resided for that day and time. Numerous mentions of him are present in the Court Order records of Bedford County. For instance, he was appointed to allot hands to work the roads,[29] he was qualified by the court to be an "overseer of the poor,"[30] and was "exempted from payment of levies on an infirm Negro girl Nelly."[31] He also made brandy as "custom work" and the sale of several gallons of it as well as a still may be noted in the inventory of his property sold after his demise.

Michael was a well-known hatter who made fine beaver hats for the public, and young men were apprenticed to him by their families to learn the trade. The following is an example: December 23, 1805, Adam Drew bound his son, to Michael Debo for 10 pounds a year, "Debo to learn Drew the trade of Hatter for his keep etc." Witnesses were Mark Anthony and John Headon.[32] The tradition of being a hatter was carried on by Michael's son John, my great-great-grandfather.

After the death of Michael Debo, Sr., on November 1, 1843, a sale of his "perishable estate" was held at his residence in southside Bedford county on December 8, 1843, to wit.[33]

"A List of property sold of the property of Michael Debo Snr Deceased sold the 8th day of December 1843.

List of property taken by Katharine Debo

To	6 Split bottom chairs	1.50
To	1 Large chest	.75
To	1 Candle stand	.50
To	1 Dressing table	1.00
To	1 Bed stead & furniture	15.00
To	1 Mettle clock	13.50
To	1 cupboard & contents	12.00
To	1 Looking glass	.12
To	1 Bureau	9.00
To	1 Walnut Table	4.50
To	2 Large Dishes	.75
To	1 Set of Cups, saucers teapot & 5 tumblers	.75
To	1 Bed stead & furniture	9.00
To	1 Bed stead & furniture	9.00
To	1 Flax wheel	1.75
To	1 Candle stick	.25
To	2 empty barrels	.50
To	1 wine cask & brandy	7.20
To	2 old boxes	.25
To	1 keg vinegar & vinegar	.75
To	1 empty barrel & 3 empty tubs	.25
To	1 Lard tub & measuring tub	.50
To	2 Mowing scythes	1.00
To	1 Coulter & Stock	.37 ½
To	2 Shovel ploughs & stocks	.50
To	1 Singletree 2 Clivises pins hand axe, etc.	.75
To	1 grindstone & Crank	2.50
To	1 Drawing knife & Auger	.62 ½
To	2 pole axes	1.25
To	1 par of steelyards & J plain	1.25
To	1 Wheat pan	3.00
To	1 Cutting knife	.25
To	1 Wheat sieve	.50
To	2 hogsheads at barn	1.00
To	1 still & worm	10.00

		111.82
To 3 hay & pitchfork		1.00
To 5 Bee stands		2.50
To 1 Lot of empty gums		.25
To 1 Spade		.50
To 2 pots 3 ovens 2 lids & hooks		1.50
To 2 pot Racks		1.00
To 1 Shovel & tong		1.00
To 1 Friing Pan		.50
To 1 Water pail & noggin		.37
To 1 Square table		.25
To 1 Stone churn		.75
To 1 Jug		.06
To 1 Coffee Mill		.25
To 1 barrel & chest upstairs		.50
To 1 par of fire Irons		.75
To 1 sow & shoats		5.00
To 1 Smoothing Iron		.50
To 1 set of plough gear		1.80
To 1 Lock chain		.30
To 1 par stretchers		.51
To 1 Dagon plough		2.00
To 4 Shoats first choice		2.05
To 4 Shoats second choice		2.00
To 1 White pided cow		7.80
To 2 Empty barrels		.12
		145.08

"List of property sale of the property of Michael Debo Sen. Decease 8 December 1843

To 1 Coulter	Samuel Martin	.25	
To 1 half bushel measure	Samuel Martin	.14	
To 1 set of knives & forks	Samuel Martin	1.30	1.69
To 1 Coulter	Henry Boyce	.26	
To 1 Dagon plough	Henry Boyce	.75	1.01
To Iron tooth harrow	Wm. Hare	.40	.40
To 1 foot Adze	Christopher Morgan	.60	
To 1 Mattock	Christopher Morgan	.58	
To 1 fifth chain	Christopher Morgan	.75	1.93
To 1 Collar Backban & traces	Michael J. Blankenship	1.55	
To 1 Singletree Clivis & lap ring	Michael J. Blankenship	.25	
To 1 Looking glass	Michael J. Blankenship	.50	
To 5 gallons Brandy at 65 cts	Michael J. Blankenship	3.25	
To 5 gallons Brandy at 67 cts	Michael J. Blankenship	3.35	

To 5 gallons Brandy at 62 cts	Michael J. Blankenship	3.10	
To 1 Barrel	Michael J. Blankenship	.37 ½	12.37 ½
To 1 hammer & trowel	Ora B. Kennet	.25	
To 1 Iron Wedge	James Ayres	.28	
To 2 Reap Hooks	Wesley Mattox	.14	
To 1 Breed Hook	Wesley Mattox	.06 ¼	
To 1 grid Iron & round stave	Wesley Mattox	.12 ½	
To 2 Coffee Mills	Wesley Mattox	.06	
To 1 Still not appraised	Wesley Mattox	10.00	
To 3 Winsor chairs	Wesley Mattox	1.55	11.93 ¾
To 1 Handrow	Alfred Tatae	.50	.50
To 1 Large chisel	T. G. Hubbard	.07	
To 1 cross cut saw	T. G. Hubbard	4.15	
To 1 arm chair	T. G. Hubbard	.40	4.62
To 1 Singletree & stretchers	Henry H. Murphy	.06 ¼	.06 ¼
To 1 Large Jointer	Lindsay Arthur	.50	.50
To 1 Cut reel	Clifton C Peters	.60	.60
To 1 Lot of old irons	Jno. M. Ayres	.06 ¼	.06 ¼
To 1 Steel trap & windlass	Ally Payne	.27	.27
To 1 tin Bucket `	Michael Debo, Jr.	.90	
To 1 hire of negro girl Elendor	Michael Debo, Jr.	.55	1.05
To 1 half gallon pot & funnel	Wesley Hackworth	.25	.25
To 1 Cotton wheel	James Franklin	1.75	1.75
To 2 Empty barrels	Elijah Swain	.10	.10
To 1 Old Stove	Milton Franklin	8.20	8.20
To 1 Smooth bore rifle	Daniel P. Debo	4.55	4.55
To 1 Parcel of shingles	Thomas Phelps	1.65	
To 1 Red Heifer	Thomas Phelps	7.00	
To 1 red bull	Thomas Phelps	3.05	
To 1 old cow	Thomas Phelps	6.75	18.45
To 3 sheep 1 choice	Henry H. Mixby	3.70	
To 3 Sheep 2 choice	Henry H. Mixby	3.45	7.15
To 5 gallons of Brandy at 57 cts	Meredith Ashwill	2.85	
To 3 ½ gallons of Brandy at 57 cts	Meredith Ashwill	1.99 ½	
To 1 old waggon not appraised	Meredith Ashwill	15.55	20.39 ½
To 1 Dollar Left in money	Michael Debo Jun.	1.00	1.00
			99.38 ¼

Add Catharine Debo's purchases   145.08

                                                                      244.46 ¼

I William C. Kasey do hereby certify that I acted as clerk at the sale of the perishable estate of Michael Debo decd. Made by Taliaferro G. Hubbard his administrator on the 8th day of December 1843, at the late residence of said decedent on a credit of 12 months & that the foregoing is a correct list thereof.

W C Kasey

At a Court held for Bedford County the 22nd day of July 1844 This List of sales of the estate of Michael Debo Snr. Deceased was produced in Court & ordered to be recorded.

Teste   R. C. Mitchell   C.B.C.

Debo Michaels
List of sales
1844 July 22nd
Returned & ord.
Recorded page 504
Book 11 Exd.

* * * * * *

The children of Michael and Katharine Debo are as follows:

1. HENRY, born circa 1796-97 probably in Pittsylvania County, Virginia. He was first married Dec. 14, 1830,[34] in Bedford County, Virginia, to Elizabeth Kennott, daughter of John Kennott. She died circa 1832, probably in childbirth or shortly thereafter. Henry then married Malinda H Turner, daughter of Elijah Turner, on March 23, 1833,[35] in Bedford County. Henry died in 1837[36] in Bedford County (burial site uncertain). He had one child by Elizabeth and two by Malinda.

2. JOHN, born April 11, 1799,[37] in either Pittsylvania County or Bedford County, Virginia. He married Jane Nichols Dec. 21, 1830,[38] in Bedford County. She was the daughter of Jesse and Sarah Field Nichols, was born April 20, 1809,[39] in Bedford County, and died May 22, 1873,[40] in the same county with burial in the Debo family cemetery. After her death John went to Missouri where son Reed lived; he died Aug. 29, 1878,[41] in Cooper County, Missouri, and was buried at Clark's Chapel Cemetery across the Missouri River in Howard County. He and Jane had ten children.

3. ELIZABETH, born circa 1801 in Bedford County. She was married Feb. 6, 1816,[42] in Bedford County to Abraham Blankenship, born in 1795,[43] the son of Abraham and Susan Wiatt Blanken-

ship. Elizabeth died sometime prior to 1850. She and Abraham had possibly seven children.

4. SALLY, born circa 1803, in Bedford County. She was married Jan. 26, 1818,[44] in Bedford County to Lawson Blankenship, a brother of Abraham. Nothing further is known about Sally and Lawson except the U. S. Census of 1820 shows one son and one daughter, both under ten years of age.

5. MARGARET (Peggy), born circa 1805 in Bedford County. She was married Dec. 20, 1824,[45] in Bedford County to John Rollins Saunders, who was born in 1801[46] in Campbell County, Virginia, and died April 13, 1884,[47] in Franklin County, Virginia. After Margaret's death in 1844 in Franklin County, John R. Saunders was married Aug. 4, 1845,[48] to Nancy Leftwich of Bedford County, daughter of Sarah C. Leftwich. Margaret and John had eleven children.

6. VALENTINE, born circa 1807. He was married on July 23, 1832,[49] in Bedford County to Mary Ann Bishop, Jonathan Bishop surety. Nothing else is known about what became of Valentine and Mary Ann. There are no mentions of them in Bedford County records.

7. DANIEL PERRY, born circa 1809 in Bedford County. He was never married. Daniel died Jan. 3, 1850, and was buried in the Old Hubbard Cemetery on Body Camp Creek in Bedford County.[50]

8. MARY, born May 7, 1810,[51] in Bedford County. She was married Nov. 7, 1836,[52] in Bedford County, and was probably buried beside her husband, Taliaferro Graves Hubbard, in the Old Hubbard Cemetery. Taliaferro G. Hubbard was born Sept. 25, 1800,[53] in Louisa County, Virginia, and died May 7, 1850,[54] in Bedford County. He was the son of John and Elizabeth Hubbard, who settled in Bedford County in 1811.[55] Mary and Taliaferro had six children, and he had four children by a previous marriage.

9. MICHAEL, JR., born in 1811[56] in Bedford County. He married Wilmoth Waldron Leftwich Nov. 15, 1836,[57] the ceremony being performed by William Leftwich. Michael died Aug. 19, 1883,[58] in Bedford County and was presumably buried in the Debo family cemetery. Wilmoth Leftwich was born in 1819[59] in Franklin County, Virginia, the daughter of Joel and Sarah C.

Adams Lefrwich. She died March 22, 1894,[60] in Bedford County, and was buried beside her husband. Michael and Wilmoth had twelve children.

10. SAMUEL, born in 1813 in Bedford County. He was married in the same county Sept. 26, 1842,[61] to Lucy Saunders, daughter of John Saunders, and died in April 1844,[62] in Franklin County. Lucy was born in 1818 (probably in Franklin County) and died in May 1850[63] in the same county. Samuel and Lucy had a daughter, Sophia.

A. Henry Debo

It is worthwhile for anyone to have behind him a
few generations of honest hard working ancestry.
--Marquard

Henry Debo, oldest son of Michael and Katharine Debo, was born either in 1796 or 1797, probably in Pittsylvania County, Virginia (it wasn't until 1799 when Michael bought his first land in Bedford County). He was married in Bedford County December 14, 1830,[1] to Elizabeth Kennott (Kennett), daughter of John Kennott. Elizabeth died in 1832, probably childbirth or shortly thereafter. They had one daughter, Elvira, who was born in either 1831 or 1832 and she must have died sometime after January 1845. [The only mention of Elvira is found in a list of the heirs of Michael Debo, Sr. (her grandfather, in a deed dated January 25, 1845,[2] in which she is listed first in order of the children of Henry Debo.]

After the death of Elizabeth, Henry was married on March 23, 1833,[3] in Bedford County to Malinda H. Turner, daughter of Elijah Turner. They had two children: Melissa Frances and Lodowick (Lod) Columbus, both of whom married, lived and died in Bedford County.

Henry Debo died prior to November 1, 1837, in Bedford County and was probably buried in the family cemetery. Mention is made in Bedford County Court Order books that he qualified as a 2nd Lieutenant in the 1st Regiment of Virginia militia, and that he also was appointed a surveyor. Before Henry's death, John Debo, his eldest brother, was named administrator of his estate and appointed to settle his accounts. Malinda H. Debo was qualified by the court as guardian of the orphans of Henry Debo, Melissa F. and Lodowick C. Debo (no mention is made of Elvira).[4]

After Henry's death, Malinda was married September 30, 1839,[5] to Washington Hackworth.

Following is a list of the sale of Henry Debo's "perishable property" held November 1, 1837.[6]

"November 1, 1837, amount and list of perishable property sold of Henry Debo, deed, decd. By John Debo admr. Of same.

Franklin Haden	To 1 set of Black smith tools	20.00
James M. Goad	To 4 Hilling hoes	1.12 ½
Martin Purdue	To 2 Iron wedges & Lot of old irons	.75
James M. Rader	To 1 hand saw Drawing knife & china	.55
Michael Debo Sen.	To 1 shovel Spade & fork	1.00
John Hall	To 1 Sithe & cradle	.60
Taliaferro G. Hubbard	To 1 two horse plough	2.30
Nathaniel Morgan	To 1 one horse plough	1.60
Michael Debo Sen.	To 1 shovel plough & stock	1.00
Nathaniel Morgan	To 1 Coulter & stock	.40
Joel Hart	To 1 shovel plough & stock	.50
Michael Debo Sen.	To 1 Still cap etc	20.35
Michael Debo Sen.	To 2 whiskey Barrelsw	.80
Elijah C. Cundiff	To 1 Apple mill etc.	1.00
Martin Purdue	To 1 Blade stack of fodder	2.00
John Debo	To 1 Blade stack of fodder	1.50
Michael Debo Sen.	To l Blade stack of fodder	2.00
Burnet Scott	To 1 Blade stack of fodder	2.25
Michael Debo Sen.	To 1 Blade stack of fodder	2.60
Michael Debo Sen.	To 1 work Bull	14.50
Thomas Martin	To 1 horse cart	3.05
James M. Goad	To 1 Ladle & fleshford	.30
Malinda Debo	To 3 Crocks	.50
Michael Debo Jun.	To shovel & tongs	1.10
James M. Goad	To 1 coopers axe croze & Jointer	.60
Thomas Plymale	To 1 pole axe	.85
Elijah C. Cundiff	To 1 pole axe	.40
Charles Holland	To 1 pole axe	.40
Wm. Hackworth	To 1 hand axe	.75
Perry Debo	To 1 lot of tin ware	.05
Abram Pullin	To 1 wheat Sive	.75
Malinda Debo	To 1 Lot of water vessels	.25
James Anthony	To 1 oven skillet & Baker	1.80
		86.62 ½
Malinda Debo	To 1 Large Pot	1.70
Thomas Martin	To 1 small pot hooks & chains	1.45
Michael Debo Jun.	To 1 Loom	4.40
Thomas Phelps	To 1 Lot of old Barrels	.92 ½
Henry White	To 1 Meal sifter & tray	.25
Franklin Haden	To House of tobacco	10.10
Wm. Leftwich	To House of tobacco	24.00

Abram Pullin	To 1 small calf	1.40
Garlent Morgan	To 1 stack of oats by the head	6.57
Wash W. Rees	To 1 hogshead of oats by the Bush	7.28 ½
Wm. Leftwich	To 1 parcel of straw	2.05
Michael Debo Sen.	To 1 house of chalf	.50
Daniel Tompkins	To Top fodder shucks etc.	9.00
Malinda Debo	To 2 first choice of fatted hogs	6.50
Malinda Debo	To 2 second choice of fatted hogs	5.25
John D. Carter	To 3 last choice of fatted hogs	5.80
Wm. Arthur	To 2 fourth choice of fatted hogs	4.90
Wm. I. Lukin	To 3 last choice of fatted hogs	5.35
Malinda Debo	To 1 Red Cow	10.20
Spicer Howel	To 1 Pided Cow	9.00
Burnet Scott	To 1 heifer Cow	5.30
Richard J. Phelps	To 6 sheep $1.95 a piece	11.70
Abram Pullin	To 1 set of Plough gear	.69
Daniel Tompkins	To 1 set of Plough gear	2.00
John Debo	To 1 set of 0x gear	.50
John F. Nichols	To 1 Cutting Vox etc.	.80
Malinda Debo	To 4 small shoats	2.80
John D. Carter	To 1 Blasé face horse	22.00
Malinda Debo	To 1 Sorrel Mare	25.00
Elijah C. Cundiff	To 1 Sorrel Colt	11.00
Abram Pullin	To 5 bushels of wheat @ 1.08	5.40
Malinda Debo	To 5 bushels of wheat @1.06	5.30
Garlent Morgan	To 2 Jugs	.30
Thomas Martin	To 1 set of shoe making tools	.95
Abram Pullin	To 1 pair of Chains nippers etc.	.41
		297.46 ½
Michael Debo, Sen	To 2 whiskey Barrels	.27
Elijah C. Cundiff	To 1 Saddle & sheep skin	2.70
Nathaniel Morgan	To 35 gallons of cider 9 ½ cts per	3.32 ½
Daniel Tompkins	To 5 Barrels of corn @ 2.15 per	10.75
Martin Purdue	To 5 Barrels of corn @ 2.15 per	10.75
Daniel Tompkins	To 5 Barrels of corn @ 2.10 per	10.50
Daniel Tompkins	To 5 Barrels of corn @ 2.15 per	10.75
Martin Purdue	To 5 Barrels of corn @ 2.15 per	10.75
Daniel Tompkins	To 5 Barrels of corn @ 2.20 per	11.00
Malinda Debo	To 1 Cupboard	8.00
Malinda Debo	To 1 Bed stid & furniture	22.00
John F. Nichols	To 1 Dressing table	.90
Malinda Debo	To 1 Looking glass	.35

Malinda Debo	To 1 Large Chest	.50
Malinda Debo	To 1 Cotton wheel	1.10
Leftwich Ayer	To 1 Clock Reel	.01
John F. Nichols	To 1 Flax Wheel	1.00
Wash W. Reese	To 1 small table	.12 ½
James Anthony	To 1 shot gun & rigin	6.50
Elijah C. Cundiff	To 1 Sword & Apaulette	2.00
Justice Hancock	To 1 Mattaxe	.06 ¼
James M. Goad	To 1 Coffee mill & Bottle	.35
Malinda Debo	To Lot of earthen ware	.12 ½
Martin Purdue	To 1 lot of earthen ware	.18 ¾
Malinda Debo	To 1 set knives & forks	.25
Malinda Debo	To 1 Dish	.06
Booker Smith	To 1 Large Jug	.06 ¼
John D. Carter	To 1 half gallon cup	.06 ¼
Joel Hart	To 1 Lot 1 Coulter 1 sythe etc.	.55
Richard J. Phelps	To stretchers singletrees etc.	.70
Robert Overstreet	To 1 Clivic etc.	.20
James Anthony	To Stable	.55
Booker Smith	To 1 Lot of Books	.40
Henry White	To 1 Stole	.21
Booker Smith	To 4 Chairs	1.10
Malinda Debo	To 3 Chairs	.37 ½
		426.54

John Debo Adr. Of Henry Debo

At a Court held for Bedford County at the courthouse the 22nd day of January 1838. This list of sales of the estate of Henry Debo deceased, was produced in court and ordered to be recorded.

Teste   R. C. Mitchell CBC

Debo, Henry's
List of sales
1838 January 22 d
Returned & ordered
To be recorded

Melissa Frances Debo, oldest child of Henry and Malinda Debo, was born circa 1835 and was married June 10, 1855,[7] in Bedford County to Samuel D. Patterson, born in 1839. They had at least two known children: Mary H., born February 15, 1857;[8] and William C., born December 22, 1858.[9] No other information and research has been obtained on the children of Melissa and Samuel.

Lodowick Columbus (Lod) Debo was born November 13, 1836,[10] in Bedford County. He was married in the same county to Elizabeth Mitchell, born September 7, 1861, in Bedford County, on October 24, 1857.[11] At the outbreak of the War Between the States, he enlisted in the 28th Virginia Infantry (known as the "Patty Lane Rifles") July 27, 1861, at Cub Run and was in Co. D. He was promoted from private to corporal August 30, 1864, and to sergeant in December 1864. Lod was wounded in action at Hatcher's Run toward the end of the war in 1865.[12] Lod Debo died April 21, 1913,[13] of what the Bedford County death records called "tubercular lung." He was preceded in death by his wife, Sallie Elizabeth, April 4, 1910,[14] and both were buried in Parrish Chapel Cemetery, Chamblissburg, Virginia. On one of my trips to Virginia I was visiting with Lillian Debo Ellis, granddaughter of Lodowick Debo, and as we were talking about our kinfolk, she told me that as a thirteen-year-old girl when he died she could remember him and also remembered his death. She described him as a "rather curious old gentleman."

Lodowick and Sarah Elizabeth Debo had the following children:
1. WILLIAM HENRY (Whit), born Sep. 25, 1858; married Dec.23, 1891, to Sallie James Feather, who was born Dec. 31, 1864, and died Jan. 27, 1903. Whit died Aug. 31, 1929, and both are buried in the Beaver Dam Baptist Church Cemetery, Bedford County. They had five children.
2. LAURISTON (Brud), born Nov. 9, 1859; married Dec. 8, 1897, to Dossie Payne, who was born Sept. 18, 1870, and died July 17, 1941. Lauriston used the "Deboe" spelling of the name (the only one in this family who did), died Nov. 22, 1928, and is buried in the Parrish Chapel Methodist Church Cemetery, Chamblissburg, VA. They had three daughters.
3. IDA LELIER, born Oct. 30, 1862, and died Nov. 6, 1938. She was never married and is also buried in Parrish Chapel Cemetery.
4. JAMES CARLTON (Jim), born Jan. 18, 1865, and died Feb. 24, 1934. He was postmaster for Jimbo Post Office and a partner with Whit in operation of Debo's Store in the Diamond Hill community. Jim is buried in Parrish Chapel Cemetery, and was never married.
5. RICHARD PERRY (Dick born Nov. 18, and died Oct. 21, 1922. He was never married and is buried in Parrish Chapel Cemetery.

6. LENA RIVERS, born July 8, 1870; married Nov. 27, 1912, to Victor Murry Masincup, who was born June 5, 1886. She died Nov. 7, 1942. They had one son.
7. FANNIE E., born Sept. 14, 1872; married March 16, 1898, to Frank J. Huddleston, who was born Jan. 20, 1868, and died Feb. 9, 1916. Fannie died April 3, 1940. They had three sons.

The Debo's Store (originally Debo's General Merchandise) was established in 1857 and was owned and operated by the family for 125 consecutive years. It was located at the intersection of Va. Rts. 655 and 616 about four and half miles west of Rt. 122 in the Diamond Hill community west of Moneta, VA. Lodowick Debo's son, Russell and his wife, Verna Minter Debo, ran the store till age and ill health caused its closure in 1982. In June 1992 Carl and Christine Brodt from New York bought the store, renovated and restored the old store building, and reopened it on July 4 of that year as the Diamond Hill General Store.[15]

I well remember the first time I went to Debo's Store. It was on my first trip to Bedford County, Virginia, in June1967. I had never met any of the relatives and had no idea whether any were still in Virginia or where they might live. I stopped at Hendrick's Store on Rt. 122 and inquired if anyone there knew of any Debos in the area. I was told to take Rt. 655, go west about four and a half miles, and I would come to a Debo's Store. Following these directions, I arrived at the store and went in. There was no one at the front, but a lady was at the back sitting there with a bonnet on shelling peas. I walked up to her and inquired of her if any Debos were around; she seemed rather hesitant to answer. After all, I was a rank stranger, and in those days strangers in a community were looked upon with suspicion – at least until their business was stated. I told the lady my name and explained that I was a Debo from Texas looking for possible kinfolk in Bedford County since that was the home of my great-grandfather, who had left there after the War Between the States. When I stated that I was a Debo the woman perked up considerably and we began a nice visit trying to rake up kin. You see, the lady was Verna Minter Debo, wife of Russell Debo, owner of the store, who was away at the time. We, at that time, were unable to tie our families together – mainly because we didn't have the information that would span the gap. Verna and I afterward in later years often laughed together about our first hesitant, nervous meeting.

Many subsequent visits to the store and the community only ce-

mented a close and loving relationship with the Debo relatives, especially as I met other members of the extended families who were alive
at that time. We also learned that Russell's great-grandfather, Henry
Debo, and my great-great-grandfather, John Debo, were brothers –
the two oldest sons of Michael Debo, Sr., who first settled in Bedford
County in 1799. Russell Debo's grandfather, Lodowick Debo, and my
great-grandfather Cornelius Debo, along with three of his brothers –
Reed, Dabney, and Thomas – all had served together in the 28th Virginia Regiment during the War Between the States.

In a little building just west of the store and adjacent to it was once
housed the Jimbo Post Office. It had opened in 1889 and was named
by a combination of the name of James (Jim) Debo [Jim(De)bo], the
first postmaster and brother of Whit Debo. The post office closed in
1903 and the mail was transferred to Moneta. Tradition has it that the
building was later used to store feed – and caskets too![16] The post office
building still stands today, along with an old structure across the road
called the "ice house" in which ice was stored in the long ago. I can
fondly remember sitting on the porch visiting with Grover and Lillian
Debo Ellis, looking across the road (Rt. 616), seeing and talking about
the old ice house and how it was used.

I remember an amusing incident that occurred on another later
visit to Virginia and Debo's Store. After driving up and stopping by
the side of the store, I walked up the steps to the front porch (we used
to call them "galleries" in Texas!) where I noticed Russell Debo sitting
there reading a newspaper. I approached and spoke to him. He never even looked up from his paper but uninterestedly kept reading. I
asked him if his name was Debo. He sort of grunted an affirmative
"yes," and kept reading. I then stated, "Well, I'm a Debo too, and I've
come all the way from Texas to see you!" At that, he looked up, began
grinning, and, as we used to say in Texas, "had a fit" as he said, "Come
on in and sit a spell." And we had a great visit!

I also remember well the last time I saw Russell. As I went out from
Bedford to Diamond Hill community to say goodbye before leaving
for Texas and home, I found him lying on his bed and not feeling well
at all. A few years before, the store had been robbed and Russell had
been beaten severely by an assailant. Although he finally recovered
somewhat from the attack, his health was never good thereafter. In my
own mind as I bid him farewell, I surmised it was for the last time. He
died the following month in August 1978.

As I was about to leave for home, Russell's sister, Lillian Debo Ellis, came across the road (VA. Rt. 655) with a sack filled with "goodies" for me to eat on the way back to Texas. Inside were some leftover biscuits – made from "scratch" and not canned! – a jar of freshly made strawberry preserves; and a large chunk of what Lillian called "sad cake." It was a pound cake that had "fallen" and didn't stand up naturally. As she gave it to me, she said: " Grover [her husband] said that you wouldn't want these old leftover biscuits and this old 'sad' cake, but I told him I was going to give them to you anyway." I replied, "That's just all Grover knows about me. You see, I've always loved to eat cake when it has fallen!" And did I have a feast on the way back to Texas! For breakfast I would split those biscuits, lay them on top of the toaster I carried along during the trip, daub some oleo on the warmed biscuits and smear some of those strawberry preserves on them – well, you get the idea! They were a fabulous repast. Upon arriving home I called back to Lillian to let the Virginia folks know I had made it okay, and I told her the biscuits and "sad" cake made it all the way to Texas – not in the sack but in my stomach!

Lillian had also given me some tobacco seed and flax seed in little bottles on another trip to Virginia. I was never, however, able to get the seed to sprout. I was so anxious to see if I could grow some tobacco and flax plants in Texas as my great-grandfather many, many years ago had grown some Virginia tobacco on our old home place in Burnet County, Texas. The bottles had holes punched in the tops, but I guess the seed had been stored too long. I even asked my great-aunt Jewel Debo to try to get some seed up (she was a good hand at doing such), but she could not get them to sprout either. I really hated it.

1. The children of Whit and Sallie Debo (all born in Bedford County, Virginia) were:[17]

    A. MAMIE GLADYS, born Jan. 11, 1893. She was married June 2, 1928, to Russell Davis McLain, son of William G. (Billy) and Jemmie Maxey McLain, born May 10, 1887, and died Aug. 14, 1978. Mamie died Feb. 16, 1980. She and Russell were members of Diamond Hill Methodist Church and are buried in the Diamond Hill church cemetery.

    B. WILLIAM RUSSELL, born April 21, 1895. He was married Dec. 26, 1931, to Verna Lee Minter, daughter of William Morrison Minter, born Mar. 22, 1868, and died Sept. 22, 1936, and Emma Gilbert McLain Minter, born Aug. 25, 1901, and died

Children and Descendants of William Henry Debo
Standing (L to R) Mrs. Russell (Verna) Debo; Mrs. Grover (Lillian) Ellis; Grover Ellis; Mrs. Harry (Lena) Debo; Harry Debo; Mrs. Jess (Lizzie) Minter
Middle Row Seated (L to R) Russell Debo; Mrs. Russell (Mamie) McLain; Russell McLain; Jess Minter
Front Row (L to R) Ann Debo; Roy Debo, Jr.; Mrs. Roy (Marlene) Debo; Roy Debo, Sr.

Jan. 22, 1994. Russell died Aug. 29, 1978. He and Verna operated Debo's Store until 1982. They were members of the Diamond Hill Methodist Church and are buried in the church cemetery.

C. HARRY JENNINGS, born Sept.25, 1896. He was married on July 16, 1923, to Lena Bell Hannabass, born May 23, 1898, and died Jan. 12, 1985. They lived in Roanoke in later years and had a son, William Roy Debo, who was born May 6, 1934, and lives in Roanoke. Roy was married Dec. 30, 1952, to Marlene Stevens, who was born Dec. 22, 1933. They were later divorced. Roy and Marlene had two children: William Roy, Jr., born April 13, 1954; and Ann Stevens, born Feb. 14, 1957. Harry Died April 22, 1973.

D. MARY ELIZABETH (Lizzie), born Dec. 30, 1897. She was married Aug. 17, 1932, to Jesse Carlton Minter, who was born Sept. 7, 1905, and died Dec. 11, 1981. He was a brother of Verna Lee Minter Debo and a son of William Morrison and Emma McLain Minter. Lizzie died Sept. 3, 1984. She and Jesse were members of Parrish Chapel Methodist Church at Chamblissburg, and were buried in Beaver Dam Baptist Church Cemetery.

E. LILLIAN MOZELLE, born May 9, 1900. She was married May 21, 1930, to Grover Lester Ellis, son of Zacaria T. Ellis, born Aug. 18, 1856, and died June 28, 1940, and Sara Basham Ellis, born Nov. 29, 1957, and died Jan 3, 1953. Lillian died Jan. 20, 1994. She and Grover were members of Diamond Hill Methodist church and are buried in the church cemetery.

Of the children of Whit and Sallie Debo, I met or was aquainted with Russell and Verna Debo, Lena Hannabass Debo, Lizzie Debo Minter, and Grover and Lillian Ellis. They were dear prople and I cherish the memory of each of them. They are all gone now. On my last trip to Virginia in July 1992, I visited Lillian Debo Ellis and Verna Minter Debo in Woodhaven Nursing Home at Montvale, Virginia. With their deaths within two days of each other in 1994 the chapter of the Debos in Bedford County closed as they were the last remaining members of the family in the county. The presence of the Debos in Bedford County covered a span of 195 years. None of Whit and Sallie Debo's children had offsprings except Harry.

2. The children of Lauriston and Dossie Deboe were:

A. WINNIE, born Oct. 13, 1898, and died June 30, 1990, and buried at Parrish Chapel.

B. LOLA F., born in 1901. She married a Mr. Tuck June 20, 1925, and they had one daughter, Peggy Sue.

C. MARY W., born in 1905. She married Joseph Crute June 20, 1925, and they had two children: Joseph Mark Crute, born May 20, 1927, and died May 21, 1927; and Joseph Crute, Jr. The Crutes lived in Washington, D.C.

6. The son of Lena Rivers Debo and Victor Murry Masincup was:

C. DONALD MURRY, born Aug. 8, 1914. He was married Oct. 11, 1945 to Maude Richardson.

7. The children of Fannie E. Debo and Frank Huddleston were:

A. GUY, born Sept, 1900, and died Aug. 15, 1972. He was married Aug. 14, 1926, To Geneva Robertson.

B. CURRAY (Bill), (no other information obtained).

C. DONALD BERKLEY, born September 13, 1909, and died Nov. 24, 1935.

B. John Debo

If I should live to be
The last leaf on the tree
In the spring
Then you may smile
As I do now
At the old forsaken bough
Where I cling.
        -- Oliver Wendell Holmes

[There will be more information on this branch of the Michael Debo family than all others because of availability and personal knowledge; so, I make no apology for the preponderance of emphasis.]

John Debo was the second son of Michael Debo, Sr., and Katharine Saunders Debo, and my great-great-grandfather. He was born April 11 1799,[1] eighteen years after George Washington defeated Cornwallis at Yorktown, Virginia, October 19, 1781, and eleven years after the U.S. Constitution was ratified in 1788 by enough states to form our country. His birth probably occurred in Pittsylvania County, Virginia (though this is uncertain), since father Michael did not purchase his first parcel of land in neighboring Bedford County until the fall of that year.

John was raised on the old Debo plantation on Goose and Rockcastle creeks in the southern part of Bedford County. At age 31 he was married December 21, 1830,[2] to Jane Nichols, born April 20, 1809,[3] who was 21 at the time. Jane, daughter of Jesse Nichols and Sarah Field(s) Nichols, was a Yuletide bride as were several in the Debo family. [Jesse Nichols was born June 15, 1776,[4] and died October 8, 1830,[5] in Bedford County. Sarah was born September 30, 1782,[6] and died May 8, 1858,[7] in Tennessee.] John and Jane had ten children – six sons and four daughters: Reed, Burton, Dabney, Thomas, Cornelius, and Bruce; Martha, Sallie, Bettie, and Mollie.

John Debo was a farmer, and also operated a still, making brandy for his neighbors as "custom work." He made fine hats of beaver pelts, and there was a good demand for his products. He was also a

John Debo   Jane Nichols and Mollie Debo

weaver, producing fine cloth on a loom for the public. The John Debos
were Methodists and attended the old Providence church down present-day Virginia Rt. 737 from the home place.

With the coming of the War Between the States and the secession
of Virginia from the Union April 17, 1861, five sons of John and Jane
entered the Confederate services – four of them to serve in the "Patty
Lane Rifles," Co. G, 28th Regiment, Virginia Infantry, under Captains
Augustus L. Minter and Richard Wright; one son to serve in Co. B,
18th Regiment, from adjoining Pittsylvania County.[8] The year 1862
brought the first of several great sorrows to the family. While their
brothers were away from home in Pickett's Division of Gen. Robert E.
Lee's Army of Northern Virginia, defending their Virginia home from
the invading Yankees, three of the Debo children were struck down
by what was termed "typhus fever"; I am more inclined, however, to
think it was typhoid fever since the deaths occurred within ten days
in the wintry month of January. Bettie Jane died January 12, at age 12;
John Bruce on January 20, at age 9; and Martha Prudence January 22,
at age 25.[9] They were all buried in the family graveyard north of the
Debo plantation home.

The next year, 1863, more sadness invaded the Debo home as word was received that son Dabney had been "lost at Gettysburg" on July 3.[10] He had participated in Pickett's charge against the center of the Union lines at the "bloody angle," and it was reported that the last anyone saw of him was as he stood on the Northern breastworks waving the banner of the Old South at what would later be termed the "high-water mark of the Confederacy." But his would not be the only loss for the family to endure that year, for shortly thereafter on July 15 Gillie Jane,[11] son Reed's little daughter, died and was buried in the Heptinstall graveyard. She had been named Gillie after her grandmother Heptinstall and Jane after her grandmother Debo. Reed Debo, John and Jane's oldest son, had been wounded and captured at Gettysburg and did not know of the death of his infant daughter until he came home after being incarcerated in a Yankee prison. She was less than two years old when she died.

The end of the war brought still more hardships for the Debos as well as the rest of the citizens of the Old Dominion state. Ravaged by the horrors of war, Virginia and much of the South lay prostrate to the specters of starvation, destruction of property, financial ruin, not to mention the loss of so many of her loyal sons. The other Debo men returned home from the war: Reed from captivity had recovered from his wound at Gettysburg; Thomas from ill health and time spent in the hospital while in service; and Cornelius, wounded in the foot at White Oak Road during the last few days of the war to face a slow, painful recovery after walking all the way home using his rifle for a crutch. Burton, the other son, had returned to his family in Pittsylvania County, but only lived two years before dying May 13, 1867,[12] at an early age of thirty-three, leaving a wife and young son behind.

With the conditions of the times presenting few opportunities for the Debo men, the year 1869 found Reed, Thomas, and Cornelius leaving their home state for Missouri where they settled near Boonville. The next year Cornelius went back to Virginia to bring Reed's family – his wife, Mary Jane; his children, Lee, Martha (Mattie), and Luther – and sister, Sallie, to Missouri. This left only John and Jane, along with their youngest daughter, Mollie, at their Bedford County home.

On May 22, 1873,[13] Jane Debo died at age 64 and was buried in the family graveyard alongside her three children. About 1875 John, along with daughter Mollie, pulled up stakes and left his home to also come to Missouri where he joined the rest of his family who had preceded him there, making his home with his oldest son, Reed P. Debo. The infirmities of age began to take their toll on John. He planned to go to Texas to visit his children who had moved there (Thomas, Cornelius, Sallie, and Mollie), but declining health and finally death overcame him on August 29, 1878,[14] at the age 79 and he was buried in Clark's Chapel Cemetery northwest of Boonville in Howard County.

In a letter from Reed to his brother Cornelius, Reed gives an account of John's last days:

Boonville Mo. Sept 8th 1878

Dear Bro.

I have in the first place to inform you of the death of Father. In the spring & summer he had a few chills which I soon stoped & about the 1st of Aug. he had some sort of fever for 3 days before we could check it & then he never regained his strength so as to get around & soon got helpless. So on Thursday night Aug. 29th he died at 10 o'clock. Soon after dark he became restless & tried to talk but could not & kept trying to change his cover pillow or anything he even thought he could reach. Mr. Davis & I who were sitting by him & half an hour before he died he got quiet & seemed to be resting but I soon saw it was death he spoke no more & died without a struggle in a few minutes. Several neighbors were here to attend to the usual duties & I started Lee at once to Jim Turners to get him to go to the Chapel to have the grave dug as he knew the place but he was sick in bed, so at sun up I started Lee to Jim Laughon & Tom Whitten & Ben Nance. Jim was also sick Tom gone to fayette Ben had started to Boonville but sent 2 hands on & Jno McGhee went from Whittens & he and Lee found the right place & had the grave ready by 4 o'clock. I got a nicer coffin than any of the family have ever had before him & buried at 5 that evening. Several went from this side & a very good attendance from Howard Co. I buried him at an expence all told of about 24 dollars. I mean the money expence...

Lewis Debo, grandson of Reed Debo, in a letter dated July 19, 1976, mentioned visiting his uncle, Grover Debo, youngest and only living son of Reed Debo at that time, in a nursing home at Boonville. Lewis asked him if Reed ever visited relatives in Texas. Grover replied that Reed took father John there for a visit shortly before John's death. This seems most unlikely due to statements made in the following letter written by John himself to son Cornelius in Burnet, Texas, shortly before John's demise. I was told by Aunt Jennie Debo Fisher, Cornelius' oldest daughter, that Reed made a trip to Texas, but it was after John's death when Cornelius' second son Eppa was a small infant [Eppa was born in January 1881.]. I asked her what time of year it was and she said the "corn was in the tassel" –about May or June. Grover's memory must have failed him when he stated Reed brought John with him to Texas.

John wrote this letter to his son Cornelius about a month before his death:

John Debo
(Shortly before his death)

Cooper County Missouri   July 26, 1878
Dear son,

I have bin in bad health ever since I wrote last I have been chilling some,but have not had any for three weeks past yet I am weak and feeble cant do any hard labour. I was not able to help in harvest neither at threshing, but now both them are through with and the wheat sold about twelve hundred bushels of the crop. I am at this time able to do lite work am gaining strength. I have not made any effort to start to Texas on account of my health. I am not willing to undertake the trip by my self in my present condition least I mite be left on the way but if I get sound enough by fall I am going to come and see you and maby I wont chill when I get there. Reed has bin confined to the house and bed for the last week the Doctor is attending him. I don't know what his complaint is tho he is almost helpless. Lee and Luther are both in bad health dull and stupid. We are living on the highest hill in Cooper where any body mite think health was there but somehow we don't find it so some of us are most always complaining some way. We have had the hottest weather the last five weeks that ever I went through with shorely during which time there has bin no rain not a drop until to day there was a lite shower this morning. The corn crop is not very promising, there is any amint irish potatoes and tomatoes in the garden. There was a big lot of peas and beans but they have gone dry we haint had any watermellons yet, I cant think of any thing to tell you of that you care about. I have not heard from Bedford this hole year. I have not bin off the plantation but once in two years past. I want to see you all and be with you and enjoy myself very much. As I cant think of any thing else to write I will tell how much stock Reed had on hand. He has five horses and three mules and fourteen cattle and fifty six hogs and I don't know how how many pigs. He has sixty acres in corn but it aint very good on account of the long drouth. Wheat is worth sixty cents a bushel corn is one dollar a barrel irish potatoes 10 cents a bushel pork three cents a pound.

Nothing more at present.

My best respects to you and your family

John Debo[16]

1. Reed Perry Debo

Do then as your progenitors have done
And by their virtues prove yourself their son.
--Dryden

Reed (Reediland in the family Bible) Perry Debo, oldest son of John and Jane Debo, was born in southern Bedford County, Virginia, on the old Debo home place (referred to as a plantation in Virginia) January 19, 1832.[1] There he was reared to adulthood, and by the time of his marriage he was clerking and operating a country store in the Fancy Grove neighborhood nearby. On February 18, 1860,[2] (a year before the outbreak of the War Between the States), he was wed to Mary Jane Heptinstall, the daughter of Caleb and Gillie Heptinstall (the marriage license gave his occupation as merchant). Mary Jane was born October 18, 1840,[3] in the neighboring Franklin County, Virginia, making her twenty years old and Reed twenty-eight at the time of their marriage.

The Reed Debos were of the Methodist persuasion, Reed having joined the Methodist Episcopal Church, South, in August 1850 at the age 18.[4] He reared his family as active adherents to this religion, and he served his church in many capacities during his lifetime. They attended the old Providence church in their community while living in Virginia. (The building is still standing today on Virginia Rt. 737 and is used as a feed barn, the congregation having long since disbanded in the early 1950s.)[5]

The store at Fancy Grove that Reed was running before leaving for the war was a log building. A portion of the building is still standing near the Saunders brothers' homes. On a trip to Bedford County years ago, Mr. Clyde Saunders showed it to me and I took a photo of it. Mr. Saunders also showed me some account books of the old store that were in his possession. In them were notations where Reed Debo had

Reed P. Debo

Mrs. Reed P. Debo
nee
Mary Jane Heptinstall

bought such items as calico, various food items, and other necessities of life. His grandson, Lewis C. Debo, in later years was also able to visit and photograph the old store building.

Reed and Mary Jane's first child, a little daughter (Gillie Jane), was born August 27, 1861.[6] She was named for her grandmothers Heptinstall and Debo. The infant was not to see her second birthday, however, and died July 15, 1863,[7] while her wounded father was languishing in a Yankee prison in New York harbor. She was buried in the Heptinstall graveyard.

Reed enlisted in the Confederate army March 8, 1862,[8] at Fancy Grove for the duration of the war. He was first a private in Co. G, 28th Regiment, Virginia Infantry, under Capt. Augustus L. Minter. His enlistment papers describe him as a man thirty years old, with dark complexion, dark hair, blue eyes, five feet plus (inches were illegible), and a clerk.

He left the next month for Lynchburg and arrived at camp on April 3, 1862. On May 1 he was promoted from private to second sergeant, and a month later on June 1 to first sergeant. Reed became ill with dysentery and was sent to the Chimborazo Hospital No. 1 in Richmond

August 10, 1862. His Confederate service records show he deserted for a time (cause unknown?) on September 4, and on November 1 was reduced from first sergeant to private. He participated in the various engagements in which his unit fought, having returned to camp February 9, 1863, and later being promoted to fifth sergeant on July 1 before the Gettysburg campaign.

Reed's 28th Infantry Regiment of Virginians was a part of Garnett's Brigade of George Pickett's Division, Longstreet's Corp, and participated in the famous historic Pickett's Charge. At the "highwater mark of the Confederacy" the Virginians along with their fellow North Carolinians were able to at first drive the Federals from their breastworks, but had insufficient numbers to break through the Northern lines, having been decimated by the awful torrent of shot and shell before reaching the "bloody angle" and clump of trees which was their goal. [I have stood at that spot and viewed the surroundings, all the time imagining what it must have been like for my kin on that awful and fateful day.] The Yankees received reinforcements and rallied, forcing the Southerners to either fall back or be captured. It was here that Reed Debo was shot in the right thigh and captured on July 3. He was sent to DeCamp General Hospital, Davids Island, New York Harbor, July 22, and paroled on August 24. He was received by the Confederate agent and exchanged August 28 at City Point, Virginia.

After some furlough time and further recuperation from his wound, Reed returned to duty with his unit on October 28, 1863. During his furlough visit with his family and relatives he no doubt learned of the death of his firstborn daughter in July; but also during this visit home Mary Jane became pregnant with what would be their eldest son Lee.

Serving through 1864 in the defense of Richmond and its environs, Reed became ill again with what seemed to be a common ailment among the ill-nourished Southern soldiers—dysentery—and was sent to the hospital again for a five-day stay from September 12 to 17, followed by a much appreciated forty-day furlough. His son, Perry Lee Debo, had been born in June and he got to see him for the first time. Reed returned to duty on November 17, and was promoted to fourth sergeant December 31. The next April found the remnant of the 28th Virginia along with their comrades-in-arms in other units surrounded by Union forces at Appomattox. Lee surrendered and the war was over.[9]

After the war, Reed spent some time in Bristol, Virginia, where he learned the plastering trade.[10] In 1869, he, along with his brothers Thomas and Cornelius, went west to Missouri. Virginia had been devastated by the war and opportunities were few with hard times the rule rather than the exception. They first came to Howard County, north across the Missouri River from Boonville, but a short time later moved south across the river on ice into Cooper County where they engaged in farming. The next year, 1870, Cornelius went back to Virginia to bring Reed's family (Mary Jane, his wife; and three children, Lee, Martha (Mattie), and Luther, all of whom had been born at Fancy Grove in Bedford County), to Missouri. The Debo men's sister Sallie, also came, and was married later that year in September to Henry Clay Bowmer. In 1872 (two years later), Cornelius and Thomas Debo and the Bowmer family left for Texas,[11] leaving the Reed Debo family alone in Cooper County.

On May 23, 1873,[12] Reed's mother, Jane Nichols Debo, died in Virginia at the age 64, and was buried in the family cemetery. By 1875 advancing age and deteriorating health caused John Debo to make the decision to leave the old Virginia home, and he and his youngest daughter, Marie Eliza (Mollie), came to Missouri to make their home with the Reed Debos. (John died three years later in August 1878 at age 79.).[13]

Between 1872 and 1885 Reed's family would increase with the addition of four more daughters and a son: Julia, Ida, Daisy (who lived less than three years), Serena Pearl, and Grover. In the summer of 1889 Reed, Mary Jane, and Grover (now five years old) went back to Virginia on a visit – twenty years after Reed had left. While there visiting Mary Jane's sister, Mary Jane contracted typhoid fever and died July 23.[14] The next day she was buried alongside little Gillie Jane in the Heptinstall burial grounds. Reed sent the following letter to his children back in Missouri:

(The letter was in the possession of Grover Debo, was postmarked Liberty (Bedford), Virginia, July 23, 1889, and addressed to Lee Debo, Boonville, Missouri.)

Fancy Grove, Va.
July 23rd

Dear Children:
I have the painful task of telling you of the death of your mother who died ten minutes till seven this morning. She will be buried tomorrow by her mother

Lee or Luther if you open this sad letter in town may be you had better get (Dr.) Evans to go home with you on Ida's account.

Grover and I will go home in a few days though I may go to Lynchburg and get a tombstone. If I do we start home Monday.

R. P. Debo[15]

The next year (1890) Reed decided to sell out and move to Bedford, Missouri, in Livingston County. Bedford had been settled by some Virginians, including Daniel Green Saunders, some of the Turners, and other former Bedford County, Virginia, residents and friends of Reed. He was to stay here about nine years. In letters to brother Cornelius in Texas in 1894 and 1896[16] he sets forth some of his activities. Not only did he farm, raising corn and wheat crops, but was a "road overseer" and served as a justice of the peace.[17] He engaged in his plastering trade, built flues, and painted the church building as well as homes in the community. Always active in his church, he served as Sunday school superintendent, steward, and represented the church at conferences. His daughter Julia was one of the organists as well as a teacher and worker. She died, however, of "quick consumption" on January 31, 1898,[18] and was buried in the cemetery there.

After moving back to Cooper County, Reed lost another daughter, Ida, in 1905. The toils, sorrows, and wear of the years began to exact their toll and he passed from the scenes of earth April 21, 1911,[19] at age 79 – the same age of his father when he died. The following obituary appeared in the Boonville (Mo.) paper.[20]

A GOOD MAN GONE

Captain Reed P. Debo, who for many years lived four miles southeast of Boonville, died last Friday morning. His death was not unexpected, as his friends had known for sometime that he was very feeble. He was just a little past eighty years of age. He leaves three sons and two daughters, highly respected citizens of the community.

Captain Debo came to Cooper county in 1869 from Bedford county, Virginia, where he was born, and has remained in Missouri since that time, though for a number of years he resided outside this county. Twenty years after he came to this state he and his wife made a visit to their old Virginia home, and during this visit the wife died while visiting a sister in the home where she was reared. Brother Debo sadly turned his face toward his Missouri home. Here he has reared an honorable family, and grew to ripe old age, honored and loved by all who know him.

Early in the war he enlisted in the Confederate army and saw much

*service as a soldier under Longstreet in the army of Virginia. He was
a member of General Pickett's division at the battle of Gettysburg, and
was one of the few survivors of that famous charge. He was a brave soldier, but it was in the great battles of life as a Christian that he excelled.*

*Sixty-one years ago this August he made a profession of religion
and united with the Methodist church. During this long service in the
church he ever remained loyal to God. Many times had his church honored him by electing him to represent the local congregation in the District conference, and several times has he been elected by the District
conference to represent his church in the annual conference. He regarded any service that he could render his church as an honorable service,
and he always gave himself to it willingly.*

*His children and his friends believed in his integrity of character,
and in his Christian life. What was said of Barnabas, "that he was a
good man, full of the Holy Ghost, and of faith," might be said of Reed P.
Debo. A good man has gone. Peace to his dust. He leaves to his children
and all who know him the legacy of a good life. The world is always
better by such lives having been lived in it. He came, in great feebleness,
down to the shore of death's river, but there is no question that he met
his "pilot face to face" and was carried safely over.*

There are at least two factual errors in the above obituary. Reed
was never a captain in fact. Perhaps the term was used in an affec-
tionate way as was often done in those days when referring to an old
soldier. Also, it is stated that he was "a little past eighty years of age."
The fact remains that Reed had passed his seventy-ninth birthday by
only three months.

The children of Reed and Mary Jane Debo were:
1. GILLIE JANE, born August 27, 1861, Bedford County, Virginia;
   and died July 15, 1863. She was buried in the Heptinstall family
   cemetery in southern Bedford County.
2. PERRY LEE, born June 6, 1864, Fancy Grove, Bedford County,
   Virginia, and died Aug 3, 1947, in Cooper County, Missouri. He
   was married Jan. 20, 1890, to Alice George, who was born Sept.
   6, 1870, and died Sept. 23, 1945, Cooper County, Missouri, and
   they were buried in Walnut Grove Cemetery, Boonville. They
   had two children.
3. MARTHA JAMES (Mattie), born Nov.25, 1866, Fancy Grove,
   Virginia, and died Aug. 27, 1958, Cooper County, Missouri. She
   never married, and lived to be 92 years of age.

4. LUTHER CLINTON, born Nov. 9, 1869, Fancy Grove, Virginia. He was married Jan. 3, 1909, to Elizabeth E. (Bessie) McFarland, who was born Sept.28, 1875, and died Jan. 17, 1959. (She was a sister to Hattie M. McFarland, who married Luther's brother, Grover Debo. They were the daughters of Truman Warren and Melvina Wear McFarland of Cooper County, Missouri.) Luther died Dec. 26, 1967, at age 98 and he and Bessie were buried in Walnut Grove Cemetery, Boonville. They had three children.
5. JULIA MARY, born Aug. 19, 1872, in Cooper County, Missouri; died Jan. 31, 1898, at Bedford, Livingston County, Missouri, where she was also buried. Julia never married.
6. IDA LAURA, born Feb. 1, 1876, Cooper County; died Jan. 28, 1905, Cooper County, Missouri. She never married.
7. DAISEY DELLA, born Nov. 12, 1878, died July 16, 1881, Cooper County, Missouri.
8. SERENA PEARL, born June 2, 1881, died June 7, 1912, Cooper County, Missouri. She never married.
9. GROVER EVANS, born April 22, 1884, Cooper County. He was married Aug 15, 1908, to Hattie M. McFarland Debo, a sister of Luther's wife. (See above.) Grover died Oct. 29, 1976. They had three children.[21]

The three sons of Reed Debo: Lee, Luther and Grover were the only ones of his family having descendants, none of the daughters were married. Grover and Hattie were the only members of that generation who were yet alive when I made my first trip to Missouri in 1968, and I was fortunate to make their acquaintance. Other later jaunts through the Show Me state in 1970, 1973, and 1976 cemented a wonderful relationship with these relatives. I remember so well how lonely Grover was after Hattie's death in 1971, and his deterioration from cancer in the nursing home at Boonville when my parents and I visited him in Aug. 1976 before his death in October of that year.

2. Lee Debo and his brother Luther were partners in farming, and the operation of a steam-powered threshing machine and sawmill around the turn of the century (1900). Lee owned the first Chevrolet automobile brought to Cooper County. He built a house of concrete blocks that continues as a landmark on the Rankin Mill Road three miles south of Boonville. For a time in the 1920s he was a rartner in operating a garage on the present site of the Boonslick Regional library.

The children of Lee and Alice were:

A. MARY L., born March 5, 1893, and died four weeks later on April 7, 1893.

B. THELMA L., born May 10, 1904. She married J. Albert Cowan of Pittsburgh on March 21, 1925, who was born Aug. 1, 1900, and his death is unknown. Thelma died Sept. 18, 1945, at the young age of 41, five days prior to the death of her mother. She and Albert had no children.

4. LUTHER Debo farmed his wife's portion of the McFarland estate about five miles southeast of Boonville. He served forty years as a director of the Hail Ridge School District. About 1905 he made a trip to Texas to visit his relatives there, and was well remembered by my grandparent during that time.

The children of Luther and Bessie were:

A. ELIZABETH LEE, born Dec 10, 1911. She was married Dec. 4, 1943, to Frank Pickett, who was born May 22, 1904. They lived in Clinton, Missouri, and had a daughter, Elizabeth Ann, born Jan. 14, 1946, who was married June 3, 1967, to Charles Robert (Bob) Greer. They had two children; Stacy Lynn, born Sept 24, 1969; and John Anthony, born March 6, 1977. Elizabeth Debo Pickett died Feb. 6, 1986.

B. LEWIS CLINTON, born Feb. 22, 1913. He was married June 13, 1936, at Prairie Home, Missouri, to Virginia Carpenter, who was born July 29, 1912, and died June 28, 1983. She was a registered nurse. After their marriage, Lewis and Virginia moved to Creston, Iowa, where he joined the staff of the *Creston News Advertiser*. In 1944 they moved to Ottumwa, Iowa, where he later became editor of the *Ottumwa Courier*. After his retirement in 1974, he became public information director for the Indian Hills Community College the next year retiring, in 1981.[22] Lewis traveled extensively after the death of his wife and was planning a trip to Germany at the time of his death June 18, 1991. He was keenly interested in the Debo family history and supplied most of the data on the Reed Debo family to this author. I only wish he could have lived to enjoy the fruits of the finished product. Lewis and Virginia had two sons:

1. JOHN CLINTON, born May 29, 1941. John is single and lives in Jacksonville, Flordia. He worked at Cape Canaveral for a number of years, taught at the University of Central Florida in Orlando, and is presently teaching in Jacksonville.

2. JAMES WARREN (Jim), born Feb. 24, 1944. He was married Aug. 28, 1971, to Regina Diane Sego, who was born Feb. 20,

1948. They live in Memphis, Tennessee, where Jim works in the field of nutrition. Jim and Diane have four children: Elizabeth Ann, born Nov. 12, 1974; Clinton Jamesson, Feb. 1, 1977; Martha Virginia, born Jan. 24, 1980; and Jean Marie, born Dec. 5, 1982.

C. TRUMAN REED, born Oct.26, 1914. He was first married to Irene Schrader on July 14, 1940. He was later married on Feb. 22, 1948,to Marguerite Patrick Korsen, who was born March 18, 1914. She had a daughter, Nancy Helen Korsen, born May 4, 1942. Truman was a veteran of World War II, having served in the U. S. Navy. He was in the farm implement business in Boonville for many years, and later was office manager for Missouri River Sand and Gravel Co. His wife, Marguerite, is a registered nurse, as is her daughter, Nancy Korsen Reichel, who resides in Kansas City. Truman died March 27, 1978.

9. Grover Debo lived in and around Boonville all his life. After leaving the farm, he was employed in road maintenance for many years, and was street commissioner in Boonville, a member of the police force, and a guard at Missouri Training School for boys.

Grover and Hattie had the following children:

A. MARY MALVINA, born Oct. 12, 1909. She was married June 1, 1926, to Calvin Huff, who was born March 25, 1907. They live in Boonville and had four children.

1. WILLIAM CALVIN, born April 29, 1927, and died Sept. 1, 1979. He was married March 2, 1946, to Arlene Goetz, who was born March 7, 1929. They had two children: Lois Jean, born Dec. 5, 1950, who was married Jan. 4, 1975, to Brice Lambert, born Jan. 24, 1945; and James Edward, born March 26, 1954, died June 6, 1978, who was married April 6, 1972, to Karla Kraft. They had two sons, Mark, born Nov. 7, 1972, and Dave, born Sept. 7, 1974.

2. THOMAS EUGENE (Gene), born Oct. 6, 1931. He was married to LeAnn Thomas, who was born Sept. 13, 1934. They had two daughters: Joy Rena, born Dec. 27, 1960; and Jennie Lee, born Jan. 25, 1974.

3. DORIS MAE, born July 2, 1935. She married Don J. Vail, and they had two children: Robin Jo, born April 6, 1960; Forrest Lee, born March 30, 1962.

4. DONALD ROY, born Dec. 14, 1940. He married Tina Kemper, who was born Feb. 28, 1942. They had a son, Roy Wayne, born

Oct. 6, 1960.

B. GROVER GLENN, born Dec. 6 1910, and died Sept. 26, 1930.

C. ETHEL LOUISE, born Nov. 20, 1915. She was married Nov. 24, 1935, to Weesen Huff, who was born Oct., 27 1911, and died Sept. 14, 1974. (Weesen Huff and Calvin Huff, husband of Mary Malvina, were brothers.) Louise and Weesen had two children:

    1. ROBERT MICHAEL, born Dec. 10, 1946, who was married Jan. 15, 1965, to Anna Mae Hunger, born May 20, 1942, and they had two children: Michael Christopher, born Feb. 26, 1972; and Jill Ann, born Nov. 4, 1976.

    2. DENNIS DALE, born March 23, 1953.[23]

2. Allen Burton Debo

Ancestral glory is as it were, a lamp to posterity.
--Sallust

Allen Burton Debo, second son of John and Jane Debo, was born on the old Debo homeplace in southern Bedford County January 6, 1834.[1] Reared to adulthood there, Burton was twenty-seven years old when the War Between the States began April 1861.

Burton evidently had taken up residence in neighboring Pittsylvania County before the beginning of the war. In the 1860 Census he is listed as a tanner, and was living in the home of John B. Hardwick, a Missionary Baptist preacher. When at age 28 he enlisted in the Confederate army at Richmond, Virginia, August 14, 1862,[2] he was enrolled by Major George Craighead Cabell for three years as a private in Company B (the "Danville Grays" from Pittsylvania County) in the 18th Regiment, Virginia Infantry. Burton was the only one of John Debo's sons who did not serve in the 28th Virginia Regiment.

Confederate service records show that Burton was admitted to General Hospital, Charlottesville, Virginia, on November 9, 1862, though the cause is not specified. He no doubt received a furlough afterward for he was married November 30, 1862,[3] to Katherine I. (Kate) Dove, daughter of James and Martha Dove. Kate was born circa 1836-37 in Pittsylvania County and died there sometime after 1880, the burial place is presently unknown.

After returning to his unit, records show he was "sent to the hospital sick" June 2, 1863. It is not known for sure whether he had rejoined the 18th Regiment in time for the Gettysburg campaign the first of the next month. The 18th Virginia was a constituent part of Pickett's Division and took part in the famous charge, suffering terrible losses in killed, wounded, or captured. It is presumed that Burton survived the battle and remained healthy the remainder of the war. The records show him present with his capture at Hatcher's Run, or White Oak Road, on March 31, 1865. He arrived at City Point, Virginia, on April 2 and was taken to Point Lookout, Maryland, for incarceration. He took the oath of allegiance to the United States on June 11, 1865, and was released to return to his home in Pittsylvania County.

Burton's army record describe him as having dark complexion, dark hair, dark blue eyes, and having a height of 5 feet, 11 ½ inches. He died May 13, 1867[4] (cause unknown), at the young age of thirty-three years. A son, Dabney Debo, named after Burton's brother of that name "lost at Gettysburg," was born in April 1866.[5]

After Burton's death and five years later, Kate Dove Debo was married on May 9, 1872,[6] in Pittsylvania County to Joel Mayhew, born in 1812, son of Drury and Celia Mayhew. The 1880 U. S. Census shows three children of Joel Mayhew by a previous wife (presumed deceased): Jacob, born in 1857; Drucila, born in 1861; and Martha F., born in 1866. The census furthr shows Joel and Kate having four children in the household: Joel F., born in 1873; Mary and Laura, both born in 1876; Lilia W., born in July 1880. Dabney Debo is shown to be a stepson 13 years of age.

In later years, Dabney came to Texas and visited his Debo relatives there. In a letter dated December 25, 1891,[7] from Burnet, Texas, to his brother Reed Debo, in Boonville, Missouri, Cornelius Debo mentions that Dabney and some of Clay and Sallie Debo Bowmer's girls and a son-in-law were all expected to spend the holidays with Cornelius and family in Burnet County. Later, in another letter from Cornelius to Reed Debo dated December 10, 1894,[8] he said, "We have had several letters from Dabney this fall. He is still in Arizona but thinks he will come back to Texas this winter and settle down for good." I have tried through the State Archives of Arizona, the Mormon church records, and genealogical societies there to find some authentic record on Dabney in Arizona, but no information was obtained. He is listed in the 1900 Census as a teamster in Mojer Precinct, Yavapai County, Arizona, in the Prescott area.[9]

My understanding is (from family tradition told me by various children of Cornelius Debo) that Dabney Debo never returned from

Arizona to Texas. The story goes that he had got into some trouble with the authorities in Bell County, Texas (where his aunt and uncle, Sallie and Clay Bowmer lived), over the treatment of a black man and had to leave the country.

Dabney returned to Pittsylvania County, Virginia, sometime between 1920 and 1930. He is listed in the 1930 Census (Tunstall Dist.) as a 64-year-old widower and a boarder in the Daniel R. Yeatts home, having been married at age 46 (1912). The Census for Arizona lists a "Dan" Debo, age 53, born in Virginia and I'm sure the census taker miswrote the given name and that "Dan" is actually Dabney since the place of birth and approximate age fit exactly. He is found to be living in Lowell, Cochise County, Arizona at that time with a wife Jeanette, 64 years of age, who was a native of Scotland and came to the United States in 1917. Later information on Dabney or Jeanette has not been found. My guess is that Jeanette died and Dabney went back to his native Pittsylvania County, Virginia, to spend the rest of his days.

3. Dabney Claybourn Debo

Posterity gives to every man his true honor
--Tacitus

Dabney Clabourn Debo, the third son of John and Jane Debo was born June 9, 1839,[1] on the Debo home place in Southern Bedford County, Virginia. He no doubt was educated in a rural neighborhood school, and I am including here a brief essay found in the old family Bible that he wrote February 30, 1860, at age twenty.[2]

"Fancy Grove   Bedford, Va.
February 3. 1860

Traveling

Traveling is one pleasure which brings many men to ruin. In the first place if they indulge in it too freely they will soon spend all their fortune and then they will not feel like work oweing to their long absence from it and will bum about from place to place until they will be driven off by people whom they used to visit.

The Traveler will sometimes get into bad company and will begin to dring (sic) whiskey and one friend will treat him to as much as he can drink, then another will do the same and so on until he thinks he has as much since (sic) as any of them and will

76

go with into the gaming house; they will win some of his money; he will have none: then he will have no money, no credit, nor friends. Those friends which he had, have become enemies and they will drive him off and he will have nowhere to go and then he is apt to kill himself.

The traveler will sometimes be waylayed and robbed on his journey and will not know what become of his money and he will be better off than either of the former ones.

Dabney C. Debo

On April 17, 1861, two days after President Abraham Lincoln called for volunteers to "suppress" the Southern states, Virginia's assembly voted to secede from the Union as "an alternate to making war on sister states." Colonel Robert E. Lee resigned his U. S. Army commission on April 20 and accepted the rank of major general. He took command of all Virginia state forces three days later. A week later, on April 27, in Bedford County, the "Patty Lane Rifles" enrolled volunteers at Chestnut Fork, located where Virginia Routes 731 and 732 come together, where the company drilled on what later came to be known as the "mustering ground." The Bedford volunteers were some of the first to respond to the call by Virginia's governor.

Dabney Debo at age 21 was one of the first volunteers to enlist on April 27, 1861,[3] in the Patty Lane Rifles [later changed to Co. G, 28th Virginia Regiment] under Capt. Augustus L. Minter for a twelve-month period. In late May the company left for Lynchburg and on June 1, 1861, it was mustered into the Confederate service by Col. D. A. Laughon. On June 19, ten days after his twenty-second birthday. Dabney was promoted from private to third corporal.

Later in the next month, the new corporal was struck by the measles and entered General Hospital in Charlottesville on July 15, 1861. He returned to his unit from the hospital August 7, but was left at Centreville August 29 unable to march. Another promotion came on October 1 when Dabney was advanced to second corporal. He left camp on November 26 due to illness, was granted a furlough, and the record states he was "sick at home."

Dabney returned to camp February 21, 1862, and shortly thereafter on February 25 reenlisted for the remainder of the war, receiving a bounty of fifty dollars. When the 28th Virginia was moved to the Peninsula in April to take part in the defense of Richmond against the 100,000-man force of Union Gen. George McClellan, a defensive line was thrown up at Williamsburg. It was at the battle there that Dabney was taken prisoner on May 5 and imprisoned at Old Capitol Prison, Washington, D. C., July 28, 1862. August 1 he was moved to Fort Monroe from which he was exchanged. He returned to his company about August 5 after being received at Aiken's Landing by the Confederate agent for exchange.

After McClellan's horde was driven away from Richmond by Gen. Lee's forces, the 28th Virginia was moved back northward to thwart another invasion by Federal forces under John Pope. The adversaries clashed at the Second Battle of Manassas and during this battle on August 20 Dabney was wounded and sent to the hospital. He wasn't able to return to his comrades in arms until November 20. In December, the 28th Virginia was entrenched at Marye's Heights before Fredericksburg, but the battle on the thirteenth did not extend to its position in the line and no casualties were sustained.

In 1863 Dabney Debo took part in all of the actions in which the 28th participated: a transfer to North Carolina to aid in battles at Washington and New Bern in March and April; and then to begin the journey north the latter part of June as Gen. Lee's forces penetrated the North via Maryland and into Pennsylvania for the inevitable clash with Gen. Meade's Yankees at the small crossroads town of Gettysburg. Here on July 3 Gen. George Pickett's Division assailed the Union center. Dabney Debo and his four brothers all took part in the famous "Pickett's charge," and three survived it while one was wounded and captured. All of my life I have heard varous ones of Cornelius Debo's children relate what they had heard their father tell, how that the last any of them saw of Dabney was that he was standing on the Yankee breastworks at the "bloody angle" waving the Confederate flag after so many of the flagbearers had been shot down. In the family Bible it was simply recorded under the deaths column that Dabney was "lost at Gettysburg July 3, 1863."[4] In his Confederate records it is stated, "Taken prisoner at Gettysburg; supposed to be dead."[5] No one really knows for sure what happened to him at Gettysburg. Was he wounded on the breastworks, taken prisoner, and died? No one will ever be able to solve the puzzle of Dabney's final hours.

To make matters worse in understanding the reality of the situation, a story told me by Cornelius Debo's son, Hardy Debo, who was born in 1889 Burnet County, Texas, further mystifies one concerning Dabney Debo. Uncle Hardy told me that as a very young child he was with his father in the Burnet County Courthouse in Burnet, Texas, at which time his father, Cornelius, saw a man that he thought looked like his brother Dabney. Remember, he had not seen him for twenty-six years, the last time being at Gettysburg. He walked up to the man and tried to engage him in conversation, but the man was hesitant to converse and was very distant in manner. The whole episode troubled Cornelius. After returning home and thinking over the occurrence, he determined to try to find the man and talk to him some more. The next time he came in from his home in the country to the county seat he began to look for the man – but he was gone! He had left the country and no one knew what had become of him. Was this actually and really brother Dabney, and did he really survive at Gettysburg?

4. Thomas Benton Debo

Study the past if you would divine the future.
--Confucius

Thomas Benton Debo, fourth son of John and Jane Debo, was born December 8, 1841,[1] on the Debo home place in southern Bedford County, Virginia. Reared along with his older brothers, Thomas was just reaching manhood when the War Between the States broke out in April 1861. It was not till the next year on March 8, 1862, however, that he enlisted at Fancy Grove community under Capt. A. L. Minter in Co. G, 28th Virginia, for the duration of the war. At that time he was described as being five feet, six inches tall, having a light complexion, light hair, blue eyes, and was listed as a farmer.[2]

Thomas came to camp April 3, 1862, and shortly thereafter on April 15 was sent to a hospital with an unnamed illness. He was not able to return to his company in camp until July 12. The next month on August 10 he was sent to Chimborazo Hospital #1 in Richmond with parotitis [described in the dictionary as "inflammation of the parotid or salivary glands located below and in front of each ear, as in mumps"]. Then Thomas was furloughed from August 29, 1862, for fifteen days, but did not return to camp till October 14.

Ill health seems to have been Thomas' lot for he was sent back to Chimborazo Hospital in Richmond June 7, 1863, with pleurodynia, a lung ailment. He was transferred to the Receiving and Wayside Hospital (or General Hospital #9) in Richmond July 11, but sent back to Chimborazo the next day, and presumably missed the Gettysburg campaign because he did not return to duty till October 8.

The Confederate records show Thomas present and on duty the remainder of the war. His brother, Cornelius Debo, younger than Thomas, always related how that in the double battle line ranks he always stood behind his older brother Thomas. After Thomas would fire his weapon he would kneel and Cornelius would fire his over him.

Near the conclusion of the conflict, Thomas was captured by Federals at Harper's Farm on April 6, 1865, and as a prisoner of war arrived at City Point, Virginia, April 14. He was imprisoned at Point Lookout, Maryland, but took the oath of allegiance June 11 and was released to return home, which was less than 200 miles away. His relatives there thought he was dead. Three and a half months later, he reached home – barefooted! He had walked the entire way. At the close of the war his military records describe him with dark complexion, dark sandy hair, blue eyes, and five feet, seven inches tall.[3] Quite a contrast to the description given at enlistment time. And he must have grown an inch!

After the war, Thomas Debo accompanied brothers Reed and Cornelius to Missouri in 1869. There is some discrepancy as to when he left there and came to Texas. I have always understood that he came in 1872 with the Clay Bowmer family and Cornelius

The Thomas B. Debo Family
Standing: Bettie Lou; Cornelius W. (Pat); Eliza Olive (Ollie); Front Row: Thomas B. Debo; Sallie Myrtle; Fannie Wilson Debo.

Debo; another source, however declared that he came two years later in 1874.

Thomas worked after coming to Texas and accompanied Cornelius and family when they moved to Burnet County in 1875, helping to prepare a place to live and the building of fences and corrals for the stock.

After working and saving for a number of years, he sent back to Virginia for his sweetheart, Fannie Wilson. She arrived by train at Georgetown, Texas, January 22, 1882,[4] at which time Thomas met her and they were married by County Judge George W. Glasscock. Fannie was born in Virginia October 3, 1853, and died February 3, 1946, in Winters, Runnels County, Texas, where she and Thomas were buried in the local cemetery. She was preceded in death by her husband June 28, 1930.[5]

For a number of years Thomas and Fannie lived on the Lampasas River in Bell County and later in Killeen (in the same county). They, in later years, moved to Winters, Texas, where they resided the rest of their days. The following letter was written by Fannie to her niece, Martha (Mattie) Debo, who lived in Boonville, Missouri:[6]

"Killeen, Texas
Dec. 29-13

Miss Mattie Debo
My Dear Neice
We received your card some days ago, glad to know we are not forgotten. We have enjoyed the holidays fine considering your Uncle Thomas has been almost laid up with Lagrippe for two weeks, not in bed, but just able to sit around the fire. He has suffered a great deal with his head & neck. We had the Dr. to come yesterday first time he had been for several days. He left some powders that eased his head some, so he had a very good nights rest. We had only one of the children with us during the last week. Bettie Lou is telephone operator, & you know they get no holidays at all, but she seemed to enjoy the time all right.

Myrtle spent last week in Burnet, said she had a good time with the folks, left them all well.

Myrtle sets type at the printing office & she got one week off. She came in last night on the midnight train, so of course she feels a little stupid today, but she went to work this morning. Cornelius is still working for the Santa Fe, so he didn't get any holiday to come home. Ollie lives west of Ft. Worth & she didn't get to come, but sent me a Xmas gift. I haven't had a letter from your Aunt Sallie for quite awhile. They were doing very well when she wrote last. Emmets widow, Ethel Bowmer, is living about one block from us, so we can see her most every day. She got a card from Prunie saying they had a new girl at her house, so Prunie has one girl & one boy.

Your Aunt Mollie wrote just before Xmas, said Tot had spent a week at home but had gone back to her own home for the holidays. Mollie seems real proud of her soninlaw; we have never seen him. I hope he is worthy of Tot, for I think she is such a sweet girl.

Have you had plenty of rain up there this winter? My, if we haven't had plenty down here, but I guess you folks read it in the papers. The floods were not bad in Killeen, tho it took one bridge & several families moved from below the Railroad, but there was no one drowned here & no property destroyed by the water, but we sure have had the mud, yes plenty of mud. We are having nice cool weather now, which we are very thankful for.

Do you ever hear from old Va? My sister writes me sometimes. She & my oldest brother & youngest brother are all that are living of our family. My sister married about two months ago. She married Wm. N. Reece, he is a nice man & a good Christian, I don't suppose any of you folks remember him unless you heard Papa speak of him, I knew him well, but I was a little surprised at my sister marrying after waiting so long, but it was her wish of course. I get letters from Cassie sometimes, & when I read her letter I imagine I can almost hear her Talking.

Mattie I wish you could make up your mind to visit down in Texas awhile I believe it would do you good, Its true your Uncle & I are getting old, but I don't feel old. I can go all day & sit up half the night. I go to S. S. & church every Sunday & most every Sunday night, prayer meeting Tuesday & Wednesday night, Ladies Aid every Monday, & visit the sick that are near enough.

Well I will make you Tired so you will not want to read any more of my scriblings so I will stop for this time and try to write again some day. We would be glad to have a letter from any of you folks. Wishing you a happy new year, I am your devoted Aunt much love to each one.

Fannie"

The following appeared in a Baptist church paper near the end of Fannie's life:

Mrs. F. W. Debo celebrated her 92nd birthday October 3, 1945. She has been a member of the Baptist church for 77 years, and is an active member of the Baptist Training Union in First Church, Winters. She recently said, "My greatest joy is reading my Bible, attending the services of my church and visiting the sick."[7]

Thomas and Fannie Debo had the following children:[8]

1. CLAUDE, born Nov. 25, 1882, and died Sept. 5, 1900. He was working in the field and some unknown person at a faraway distance fired a gun and it accidentally hit Claude, killing him. He was buried in Bell County in the Maxdale Cemetery.
2. ELIZA OLIVE (Ollie), born March 25, 1884, in Bell County, and died July 23, 1973. She was married Nov. 5, 1905, to Robert Jeffreys. They had four children.
3. CORNELIUS WILSON (Pat), born Oct. 9, 1885, in Bell County, and died Jan. 7, 1978, in Abilene. He was buried in Elmwood Memorial Park there. Pat was named for his Uncle Cornelius and Wilson was his mother's maiden name. The nickname "Pat" was given him by a teacher when he was in school, and the name stuck. He was first married Nov. 8, 1909, to Alice Long, born Feb. 9, 1886, and died April 6, 1920. He was later married Sept. 11, 1926, to Bessie Little, born May 1, 1902, and died on March 12, 1968. They had one daughter. Pat and Bessie used to enjoy coming to Burnet to attend the Debo reunion. The following obituary appeared in an Abilene paper:

C. W. Debo

Services for C. W. (Pat) Debo 92, of 2826 S. 28th St., who died Saturday evening at Hendrick Medical Center, will be at 2 p.m. Monday in St. James United Methodist Church, at 3100 Barrow.

The Rev. M. Ronald Hamby, pastor, will officiate. Burial will be at Elmwood Memorial Park, directed by Elliott-Hamil Funeral Home, 542 Hickory.

Survivors include a daughter, Mrs. John (Amelia) Gambill of Dallas, and several nieces and nephews.

Pallbearers will be Paul E. Lack, Harold Girdner, Robert Aiken, Curtis Redman, Dr. Virgil Bottom , and Dr. Robert Sledge.

4. BETTIE LOU, born April 22, 1887, in Bell County, died Nov. 14,

1987, in Dallas. She was first married July 14, 1922, to Dennis Nance, born Jan. 30, 1886, and died Aug. 10, 1923; they had one daughter. Bettie Lou was later married Oct. 15, 1925, to C. F. Hendricks, born Oct. 13, 1881. They were divorced in 1937.

    5. SALLIE MYRTLE, born Dec. 21, 1893, in Bell County, died Aug. 22, 1928. She was married June 3, 1926, to Frank C. Johnson, born in 1886. They had no children.

*   *   *   *

2. The children of Ollie and Roberty Jeffreys were:
- A. VELMA, born Sept. 24, 1907; she married Pat Neill.
- B. MYRTLE, born June 3, 1910; she married Butcher Caudle.
- C. TRUMAN, born March 20, 1920; died in action in China during World War II Aug. 20, 1943.
- D. OLLIE MAYE, born Aug. 24, 1924; she married Ambers E. (Amby) Mayfield.

3. The daughter of C. W. (Pat) and Bessie Debo is:
- A. AMELIA, born Feb 7, 1928, She was first married to Bobby Dee Williams, and later to John Gambill. They live in Dallas.

4. The daughter of Bettie Lou and Dennis Nance is: MARJORIE, born July 29, 1923. She married E. C. Boniface. She was later married to a Mr. Balz, and they lived near Temple, Texas.

5. Cornelius (Patrick) Debo

If you could meet your ancestors
All standing in a row
There might be some of them perhaps
You wouldn't care to know.

But here's another question
Which requires a different view.
If you could meet your ancestors
Would they be proud of you?
                                        -- Author Unknown

Cornelius Debo, my great-grandfather, fifth son of John and Jane Debo, was born April 26, 1844,[1] at the Debo home place in southern Bedford County, Virginia. He always called himself the "ragtag" of the family.[2] Reared in the home with four older brothers and a sister older than he, one might discern his reasoning.

Cornelius never used the name "Patrick." The name listed in the family Bible was "Cornelious" with a "P" penciled in following.[3] Who penciled it in is unknown. His Confederate army records list him as "C. P. Debo."[4] He always signed his name "C. Debo."

Reared in the Fancy Grove community of southern Bedford County, Cornelius was educated in neighborhood rural schools. At the age of thirteen (in 1857) he joined the Methodist Church,[5] and attended the old Providence church near the home place on present-day Virginia Rt. 737. [The date of organization of this church is unknown, but the property was deeded to the Virginia Conference in 1848 and a one-room building was erected.[6] The building was sold at auction in June 1958 after the congregation had disbanded in the early 1950s.[7]]

After Fort Sumter was fired on and the War Between the States began in April 1861, Cornelius soon reached his seventeenth year. [Here begins a puzzle that I have never been able to solve.] The Confederate records say that he enlisted as a private in Co. G, 28th Virginia Infantry, on April 15, 1863, at Greenville, North Carolina, and was enrolled by Lieutenant Thomas C. Holland for the duration of the war.[8] All of my life, however, I have understood that he served the entire four years of the war. This fact is verified by two written reports: (1) Cornelius' own words in a newspaper article written by him; and (2) his obituary printed in the same newspaper. At the close of his article titled "A War Experience for the Boys," he stated: "When I left [home] I was the ragtag of the family. I had seen nearly four years of actual service and had made a record that even the neighbors were proud of."[9] Col. James A. Stevens, editor of the *Burnet Bulletin*, related in Cornelius' obituary: "When a mere boy he enlisted as a Confederate soldier in the 26th [sic] Virginia Infantry, and was in nearly all of the terrible battles of that incomparable army from the First Manassas to the engagement a short while before the surrender…in which his foot was partially crushed by a shell. He had one or two brothers killed from his regiment. If written out, his experience of <u>four years</u> [my emphasis, D.D.] would read like a table and be a rich inheritance to his descendants."[10] The only plausible solution seems to me is that he began serving with his brothers in Co. G, 28th Infantry, near the onset of the conflict but was not enrolled in the company until a formal enlistment near his nineteenth birthday. Could it have been because of his young age that he was not enrolled earlier?

The Confederate records show that Cornelius was sent to Chimborazo Hospital #1 in Richmond May 15th, 1863,[11] with typhoid fever. I have in my possession, however, a copy of a letter written May 9[12] by an unnamed but admiring Confederate soldier to Sallie Debo, sister of Cornelius, who had been frequenting the hospital and caring for her brother during his illness. He was furloughed June 18 for fifty days,[13] but he evidently did not avail himself of the leave, for the 28th Virginia left Culpeper, Virginia, on June 15 and was nearing Hagerstown, Maryland, by June 25 on the way toward the confrontation with the Federals at Gettysburg.[14] Cornelius participated in Pickett's Charge, along with his four older brothers. Luther Debo, of Boonville, Missouri, father of Lewis C. Debo and son of Cornelius' brother, Reed Debo, in an interview with Lewis told him that Cornelius buried a Yankee soldier he killed at Gettysburg, probably interring him on the field.

After Cornelius came to Texas and in the latter part of his life, there arose a controversy in some Texas newspapers about whether Gen. George E. Pickett led the charge at Gettysburg, and it seems a "prominent" Texan was denying that he did. A former member of Pickett's Division, J.H. Holt, who lived in Round Rock, Texas, wrote the following letter to Cornelius:

> I was with Picketts Division all during the War, & don't remember one single fight that said Division was in that Genl Pickett was not its leader. At Gains Mill when shot through the left shoulder he refused to leave the battlefield until the fight was

over. Well the charge you rifer to is too absurd to notice, I know personally that he did lead the charge at Gettysburg and so does all the survivors of his Division.[15]

Yours truly

J. H. Holt

Also, Cornelius' brother, Reed Debo, then living in Bedford, Missouri, sent the following notarized statement to the editor of the *Burnet Bulletin*:

Ed. Bulletin:

I understand that it has been publicly stated by a Texan of prominence, that Gen. Geo. E. Pickett did not lead the charge made by his division at Gettysburg, Pa. on July 3, 1863. That he was too drunk to lead, and that it was led by Brigadier General Armstead.

Now, in justice to the dead general, and to gratify my own feeling, I wish to state that such was not the case.

I was a member of the Twenty-eighth Virginia regiment of Garnett's Brigade of Pickett's Division. Was present at the battle of Gettysburg; was in the charge from the beginning to end. Was one of the last to leave the Federal breast-works. I saw Gen. Pickett before the fight, I saw him in the fight, and I saw him come off the field in rear of us. I remember how he looked when we started on the charge and how sad he looked as he came off the field.

Gen. Armstead did all that was required of him until he fell, and that was to support Generals Kemper and Garnett, who were in front.

Gen. Corse, who commanded Gen. Pickett's other brigade, was left at Richmond, so was not at Gettysburg.

R.P. Debo

May 14, 1896. Bedford, MO.

Subscribed and sworn to before me, a Notary Public of the county of Livingston in state of Missouri, this 14th day of May, 1898. My term expires June 3rd, 1899.

E.S. Campbell

Notary Public[16]

Following Gettysburg, Pickett's determined division was sent to the Richmond area for rest and recruitment, and to help guard the Confederate capital from attack on the east and southwest toward Petersburg. The 28th Regiment had been led by Brig. Gen. Robert B. Garnett, who was slain at Gettsburg, and in August 1863 Col. Eppa Hunton, who had been wounded at Gettysburg and now was recovered, was elevated to the rank of brigadier general and given command of the brigade. Cornelius Debo in later years would name his second son , Eppa Debo, after his last commander of his unit, a unit which would spend the winter of 1863-64 at Chaffin's Bluff near Richmond. Of some 376 of Co. G, 28th Virginia, engaged at Gettysburg, 36 had been killed 44 wounded, 49 wounded and captured, and 42 captured, making a total of 171 casualties, a 45.5% loss for the company.[17]

As Union Gen. U.S. Grant began his relentless campaign to overwhelm Gen. Lee's diminishing strength, he began moving closer to the Confederate capital at Richmond by side-stepping the defensive positions established by Lee in battles at the Wilderness, Spotsylvania, and the North Anna River without regard to the terrific losses inflicted by the Southerners on the Federals. By June 1, 1864, the battle lines had reached the site at old Cold Harbor to Sydnor's Saw Mill. Gen. Eppa Hunton's 28th Virginia Regiment was called upon to assist in stemming the onslaught as Union Gen. Meade launched his divisions against the Gray forces of Generals Hoke and Kershaw.[18] The Yankees at first penetrated Hoke's lines, but Hunton's Virginians were hurled into action to support the battered North Carolinians – and Cornelius Debo was in the midst of the fray and gave the following account of the action in a story to the *Burnet Bulletin*, May 14, 1896, titled "Gen. Clingman at Cold Harbor":[19]

EDITOR BULLETIN:

I saw a notice in your paper last week about General Clingman that reminded me of a little incident I happened to see in 1864, back in old Virginia. It was at Cold Harbor after Gen. Grant's last chance at Richmond from the north side of the river. There is a ridge lies on the north side of the Chickahominy river that extends clear to Richmond and if Gen. Grant could have occupied that ridge no force could have kept him out of Richmond. He saw the importance of that position and tried to seize it but failed. That night he concentrated over thirty thousand of his best troops from their position on the heights of Cold Harbor. Gen. Lee of course knew what his intention was and prepared to meet him.

Gen. Hoke's division of North Carolinians was placed in

front to hold the heights and our brigade (Hunton's) of Virginians was held in reserve to support them. Just before sundown the ball opened. 'My stars alive!' Colonel, did you ever sit in a box car and listen to a first class Texas hailstorm falling on the roof with claps of thunder as fast you could count? In about an hour they came for us to go to the front. Gen. Meade had broken the line. Our General put his big iron gray stallion off at a brisk trot and we kept up with him a foot. He threw us into line and hurled us against Meade's front, four thousand of us, and thirty thousand of the enemy.

It was pitch dark, only the light of burning powder to shoot at. I don't know how close they were, but I often felt the heat of their powder on my face. I don't suppose it lasted that way more than five or ten minutes till Meade's men broke and fell back in confusion. We forced them back through the gap they made in Hoke's line. As soon as the excitement had calmed a little, I found that we were mixed up with other troops, but I soon saw that they could be depended on, so we stayed with them in the ditch that night.

Gen. Meade charged us at that place nine times in the next twelve hours, with from three to five lines of battle, but they never broke that line again. All the time, an old man sat close to me in the ditch who kept continually speaking words of cheer and comfort to the boys just like they were his own children. About eight o'clock next morning, they made their last effort to break the line and failed. I noticed that the old man had got half of his hat brim shot off close to his head in that last charge. As soon as they had got out of shooting range, he turned to me and asked me if I had any grub. I had some mouldy corn dodger that was three days old, and a piece of raw middling. I gave him part of it and while he was eating it he unbuttoned the old black slicker he had on, and I saw by the stars on his collar that he was a Brigadier General. Colonel, that was Gen. Clingman! That man with less than seven thousand men, including our brigade, had successfully held his ground against Meade's thirty thousand in nine determined efforts to break his line. That's all I know about Gen. Clingman. Gen Grant admitted the loss of thirteen thousand in that fight, while Gen. Lee praised God that our loss was scarcely twelve hundred.

Our school histories don't tell it that way, but I have a copy of Gen. Grant's report and also of Gen. Lee's made at the time.

We never called Gen. Clingman's boys 'tarheels' or 'conscripts' or 'hospital rats' after that night. There is a lot more connected with that fight this history don't tell I would like to tell you, but it wouldn't look well in print this long after it happened.

Colonel, if you think this would interest any body you can publish it. It seems to me if our people would read and talk more of this kind and less politics we would like each other better and be happier. If there is a man in Burnet county who was in that night's scrape on either side, if he will write me a card, I'll go and see him.

Yours Respectfully,
"OLD VIRGINIA"

The losses to the Northern forces during that battle and Gen. Grant's seeming unconcern about their magnitude earned him the sobriquet even in the Northern press of "The Butcher." He had learned in a most difficult fashion that he could not vanquish Lee's depleted forces by direct frontal assaults, and he began other tactics – the stretching of the battle lines until his superior numbers of men would break through Gen. Lee's lines.

Cornelius Debo received a fifteen-day furlough of indulgence October 17, 1864, and returned to duty November 1, 1864.[20] The latter part of 1864 and first part of 1865 the 28th Virginia had been entrenched on the Howlett line in defense of Richmond. By the end of March Gen. Grant had extended the Northern lines farther and farther south and west of Petersburg until his overwhelming strength had stretched the forces of Gen. Lee to the breaking point. Gen. Eppa Hunton's brigade, along with McGowan's, was situated on the White Oak Road south of Hatcher's Run awaiting the Federals and the Debo brothers were among the defenders. As Hunton's 2,000 men formed a line of battle, men in the 28th Virginia could see their beloved leader, Gen. Lee Standing erect "with his hat off, one of the noblest looking men [their] eyes ever fell upon, grand and stalwart.[21] One veteran noted, "If there was ever a man, the very sight of whom could fill despaired men with the determination to win or die, that man was Lee."[22]

What transpired next was described as an eyewitness participant by Pvt. Cornelius Debo in "A War Experience for the Boys," not only giving an account of the battle and his wounding, but the last days of the Confederacy and his footsore walk home to Bedford County:[23]

"(By a Confederate Soldier in the Virginia Army)

It's not a Georgia possum tale, but the actual experience of a boy 19 years old during the last ten days of the Confederacy. The men of middle age and old selfish croakers will not believe it, but I don't care. I don't want them to even read it, it's for the boys, and when they see that it's not a Georgia tale they will believe every word of it. I will use the first person singular because I was the boy.

On the 31st of March, 1865, after four hours sound sleep in the mud nine miles S. W. of Petersburg, eight thousand of us under Bushrod Johnson marched out in the pine thicket in front of the breastworks and formed a line of battle. Johnson gave the order, 'Forward, guide centre, double quick, march!' As we emerged from the thicket into an open field 90 yards wide we saw three solid lines of blue coats coming from the other side at a double quick, trail arms. Neither side fired till we were within 25 yards of them, then we gave them one volley. It sounded like as if you take a piece of ducking and tear it from one side to the other, only louder of course. There was nothing between us except a crop of young corn about knee high. Boys, that volley just covered the ground with men; it seemed like every shot found a victim. They just stampeded and never returned the fire till they rallied at their breastworks, and then came our time to run. I had just put down my fortieth and last cartridge and was putting a cap on my rifle when a shell from the enemy's guns struck my right foot and crushed it. Boys, you just ought to have seen me coming out of that—my gun under my arm for a crutch and my well foot on the other side. I came out in a lope, like a buzzard of a cold morning. That night they sent the wounded to an old winter camp in the pine woods close by a cane-break swamp, and left us there without surgeon or a nurse. They put five of us in a log hut 8x12 and next morning Jack Steward, Bige Douglas and Henry Thomas were dead and left Jess Johnson and me alive, but not able to walk. During the night I went on my hands and knees to a well about 100 yards to get water for the dying men. Henry Thomas drank over two quarts of water at one draught and died in a few minutes. We had no candle or light of any kind. Boys, how do you like that for a night in the army?

April 1st two negroes came in a wagon and took the dead away. After noon I heard a feeble voice calling me from the other side of the camp; it said, 'If you can get here, come to me.' I crawled over there, and there lay poor old Jerry Overstreet on a plank, shot through the lungs. The ball went in the right breast and came out below the shoulder blade. He wanted to send a dying message to his wife and seven children; he never got off that plank.

April 2nd. Lay on my plank nearly all day pouring cold water on my crushed foot and not a bite of anything to eat for two days.

April 3rd. Found out that our army had gone and left us to the mercy of the enemy. About 8 o'clock I looked and saw some of the blue coats coming up the hill. I got a stick I could use for a crutch and pulled out to the canebrake. That night I heard a mule eating corn in a box. He let me have an ear of corn and I thanked the mule, and took my corn to the thicket, and ate the first meal I had had for three days. (My teeth were better then than now.)

April 4th. Kept hid mostly till night, but every chance I got I'd move up a mile or so in the direction of home. Just before night found a corn hoecake lying in the trail; didn't try to find out how it came there, but took it to the creek and had a square meal; travelled nearly all night.

April 5th. Met up with another wounded Reb, went to the mansion of the old planter to get some grub; he had no sympathy for the Rebs, and wouldn't let us have anything. We traded him a gold ring for $2.50 worth of provisions. That ring was made out of a brass bombscrew. We met five other wounded Rebs, and all had a square meal from that home-made brass ring. I took Jess Johnson and we two pulled out toward the setting sun and travelled all night mostly.

April 6th. We found a brigade of our men in line of battle waiting for Sheridan to come up from the way we came. They gave us a rousing cheer and we moved on feeling that we are among our friends. Pretty soon we fell in with General Gordon's wagon train. We thought to stay with that and we would have protection, but in less than two hours I heard a great commotion ahead of us and the noise of battle. A band of Sheridan's cavalry had made a dash on the train and were killing the mules and setting fire to the wagons as they came to them. I took to the thicket of scrubby pines and briars, and hid in a deep gully about thirty yards from the road and went to sleep. When I woke all was quiet. I crept out on a high place to see if the way was clear, and from there I saw over three miles of solid wagon train on fire at one time. I saw a big fine mansion about a mile off the road and went over there to try to get something to eat. There was a big yellow flag waving over the house and a little negro girl met us at the door and said, 'Master says don't come inside, cause him and all de rest is got de small pox.' I sent him word I was not afraid of small pox but would like to get something to eat. He sent us two cups of tea, two slices of baked ham, and two of light bread. I thanked him and asked him if he couldn't give us something more solid. He then sent us a bountiful supply of boiled middling, ash cake, and butter milk with the request to get away from the house to eat it; of course, we gladly obliged him. That night we travelled nearly all night in the rain and I found a whole plug of good navy tobacco, that some good Yankee had lost. I hadn't had a chew for over a week.

April 7th. Kept moving nearly all the time but had to keep away from the public roads. Went to an old man's house to try to get something to eat. I asked a negro wench where the proprietor was. He saw me and gave me a genteel cursing for speaking to a negro. He wouldn't give us a bite to eat but ordered us to leave his premises. I shed a few tears and left. Boys, inside of three hours I had fooled that old sinner out of three square meals of ash cake and middling for Jess and me both. I will tell you how it was done if you will ask me privately. It wouldn't look well on paper. I think he had as much of old Satan in him as any man I ever saw. That evening we came to a train of cars loaded with government plunder, steam up, headed for Lynchburg 30 miles ahead. We stored ourselves away among the other government stuff and went to sleep. Ten miles from there the cars stopped and I heard firing a few hundred years ahead. I crawled off and took to the woods. A half hour after I left it that train was captured and burned. We travelled all night and next morning.

April 8th found me 40 miles from home with my foot so badly swollen that the skin had bursted between my toes, and the blue coats in possession of every town and crossing between me and home, with bands of men scouting the whole country over.

We kept away from the roads and kept moving. The day passed without incident. I traded a hatchet that I had carried through the war to a little negro for a quart of meal. Later on I gave a poor old woman a pint of green coffee for what buttermilk we could drink. At 11 o'clock that night we came to Otter river at old Charles Anthony's. The bridge was burned; it was 80 yards wide and 12 feet deep. On the hill the other side of the river was a negro cabin, a bright light was shining in the cabin; we guessed that Old Randal was giving a negro hoedown. Jess could imitate the negro voice exactly. He gave four or five big negro yells and then called out 'Ran!' as loud as he could bawl, and said 'Come and help me over!' Old Ran thought it was another negro coming to his hoedown. Soon we heard the noise of his canoe. I hid close to the water's edge and Jess stood out on the bank talking negro talk to him. When his canoe struck the sand, I caught hold of the chain and told him to hold up. Old Ran was fooled but we made him set us over. We went four miles along a trail up the mountain and laid down and slept till sun-up.

April 9th, we went to George White's. There I washed my face and combed my hair for the first time in 12 days. At noon I got home. When I left I was the rag-tag of the family. I had seen nearly four years of actual service and had made a record that even the neighbors were proud of.

Boys, this was my actual experience during that time. If you enjoy it tell me so, and I'll tell you another. I don't care whether the old men believe it or not; it's the truth all the way through all the same.

Your friend,
C. DEBO"

When Cornelius arrived at home, as he approached the house he could see his father sitting in the front room reading a newspaper while some of the womenfolk were quilting a quilt. Rather than enter the house at the front door, he went around to the back and came in at the back door for fear that in all the excitement of his homecoming some of his loved ones, not knowing of his severe wound, would injure his split and swollen foot.[24]

The story has been told among the family through the years that as Cornelius was hobbling along using his gun for a crutch to get out of the line of battle after being wounded that he met Gen. Lee, who proffered words of inquiry concerning his wound and extended to him sympathy for his injury. This fact was repeated in his obituary.[25]

While Cornelius was rejoining his family in Bedford County, the survivors of the 28th Virginia were stacking their muskets and rolling up their battle flags in preparation for the surrender at Appomattox Court House. Many wept openly as Gen. Lee returned from the McLean house, announcing the surrender and bidding his soldiers farewell. Few of the men in the 28th who surrendered on that sad and fateful day had been present four years before, but among them was Cornelius Debo. Hundreds of other of Virginia's patriots who had gathered on the muster grounds in western Virginia counties had found their resting place on the battlefields of Virginia, Maryland, and Pennsylvania. One Debo brother was "lost at Gettysburg" and four survived the war. Since he was not present at Appomattox for the surrender but had gone home, Cornelius never surrendered and as far as has been ascertained never took the oath of allegiance as some of his brothers who had been taken prisoner were required to do. Maybe he was in reality a genuine "unreconstructed Rebel"!

Recuperating from his wound and recovering physically as well as emotionally from the ravages and privations of the past four years of conflict no doubt occupied the next period of time in Cornelius Debo's life. From a letter later in life we learn he learned the trade of plastering probably from his brother Reed, who went down to Bristol, Virginia, on the Tennessee border to learn the art.[26] (Whether Cornelius learned how to plaster at this time or later after they had gone to Missouri is unknown.)

In 1869 the three brothers, Reed, Thomas, and Cornelius, all went to Missouri for new opportunities and a new start. Times were hard in Bedford County and Virginia had been so devastated by the war that the future appeared anything but bright in those years following the conflict. Out west where not so much destruction had occurred presented a more favorable scenario for a new beginning, so the brothers settled for a short time in Howard County, Missouri.

Cornelius did not remain in Missouri very long, however, for he had his eyes on Texas, no doubt influenced by his brother-in-law, Clay Bowmer, who had come to Texas in 1859.[27] Bowmer had served with the Texas Confederate forces during the war, but had returned afterward in 1868 to Missouri where he met and married Cornelius' sister Sallie in 1870.[28] In 1872 Cornelius, Mr. and Mrs. Clay Bowmer and young daughter Elsie, and Thomas Debo left Cooper County by wagon and on horseback for the state of Texas, the Missouri relatives riding out south of Boonville to bid them Godspeed and farewell. In June 1970 while visiting Mrs. Elsie Bowmer Cook(e) in a nursing home in Monroe, Louisiana, she laughingly told me, "Uncle Tenie [Cornelius] nursed me on his lap half the way from Missouri to Texas! He was my favorite Uncle." (Elsie was about one year old at the time, but had no doubt heard about it from her mother.)

While crossing the Indian Territory (Oklahoma), the travelers one day noticed a dark cloud up ahead of them and surmised that they were facing a tremendous storm. A closer investigation, however, revealed an approaching prairie fire, and the wagons turned aside to hurriedly run parallel to the conflagration to avoid it. Later, as the wagons reached the Red River, the travelers camped for the night in the dry bed of the river – what would today seem a very hazardous practice, knowing the results that can come from a sudden, severe Texas thunderstorm! When the wagons approached the city of Waco (with a population of 3,000 in 1870), Cornelius later described the place as "a very small city," with little of substantial nature between there and Williamson County – their destination – except the little village of Belton, population 777. Cornelius described the journey from Missouri to Texas in a letter to his brother Reed:[29]

Williamson County, Texas
November 5, 1872

Mr. Reed P. Debo
Dear Brother
If you would like to know what I am doin and where I am just be patient and read this.

I could not begin to give you all the details of the trip. I can only tell you which way we came and that we had no axidents except such as one common to people traveling in that route. We came by Baxter Springs [Kansas] and crossed the Arkansas river at Fort Gibson and crossed the Red river at Colbert's ferry and on to Sherman, Texas. With these leading points any one who has ever went that rout can tell you any thing you want to know about the places we passed by.

Our teams all held out finely and we did not suffer on the road for any thing except water and not much for that. We stoped in Tarrant county a week and such as were able hitched up and rolled down here where I believe all are pleased with the country and the people.

Clay has rented a farm and is sowing wheat and seems to be well pleased with the prospect. Sallie is wonderfully pleased with her 1000 new aunts and cousins and uncles and so forth that she found in this county.

Thomas has hired to a farmer for $20 in gold a month. I went to Austin last Saturday to see how plastering is and I found plasterers enough there to put work at 8 cts. I went to the old plasterers and they told me they had not had a job for four months because they wouldn't work for less than 12 cts and the new comers would work at 8. I have been asking at all the towns away from the R.R. how plastering is and I know of several places where business is lively at 25 cts for g(undecipherable) any town off from the R.R. its 25 cts for brown work.

I took my mules to Austin to see what I could do with them. I found big mules very dull sale because money is mighty scarce in Texas. I managed to sell them for $375 in gold cash. I sold my wagon for $80 in gold so now I have nothing left to trade on except the saddle and it attracts more attention than anything else.

From the time I began to buy up my outfit counting all of my expences up to the time I got here with the sales I have made after taking out the expences I have all my money back in gold and $80 over all in gold.

There is no Greenback in circulation here but when a man says dollars here he means gold or silver. They take Greenback at 90 cts at stores but brokers must have it at 87 ½ cts.

Reed I wish you would find out exactly where the Tinsley boys are and let me know as soon as possible so I can call on them when I pass that way. My address will be Bagdad for the present but I dont know how long but just direct to Bagdad Texas and Ill get it some time or other.

I have no more to write so I close.

As ever   Cornelius Debo

To R. P. Debo

(Note: Baxter Springs was in Kansas, and Fort Gibson was in Indian Territory, later to be Oklahoma. The Tinsley "boys" were from Virginia and had served in the same regiment with the Debo brothers).

When the Bowmers and Debos arrived in Williamson County, they

Cornelius and Mary Debo with younger children (Standing: Frank and Hardy); (Girls: Sallie and Nell)

drove their wagons up to the home of William S. Schooley near Bagdad (present day Leander). Clay Bowmer threw some apples against the front door of the Schooley home and hollered loudly, "Billy Schooley, Billy Schooley! Come out here, for this is Clay Bowmer all the way from Missouri!" This W. S. Schooley had a young daughter who caught the eye of Cornelius Debo, and by May 28, 1873 (the next year), he was married at the Schooley home by R. B. (Bob) Davis, a Cumberland Presbyterian preacher, to Miss Mary Ruth Schooley, who was just sixteen years old, having been born December 3, 1857.

(Cornelius was twenty-nine,) The newly-married couple set up housekeeping on the banks of Brushy Creek and stayed long enough to "make a corn crop"[30] in 1874 and for the birth of their first child, Jennie Prudence, on November 3, of that year. The next year the young family moved about thirty-five miles northwest into Burnet County where Cornelius for $330 purchased 220 acres in the Spring Creek community about five miles northwest of the city of Burnet (he later purchased 320 adjoining acres on the north).[31] Here the "fireplace room," with a fireplace built by a "Dutchman named Schultz,"[32] had been built, and it served as the first home for the family for several years with Mary Debo having only the fireplace on which to cook the meals. (How happy Mary was in later years when she had obtained a wood range on which to prepare her meals.) Thomas Debo was with the family and marked the height of little Jennie on the door-facing the day the family moved into their new home. Thomas helped his brother clear land for his fields and with the arduous task of building rock fences as well as a barn, granary, and other out-buildings such as a corn crib, smoke house, and so forth.

While most of the children were still at home, a number of them had a sort of a little family band. Eppa and Frank could play the fiddle, Nell played the guitar, Sallie "chorded" on the organ, and my grandfather, Lilbon, beat time on a triangle. My grandfather always said the reason he couldn't play the fiddle, was that he couldn't keep his foot patting! He said he could start a tune but that his foot wouldn't keep up!

Cornelius would spend the next number of years farming and participating in activities of the communities. Mr. E. F. Thomas deeded an acre of land on December 3, 1877,[33] to the Spring Creek School District and a frame building was erected in the Thomas pasture. The building was used for school, religious, and community affairs. One Sunday morning in the early days Cornelius and family headed for the schoolhouse for Sunday school with Cornelius riding horseback and the family in the wagon. He rode on ahead toward the school building and came back shortly, telling the ones in the wagon not to continue on to the school but to turn aside and go to the Roper home at Four Mile Spring, there to wait for him. He had found the body of a man at the school who had been killed, and wanted to spare his family seeing such a sight. While Mary Debo and the children were at the house at Four Mile Spring a man appeared at the back door asking for food. The lady of the house gave him some and he hurriedly left, heading west. The family always thought that man was the killer. Those were still tough days in early Texas.

The Spring Creek neighborhood later built a new schoolhouse only about a mile from the Debo home. The land was deeded to the school district by J. F. Banks on September 19, 1891,[34] and the building was situated north of where it was formerly, being now near what was known as the Ed Magill home. Cornelius mentions this new schoolhouse in a letter to brother Reed dated December 25, 1891.[35]

When the Methodist church in Burnet was organized in March 1877 Cornelius and Mary Debo were among the charter members.[36]

On September 9, 1887,[37] Cornelius was licensed by the quarterly conference to preach, which license was renewed yearly until November 25, 1894, when he was ordained a deacon by Bishop Joseph S. Key at Castell, Texas.[38] He preached in the country schoolhouses throughout the county and area. A number of his children told me that despite the usual Methodist practice of sprinkling for baptism that Cornelius refused to do so and immersed his converts, saying, "My Bible says that baptism is a burial in water," citing examples in his New Testament. (Could this have been another example of what Miss Era Deboe described as the common family trait of stubbornness?)

Marriages performed by Cornelius in Burnet County include the following: H. N. Banks and Della Clark, Dec. 15, 1895; James A. (Jim) Fry and Ella Marx, Dec. 8, 1896; William (Will) Marx and Mabel Lanterman, April 7, 1897; J. H. Shaw and Mrs. Eva Owen, June 30, 1897; V. B. Brown and Mary Hill, Oct. 27, 1897; Thomas C. (Tom) Anthony and Maud Fry, Dec. 15, 1897; and Charles Barker and Elizabeth (Lizzie) Baker, Feb. 23, 1898.[39]

Sometime around 1890 and 1891 Cornelius Debo, while working out in the hot Texas sun, suffered what would probably be termed today a heatstroke and was never really well thereafter. My grandfather, Lilbon Debo, told me now that as the oldest son he had to quit school in the seventh grade, and as he termed it, "go to plowing." He, along with his brother Eppa and two older sisters, Jennie and Mollie, had to make the crops and do the outside work. In a letter to his brother Reed, December 25, 1991,[40] Cornelius described his condition as follows: "I can go where I please in good weather and work some but when the weather is bad I have to keep close. I take cold just like some old woman and then it sets me back again."

Cornelius Debo departed this life on Sunday morning, October 16, 1898,[41] at the early age of 54, leaving a 41-year-old wife, eleven children, and another child born the following March. He had requested to be buried north of the Debo home, and his burial was the beginning of the Debo family cemetery. It was only after I had been to Bedford County, Virginia, and had seen the old home place, its location, and the cemetery there that I realized why Grandfather Debo requested the certain burial spot. The family burial ground in old Virginia was located north of the house amid the hills; and now he would rest north of his Texas home in the shadow of the hill known in legal documents as Shin Oak Mountain and on some maps as Roper Mountain, but among some of the family as Debo Mountain.

The editor of the *Burnet Bulletin* wrote the following obituary for his paper:[42]

DEATH OF A CHRISTIAN GENTLEMAN

With much sorrow this paper records the passing away, on last Sunday, after many weeks of suffering, of Rev. C. Debo, in the 52rd or 54th year of his age, from inflammation of the stomach and bowels. Seven or eight years ago, he received something like sunstroke, and has never been well since. He met his death patiently and calmly, having lived an humble, consistent Christian life that left no room for fear of the future.

Mr. Debo was a preacher of the gospel as taught by the Methodist brethren; an eccentric man who did not court popularity, but a just, good man, husband, father and citizen.

When a mere boy he enlisted as a Confederate soldier in the 26th (sic; should be 28th D. D.) Virginia Infantry, and was in nearly all of the terrible battles of that incomparable army from the First Manassas to the engagement a short while before the surrender – we think at Richmond – in which his foot was partially crushed by a shell. He had one or two brothers killed from his regiment. If written out, his experience of four years would read like a table and be a rich inheritance to his descendants. As he hobbled out of battle with his gun for a crutch, he met General Lee, who dropped some words of inquiry and sympathy, and that was the last he ever saw of the great commander. He has at time furnished this paper several interesting sketches of his army life and often would tell the writer, he was afraid to give his experience lest it might not be believed.

Rest, brave veteran! Your last roll-call will be in Heaven. God will care for thy widow and orphans.

The following obituary written by Cornelius' preacher appeared in a Methodist paper:

DEBO. – Rev. Cornelius Debo was born in Bedford County, Va., April 26, 1844. In his thirteenth year he was converted and joined the M.E. [Methodist Episcopal} Church, South. In the winter of 1865 [should be 1869, D.D.] he moved to Missouri, where he lived till 1872, then moved to Texas. In 1873 he was happily married to Miss Mary Schooley. He settled in Burnet County,

Texas, where he lived till his death, which occurred on Sunday morning, October 16, 1898. He was licensed to preach in 1887, and ordained deacon in 1894. Bro. Debo was widely known by the itinerant ministry and laymen. He was rugged and straightforward in all he ever did - "an Israelite in whom was no guile." With few advantages in early life, he had very little opportunity in after life to become an educated man, yet he became a strong, clear, earnest preacher of the Word. He was a wise father. His children will rise up to call him blessed. He had the perfect confidence of his neighbors, without being a very popular man. He was rigid, not to say stern, in his resistance of all evil. He catered to none nor compromised his convictions at any time. Grace did much for him. Naturally high-tempered and fearless in an unregenerate state, he would have been perhaps hard to get on well with; but when he yielded his heart to God he made a complete surrender. It is a joyful reflection to me that I have known so good a man as he. God bless his widow and the children.

His Pastor[43]

No doubt the deprivations, hardships, and wound suffered in the war, along with the hard physical labors of that day and time, hastened the deterioration of Cornelius Debo's health and ushered him toward his departure from this world. Mary, his widow, was left with the burden of a large family to care for and was to live forty-five years after the death of her husband, passing from this life at the home of her daughter, Nell Debo Johnston, on January 11, 1944.[44] The inner strength of this pioneer woman is seen most vividly in what she had to endure in the six years following the death of her spouse. Beginning with and counting the death of Cornelius, she suffered the loss of six of her family in that length of time. The next month after her husband's death a son, William Clay, died (Nov. 21, 1898); her father, W. S. Schooley, two years later (Nov. 21, 1900); a little five-year-old daughter, Cora Lee, March 2, 1901; the last month of that same year, her mother, Sarah Prudence Schooley (Dec. 30, 1901; and two years later another son, John Henry (Nov. 30, 1903).[45] Her parents were buried in the Mt. Zion Cemetery near Bertram, Texas, and the three children joined their father in the family cemetery north of the Debo home.

Another manifestation of Mary's strength was related to me by her daughter Nell in an incident that occurred when she was but a girl. Mrs. Debo had her children gathered around her before the fireplace after supper and was reading the Bible to them (as was her nightly custom). A coal oil lamp gave light for her to read. The children looked up and at one of the windows at the side of the fireplace a man's face appeared, the visitor peering in at the little assembled group. Mary quietened the children, calmed them, and told them to remain very quiet as she continued her reading. The face soon disappeared and no harm came to them. A neighbor woman, whose place adjoined the Debo place on the north, had two brothers who were outlaws, and it was afterward surmised that perhaps the night visitor was one of the woman's brothers who was passing through the country. The calm demeanor of a wise pioneer woman of strength and character possibly averted tragic consequences.

Mary Debo not only displayed her strength as an adult, but even as a child she showed a character that would develop and carry her through the trials and tribulations of later years. As an eight- or nine-year-old girl, she was willing and ready to help defend her family, and home against outside invaders. She had gone visiting some nearby neighbors who lived within sight of the Schooley home in the old Bagdad community, and saw some Yankee troopers ride up to her home (this was shortly after the close of the War Between the States when Federal troops had come into Texas for occupation of the state.) Little Mary knew her mother was alone at home along with a few of the younger children, and she left the neighbor's house "by the back way" and went back home to help her mother save their home from the "invaders." An eight- or nine-year-old! Imagine that, if you will.

With the marriage of her children, the establishment of their own homes, and the marriage in 1919 of her last unmarried son, Eppa Debo, with whom she, along with her youngest daughter Julia, had been living at the home place, Mary Debo and Julia moved into Burnet while Eppa and his wife Jewel continued to live and farm the home place. Mary and Julia moved in with her daughter and son-in-law, Jennie and Lindsey Fisher, until Julia's marriage to Winter Landtroop after which Mary lived most of her remaining days with them and spent time visiting with different ones of her children. Mary and the Landtroops lived for some time at Cedar Park, but Mary was in the home of Tom and Nell Johnston during her last illness during which Miss Kate Sarrels, a practical nurse, helped care for her. As a twelve-year-old child, I remember attending a graveside service for her on a very cold January day at the family graveyard as her grandsons laid

Mary to rest beside Cornelius, who had departed this life so many years before. Sons and sons-in-law shortly after Mary's death erected a rock fence around the Debo graves in the family cemetery, which had grown throughout the years as neighbors requested to bury their dead there and had been granted permission by the family. The home place was sold on June 15, 1944,[46] and the proceeds divided among the many heirs. A one-fourth acre plot around the cemetery, however, was reserved from the sale for the benefit of the Debo family as the deed of sale specified that "excepted from this conveyance and not intended to be herein conveyed ¼ acre of land, more or less, known as the Debo Cemetery, upon which said ¼ acre of land, more or less, the bodies of C. Debo, Mary R. Debo, and others are now buried."

Mary Debo's obituary, written by the editor, Mr. Louis Chamberlain, a treasured friend, appeared in the January 13, 1944, issue of the *Burnet Bulletin*, as follows:[47]

MRS. MARY DEBO CALLED BY DEATH

Mrs. Mary Debo, a resident of Burnet County for more than a half century, was called by death at the home of her son-in-law and daughter, Mrs. Tom Johnston, early Tuesday morning, January 11th, 1944. The body was interred and the funeral service held at the Debo family cemetery in the Spring Creek community, conducted by Rev. L.D. Hardt, pastor of the Burnet Methodist church. The W. Northington Funeral Chapel of this place was in charge of the arrangements, and the pallbearers were grandsons, Clyde and Bill Debo of Burnet, Clarence and Dorr McFarland of Austin, Lewis McFarland of Cleburne, and Pfc. Wm. Johnston of Sheppard Field.

Mrs. Debo was born December 3rd, 1857, in Williamson County, Texas, but by far the greater part of her life was spent in Burnet County. She is survived by four daughters, Mrs. L. Fisher of Houston, Mrs. E. A. Simpson of Winters, Mrs. W. A. Landtroop of Austin, Mrs. Tom Johnston of Burnet; four sons, L. Debo, Eppie Debo, Frank Debo, and Hardy Debo, all of Burnet; one sister, Mrs. Ed Shuford of Rio Grande City; one brother, Dick Schooley of Houston. Her husband preceded her in death many years ago.

Mrs. Debo was a devout Christian, a member of the Methodist Church and was loved, honored, and reverenced by all who knew her. If this writer was asked to name only a few of the finest, most lovable women he had known during his entire life, one of them would be Mrs. Mary Debo. Once or twice a year for almost as far back as we can remember she would call at our office for a short friendly visit, and the day was always made brighter by her cheery, friendly presence. Had she realized how her visits were appreciated and enjoyed by us we are sure they would have been more frequent. She leaves a fine family of sons and daughters to mourn her departure, and we know they appreciated their saintly mother to the fullest extent. They have our heartfelt sympathy in their bereavement.

Cornelius and Mary Debo were the parents of twelve children – six boys and six girls. The remainder of this chapter will consist of the story of those children and their descendants.

a. Jennie Prudence Debo Fisher

Jennie Prudence Debo, the oldest child of Cornelius and Mary Debo, was born November 3, 1874,[1] in Williamson County, Texas, near old Bagdad on Brushy Creek. She was named for her grandmother Debo and Schooley. The family moved to Burnet County the next fall after gathering a corn crop and settled about five miles west of Burnet in the Spring Creek community. Jennie grew up in the typical country home of those pioneer days and as the oldest child assumed her part of the daily tasks for which she was responsible. She attended the old Spring Creek rural school when it was located in the Thomas pasture. By the time her father had his sunstroke in 1890-91 Jennie, her sister Mollie, and two oldest brothers, Lilbon and Eppa, were working in the fields picking cotton, gathering corn, and so forth, making the crops.

At the age of twenty-one Jennie was married to Peter Lindsey Fisher, who was reared in the neighboring Council Creek neighborhood. Lindsey was the son of Alexander (Zan) Fisher and the former Sarah Jane Fry, and was born December 27, 1872, in Burnet County.[2] The Fishers had come to Burnet County from Illinois in 1855 with the Fry, Johnston, and other families, settling in the Council Creek community.[3] Jennie and Lindsey were married on July 19, 1896,[4] the ceremony being performed by Jerome J. Haralson, a Methodist preacher from Burnet. The first year of their marriage they lived in a tent over on "Pull Tight" ridge – so named by "Uncle Bill" Fry because he said if one lived on the ridge he had to "pull tight" to subsist! The Fishers' first child, Otis Herman, was born September 11, 1898, but they lost their second son, who was born and died September 10, 1900, and was buried in the Fisher-Fry Cemetery west of Post Mountain west of Burnet.[5]

Jennie and Lindsey later moved into Burnet where they operated the Cowboy Café next door to the old *Burnet Bulletin* office until 1920 when they sold it to Jennie's oldest brother, Lilbon Debo. They then purchased a grocery store on the south side of the square in Burnet, which they operated until about 1929 when they sold it to Leonard Wimpy. Lindsey's health began to deteriorate, and after hearing of a doctor in Nacogdoches, Texas, whom it was thought could treat and possibly cure his ailment, the Fishers moved for a time to that city. His health only got worse and his one desire was to get back to Burnet. Upon returning to Burnet they moved into the Chamberlain house near the old football field where Lindsey departed his life on June 24, 1930,[6] and was buried in the Odd Fellows Cemetery with Silas Howell, a minister of the church of Christ, officiating. The following obituary appeared in the local paper:[7]

DEATH CALLS LINDSEY FISHER

Tuesday morning, June 24th, 1930, at his home in this place, death claimed Lindsey Fisher. Both religious and Masonic services were held over his body. The religious service was held at the Baptist Tabernacle, conducted by Silas Howell, after the Masonic Order of which the deceased was a member, took charge of the body and placed it in its last resting place in the Odd Fellows Cemetery. The pallbearers were Bunk Gibbs, Bill Chamberlain, Shaw Norris, Vert Gibbs, Herbert Norris and John Olney. The grave was literally covered with beautiful flowers from loving friends of the family.

Lindsey Fisher was born in Burnet County, Texas, on December 27th, 1872, making him at the time of his death 57 years 5 months and 27 days of age. He grew to manhood in this section and on July 19th, 1896 was united in marriage to Miss Jennie Debo, who with three children survive him, as follows: Otis Fisher of Houston, Mrs. Arch McDaniel of Houston, and Miss Ruth Fisher of Burnet. He is also survived by one sister, Mrs. W. J. Daugherty of Burnet, and four brothers, Sam and Bill Fisher of Wichita Falls, and Ed and Frank Fisher of Winters.

Everyone has his idea of what it takes to make a brave, upstanding man. The writer was perhaps as close to Lindsey Fisher as any man outside of close relatives, and I know that he possessed more of the characteristics of the true man than the average citizen. He was as Brave as a lion, but as gentle as a woman. No man, woman or child in distress ever called upon him and was turned away. He was a friend that could be counted upon in both adversity and prosperity. His word was as good as any bone, and he had the unlimited confidence of those who knew him best. He was a faithful and loving husband, a devoted father, and a citizen that any place should be proud to own. In truth and fact, Lindsey Fisher was a MAN.

Until three or four years ago Mr. Fisher had been a man of unusual physical strength, but when bad health struck him he bore his pain and suffering with fortitude. All that the best medical aid could do was rendered unto him, but of no avail. His time had come.

To the patient, faithful, heart-broken wife, and children, the sincerest sympathy of this writer is extended. The baby girl of the family, Ruth, has been my unwavering friend since she was old enough to walk, and she has a place in my heart almost equal to that of my own children. Ruth, if such things are known in heaven, your beloved father knows that as long as my life lasts you have a friend that you may call upon in happiness or adversity, and your call will be answered.

After Lindsey's death, Jennie and her youngest daughter, Ruth, moved to Houston where son Otis and her other daughter Eula were already living. She lived with Ruth and her husband, Bob Holmes, the remainder of her life. Most of that time was spent in Houston, with the exception of a few years in the early 1970s when they lived a few miles northeast of Burnet near the Eppa Debos before returning to Houston. While Jennie lived there I visited often and spent many hours with her reliving the days of yore and gathering data on the family which she remembered vividly even in old age. She called me her "preacher boy." Jennie passed away on July 24, 1976,[8] at the grand age of 101, and she was brought back to Burnet for funeral services and burial beside her husband. Her obituary from the *Burnet Bulletin* is as follows:[9]

MRS. JENNIE FISHER

Jennie Prudence Fisher, 101, of Houston, died Sunday, July 24, 1976, in Houston.

Funeral services for Mrs. Fisher were held Monday, July 26, at the Clements Chapel in Burnet, with Darrell Debo officiating.

Interment followed at the Odd Fellows Cemetery under the direction of Clements Funeral home.

Survivors of Mrs. Fisher include two daughters: Mrs. Eula Allison and Ruth Holmes, both of Houston; three sisters, Mrs.

Sallie Simpson of Clyde, Mrs. Nell Johnston of Burnet and Mrs. Julia Wolf of Austin; two grandchildren, seven great-grandchildren and two great-great-grandchildren.

Nephews of Mrs. Fisher served as pallbearers.

Mrs. Fisher was born November 3, 1874. She was a member of the Methodist Church.

Jennie and Lindsey Fisher were the parents of the following children, all of whom were born in Burnet County:

1. OTIS HERMAN, who was born Sept 11, 1898, and died May 24, 1975, in Rosenburg, Texas, with burial in Houston. He was married Jan. 31, 1924, to Nettie Mae (Nets) Hill, who was born Feb. 8, 1900, in Kentucky, and died Oct. 17, 1974, with burial in Houston. They had no children. Otis' obituary is as follows:[10]

MR. OTIS H. FISHER

Mr. Otis H. Fisher, 76, of Richmond, passed away Saturday morning, May 24, 1975, in a Rosenburg hospital. Mr. Fisher was born September 11, 1898, in Burnet County and was the son of Lindsey Fisher and the former Jennie P. Debo. Although reared in Burnet, he was a former resident of Houston, but had resided in Richmond for the past three years.

Mr. Fisher was a member of the First Methodist Church of Houston; Washington Chapter No. 2 Royal Arch Masons; Houston Council No. 1 Royal and Selected Masters; Valley Lodge No. 175 A.F.&A.M., Ft. Bend Country Club, Richmond; and a veteran of World War 1.

Funeral services were held at 2:00 p.m. Monday, May 26, at Memorial Mission chapel in Forest Park Westheimer Cemetery with Rev. Frederick Marsh officiating. Interment was in the Forest Park Westheimer Cemetery under the direction of the Forest Park Lawndale Funeral Home.

Survivors include his mother, Mrs. Jennie Fisher, of Houston; two sisters, Mrs. W. D. (Eula) Allison and Mrs. R. L. (Ruth) Holmes, both of Houston; and numerous nieces, nephews, and cousins. He was prceded in death by his wife, Mrs. Nets Fisher, on October 17, 1974.

2. INFANT SON, born and died Sept. 10, 1900, with burial in the Fisher-Fry Cemetery west of Burnet.
3. EULA LEE, who was born Feb. 20, 1902, and died Aug. 8, 1982, in Houston. She was first married Mar. 15, 1925, to William Arch McDaniel, who was born Jan. 3, 1895, in Bell County

and died Apr. 29, 1936, in Houston. She was later married in Nov. 1949 to Oliver Allison, and after his death was married in March 1964 to his brother, William D. Allison, who was born June 2, 1902. Eula and Arch McDaniel had two children:

a. WILLIAM OTIS (Bill), who was born Apr. 29, 1926, died June 5, 1989, and served many years in the U. S. Navy. He was married June 29, 1946, to Peggy Cole, who was born Oct. 24, 1927. Their children are William Douglas (born May 29, 1947), Kathryn Lee (born Oct. 7, 1951), and Betty Ann (born Nov. 14, 1961).

b. JENNIE MARIE, who was born Dec. 14, 1927. She was married Nov. 24, 1948, to Wayne Dowling, who was born Jan. 22, 1924, and died Sept. 3, 1992. Their children are Ralph Wayne (born Mar. 5, 1952), Judy Marie (born Oct. 15, 1954), Mary Ann (born Nov. 29, 1961) and Patrick Lee (born June 29, 1963). Marie lives in San Angelo.

4. SARAH RUTH, who was born Sept. 25, 1910. She was married May 18, 1937, in Burnet to Robert L. (Bob) Holmes, who was born Mar. 29, 1911, in Beeville, Texas, and died July 21, 1975. They had no children. Ruth died June 25, 2007, and was buried in Houston. Bob's obituary is as follows:

ROBERT L. HOLMES

Robert L. Holmes, 64, of 7635 El Rancho, Houston, died on Monday, July 21, 1975, in a Houston hospital. Mr. Holmes was a native of Beeville, a resident of Houston for 40 years, and a member of the Methodist church. He was married to the former Ruth Fisher of Burnet.

Funeral services were held Thursday, July 24, at Forest Park Lawndale chapel at 1:30 p.m. with Rev. Reginald C. Brock officiating. Interment followed in Forest Park Lawndale Cemetery.

Survivors include his wife, Mrs. Ruth Holmes, of Houston; a sister, Mrs. Edna Sailer, and a brother, W. C. Holmes, both of Houston; and numerous nieces and nephews.

In lieu of usual remembrances, the family requested that donations be made to the American Cancer Society or a favorite charity.[11]

b. Mary Thomas (Mollie) Debo McFarland

Mary Thomas (Mollie) McFarland, the second child of Cornelius and Mary Debo and the first to be born at the home place in Burnet County, was born December 23, 1876,[1] and was named for her mother and her uncle, Thomas Debo, Cornelius' brother. Because of their nearness in age, Mollie and Jennie grew up as close companions and classmates at the Spring Creek rural school when it was located in the Thomas pasture. With Jennie and her oldest brothers, Lilbon and Eppa, the responsibilities for growing and harvesting the crops as well as making the living for the family (after the sunstroke suffered by their father and the deterioration of his health) fell heavily upon these older children. The cotton and corn fields were common fields of labor as well as the garden and the daily chores common to the whole of rural society in that day and time.

Ray and Mollie Debo McFarland
(Possibly at Their Marriage)

Mollie did not marry until after the death of her father in 1898 because of his opposition to her suitor. She was married by J. T. Bell on April 23, 1899,[2] to Robert Ray McFarland, who was the son of Samuel King McFarland and Musadore Louisa (Lou) Rowntree, neighbors in the Spring Creek community. They made their home in the community, and later moved into Burnet where Ray was a barber. The children of Ray and Mollie McFarland were all born in Burnet County, but the family later moved to Cleburne, Texas, where

110

the children were reared.

Ray McFarland died December 1, 1944,[3] and was buried in Cleburne. Mollie had already departed this life on May 24, 1932,[4] and the following obituary appeared in the *Burnet Bulletin*.[5]

MRS. RAY McFARLAND DEAD

The sad word was received at this place Tuesday night that Mrs. Ray McFarland had died at her home in Cleburne. Lilbon, Eppa, and Frank Debo and Mr. and Mrs. Winter Landtroop left early Wednesday morning for Cleburne to attend the funeral.

Mrs. McFarland before her marriage was Miss Mollie Debo, daughter of Mrs. Mary Debo of this place. She was born in Burnet county on December 23rd, 1876 and lived in this section practically all her life up until a few years ago when she moved with her family to Cleburne. She was married thirty-three years ago to Ray McFarland. She is survived by her husband and the following children: Mrs. Flora Asberry, Dorr and Clarence McFarland of Austin, Lewis, Lora and Nell McFarland of Cleburne, her mother, Mrs. Mary Debo of Burnet, sisters, Mrs. Jennie Fisher of Houston, Mrs. Sallie Simpson of Winters, Mrs. Tom Johnston of Burnet, Mrs. Julia Lantroop of Burnet, and brothers, Lilbon, Eppa, Frank and Hardy Debo, all of Burnet County.

Mrs. McFarland had many friends in this section of by-gone years, who will deeply regret her death. She was a woman loved and honored by all who knew her and the sympathy of all our citizens go out to the husband and children, the dear mother and the sisters and brothers.

The children of Mollie and Ray McFarland were:

1. CLARA LOUISE, who was born Feb. 27, 1900, and died May 7, 1900. She was buried in the Debo Cemetery on the home place.
2. FLORA, who was born April 7, 1901, and died Aug. 26, 1986.
3. JAMES DORR, who was born Feb. 7, 1903, and died Jan. 18, 1999. He lived in Austin for many years where he taught at the University of Texas. He was married June 1, 1930, to Phyllis Short, who was born Nov. 18, 1906, and died Aug. 18, 2000. Their children were:
   a. JAMES DORR, JR., born April 20, 1935. He first married Patricia Yvonne Hill and their children were James Paul (who later changed his name to Paul Edwin Collins). Born Nov.10, 1968; James Door III: Jason; and Howard (Trey). He later married Donna Witherington; and Carol Payne.
   b. SAMUEL ROBERT, who was born July 4, 1942, died June

19, 1989, with burial in Austin. He was married May 29, 1965, to Carolyn Margaret Aldridge, who was born Dec. 3, 1943. Their children are Molly Carol, born April 16, 1968; and Joel Dorr, born May 26, 1970 .

4. CLARENCE ALEXANDER, who was born Feb. 14, 1905, and died Sept. 4, 1975. He was married to Lucille Clara Haby, who, who was born Nov. 3, 1901, and died Feb. 23, 1999. They made their home in Austin. Their children were:

   a. MARY KUHNE, born Dec. 27, 1936, who married Milton M. Stevens and they had two daughters, Charlotte Leigh, born Feb. 18, 1962, and Sharon Louise, born May 14, 1966. This entire family was tragically killed in an airplane crash in Arkansas Aug. 17, 1974.

   b. WALTER ALEXANDER, born Jan. 27, 1938, who was killed in a car accident near Leander, Texas, Oct. 1, 1938.

   c. CLARENCE ALEXANDER, JR., born April 6, 1941, and died May 22, 1988.

   d. WILLIAM HOWARD, born Sept. 17, 1942, and died Dec. 9, 1996. He married Ellen Frances Hudnall in 1966, and they had two daughters: Celia Eve, born June 1, 1967. And Amelia, born Feb. 3, 1971.

5. SAMUEL LOUIS, who was born Dec. 27, 1906, and died Dec. 11, 1982, in Cleburne. He was first married to Johnnie Mae Kent and they had a daughter, Doris Claire (Tookie), who was born July 11, 1926, and married Dec. 24, 1948, to Homer Ferguson. They had a daughter, Kimber Ann, born Oct. 18, 1951. Louis later married Mabel Bandy.

6. LORA RUTH, who was born Aug. 2, 1909, and died Jan. 20, 1982. She was first married to Chester Millican and later to Albert D. Roberts.

7. NELLIE ELVIRA, who was born Oct. 23, 1911, and died Jan. 16, 1996. She was married to James Merriman deGarmo, born Dec. 8, 1911, and died Dec. 27 1986. They had two sons:

   a. JAMES MERRIMAN, JR., born Jan. 26, 1940, and died Sept. 29, 1999, who was married July 18, 1970, to Guadalupe Soto.

   b. JACK RAY, born Jan 16, 1947, who was married March 31, 1966, to Billie Josephine Fernandez. They had two sons: Billie Matthew, born August 9, 1967, and James Robert. Jack

Ray later married Terry _____.[6]

c. *Lilbon Debo*[1]

Lilbon (Lib) Debo , third child and oldest son of Cornelius and Mary Debo, and my grandfather, was born January 9, 1879, on the home place in Burnet County. I do not know for whom he was named, and I did not have the good sense to ask him prior to his demise. It is my considered opinion, however, that he probably was named for someone his father had known during the war – as was the case in naming Lilbon's brother Eppa.

He was reared in the rural society of his day along with his siblings and attended the Spring Creek school. He had to quit school in the seventh grade, for as the oldest son he had to go to work in the fields because of the illness of his father. As he explained it, "I had to quit studying and go to plowing. I didn't graduate, but I quituated"

An interesting incident occurred in Lib's early life when he was only twelve years old. It resulted in a write-up being published by James A. Stevens, editor of the *Burnet Bulletin*, in his paper in January 1891.[2]

BRAVE LITTLE BOY

Lilburn [sic] Debo, the 12-year-old son of Mr. C. Debo, who resides five miles west of Burnet, bobs up serenely as the hero of a wild-cat killing. During the holidays, when his father was confined to his room with sickness, the youthful Nimrod venturing out with dogs, and when "deep immured" in the neighboring forest, the dogs treed a vigorous looking wild cat, a very large one. The boy, having neither axe nor gun, concluded he would climb the tree, and climb it he did. When nearly in reach of him, the "baste" made a leap for life and after a lively chase with the dogs, took to another tree; and again the fearless little fellow followed him to his perch and again the game took its flight. Again treed by the dogs and followed up the tree by Lilburn [sic], the cat concluded he was tired of the fun and when the boy approached very near him, he made fight, whereupon the youthful sportsman descended and, leaving the dogs to hold the fort, went home to tell about what had happened. His father put a light load in his gun, gave it to the lad, showing him how to manipulate it, and told him to go back and shoot the cat. That was

113

fun for the kid, and sure enough he got his game and marched home with the wild cat measuring 3 feet and 9 inches in length.

The story is reported correctly for I have heard it told by my grandfather many times. He said the measurement of the cat was from the tip of its nose to the tip of its tail. He also told how that he had to prop the muzzle-loader gun in the fork of a tree to shoot because it was too heavy for a twelve-year-old to hold up. Another unreported part of the incident that I have heard related was that Lib's sister Jennie, only four years older than he, stayed with the beast until her brother could return with the gun. Can you imagine that kind of bravery in modern children weaned on television and self-gratification?

In 1898 the Spanish-American War began. Lib intended as a patriotic 19-year-old to enlist for service, but the short war ended before his intention came to fruition. As a young man, in addition to his farming labors at home, he also took his turn in neighborhood road work, working with other men in the community on the upkeep of the area roads. Practically the entire equipment in those days were either oxen or mules, plows, and scrapers. Lib also worked his mule and scraper in helping to construct the bed for the railroad between Burnet and Lampasas in 1901. (The railroad was completed in the next year.) He told me of an incident that occurred during this time. The men were working in their shirt sleeves on a warm day when a Texas "blue norther" blew in from the north, and it hit freezing. The men all unhitched their teams and headed for home. Lib told me he nearly froze before reaching shelter and warmth.

In a day of rapid travel and communication some may find the following hard to believe. Lib was a grown man before he ever went to the city of Austin – at that time some fifty-five miles away! He has related to me how that his first journey to Texas' capital city was on a cattle drive. He, along with the other drovers, drove the herd to Cedar Park, just outside Austin, and camped there during the night. Some black folks had a revival meeting going on nearby and the drovers were entertained that night by the goings-on. The next day they drove the cattle into the city and down Congress Avenue to the railroad for transportation by train to the markets.

On October 12, 1902, Lilbon was married by L. S. Chamberlain, a Methodist preacher, to Hattie Irene Kirk, daughter of Joseph Newton Kirk, and the former Virginia Ann (Jennie) Rogers. (She was born March 7, 1881, and died February 24, 1975, with burial in the Burnet

Cemetery.) The following announcement appeared in the *Burnet Bulletin*:

On Sunday afternoon at 3:30 o'clock, in the presence of a number of friends and relatives, Mr. Lilburn [sic] Debo and Miss Hattie Kirk were united in marriage, Rev. L. S. Chamberlain officiating. The groom is the son of Mrs. C. Debo, is an energetic, sober and industrious young man. The bride is the sweet and accomplished daughter of Mr. Newt Kirk. Both bride and groom are prominent members of Spring Creek society. The Bulletin extends congratulation to this most worthy couple.

Hattie and Lilbon (lib) Debo with the author.

The Kirk family lived in the Spring Creek community at that time, and Lib and Hattie's oldest son, William Clyde, was born at their house on July 18, 1903. The Lib Debos lived on what was called the "White Eagle" place (just north of present-day Texas State Highway 29 about six miles west of Burnet and about two miles west of the Four-mile Spring) and farmed during the first year or two of their married life (I never learned where the place got its name). They then moved to the Will (Billy) Moore place in the Hairston Creek community some five miles southeast of Burnet where they farmed, raising cotton as a cash crop and corn, feed, et cetera, as was common by the tillers of the soil in that day and time. It

115

would take them an entire week to pick a bale of cotton. On Saturday while Lib took the cotton to gin, Hattie would wash and clean house. They were living there on Hairston Creek when their second son, Lewis Berton, was born October 5, 1911. The family attended church services and community gatherings at the Hairston Schoolhouse (later called sometimes the Will Moore School after Mr. Moore gave the land for the erection of a new schoolhouse).

In 1919 the family moved into Burnet and lived in an apartment upstairs in the county jail for awhile until suitable living quarters were found. In 1920 Lib purchased a restaurant just off the Burnet square from his brother-in-law, Lindsey Fisher, and he and Hattie operated it as the Cowboy Café until 1936 when it was moved to the east side of the square and sold to sons Clyde and Bert. The name was changed to Debo's Coffee Shop.

Lib worked at various jobs in later years, ranching on the Norman Brown place awhile; living at Inks Lake and operating a Sinclair service station; and serving as night watchman at Inks Dam, Buchanan Dam, and Inks Fish Hatchery, and at the Victoria Gravel Company. Lib and Hattie had bought a place from Wash Clements on South Main Street in Burnet and lived there the rest of their lives except for the times spent at the lake or on the Brown place. The old original house was torn down and a new duplex built by Roy Wear and completed in 1941 before beginning of World War II.

The union of Lib and Hattie Debo lasted 67 years, ending only with his passing on Sunday morning, August 31, 1969. That Sunday morning as the regular preacher for the Highland Lakes Church of Christ in Kingsland, Texas, I was speaking as usual and after the services were concluded I received word that my grandfather had died. I immediately returned home to be with my family, and requested that I might make the talk at his funeral service. "Pa", as we familiarly called him, was past 90 years of age when death overtook him, and the following obituary appeared in the September 4, 1969, issue of the *Burnet Bulletin*:

LONGTIME BURNET COUNTY CITIZEN SUCCUMBS

Mr. Lilbon ("Lib") Debo, resident of Burnet County for more than 90 years, passed away Sunday morning, August 31, 1969, in the Allen Clinic and Hospital.

Mr. Debo was born January 9, 1879, on the old Debo home place in the Spring Creek community of Burnet County six miles west of Burnet, and was the oldest son of Cornelius and Mary Ruth Schooley Debo. On October 12, 1902, he was united in marriage to the former Miss Hattie Kirk by L. S. Chamberlain, Methodist minister, a union which would endure for 67 years.

Mr. and Mrs. Debo lived in the Spring Creek community for only a few years, moving to the Hairston Creek community southeast of Burnet where they lived and farmed till moving to Burnet in 1920. Mr. Debo was the owner and operator of the Cowboy Café (next door to the Burnet Bulletin office) for sixteen years until he sold the business to his sons in 1936, at which time the name was changed to Debo's Coffee Shop and the location moved to the east side of the square in the present Edgar Flower and Gift Shop building. He worked as a night watchman for the old Victoria Gravel Co. and several projects of LCRA.

He was a member of the First Methodist Church and a life member of Valley Masonic Lodge No. 175 A.F.& A.M., of Burnet.

Funeral services were conducted Monday, September 1, 1969, at 2:00 p.m. in the Clements Chapel with his grandson, Darrell Debo, and Wm. E. Parrish of Fredericksburg officiating. Interment was in the Burnet Cemetery under the direction of Clements Funeral Home.

Surviving him in addition to his wife, Mrs. Hattie Debo, of Burnet are two sons, Clyde Debo and Bert Debo, both of Burnet; three grandchildren, Darrell Debo, Burnet, Jack Debo, Fort Worth, and Mrs. W. J. (Margaret Ann) Hornsby, Burnet; two brothers, Eppa Debo and Hardy Debo, both of Burnet; and four sisters, Mrs. Jennie Fisher, Houston, Mrs. Sallie Simpson, Clyde, Mrs. Nell Johnston, Burnet, and Mrs. Julia Landtroop, Austin.

Serving as pallbearers were Upton Frazer, B. Pogue, Tom Whitaker, Charles L. "Red" Wheat, Winston Magill, Melvin Kincheloe, S. H. "Pete" Elliott, and Carl Yarborough.

Tribute to L. Debo
By Darrell Debo

Lilbon Debo was affectionately known to his many friends and acquaintances as "Lib" or "Uncle Lib." His life span was less than ten years short of the century mark, during which time he was able to witness many transitions and changes of age.

In the so-called "modern age" of the present with its changing standards and values, there are some immutable and valid principles

117

which need to be emphasized and impressed upon the minds of us all. Some of these principles found in the life of my grandfather were patience, honesty, and truthfulness, and unselfishness.

Pa (as he was known to us) exhibited a greater degree of patience throughout the years than any person I have ever known, as he bore his lot in life without murmur and complaint. In all of his years among us, he had not lived long enough to learn dishonesty, deceit, or the telling of a falsehood. His standard of goodness in a man was one who was honest and told the truth. If Pa had an enemy it must have been himself in that he trusted everyone and thought them as good, honest, and truthful as he. His confidence was destroyed if he found a person dishonest or untruthful. He gave unselfishly of himself and what he had to the happiness and good of his family and others.

These old fundamental ethics he learned from his father and mother, who were sturdy pioneer stock of Burnet County. He did not besmirch the good name of his father, but built on the foundation they laid and left the younger generation of the family a worthy heritage. A good name is to be chosen more than great riches.

Pa and I were perhaps as close as any grandfather and grandson ever were, and we derived much pleasure from the years of association and our conversations concerning mutual interests. There was no generation gap or communication gap here! I am most grateful for those many years together, and a rich heritage is mine indeed. I shall miss him – his daily presence, words of advice and wisdom, and his encouragement in that which was right.

Hattie Debo lived six years after Lib's demise, departing this life Monday, February 24, 1975, at age 93. The following obituary was in the local newspaper:

MRS. HATTIE KIRK DEBO

Mrs. Hattie Kirk Debo, 93, of Burnet, died Monday, February 24, 1975, in Burnet. Mrs. Debo was born March 7, 1881, in the Shady Grove-Providence section of Burnet County, and was the daughter of Joseph Newton Kirk and the former Virginia Ann (Jennie) Rogers. She was a life-long resident of Burnet County, and was a member of the First United Methodist Church in Burnet. Mrs. Debo held a lifetime membership in the Order of the Eastern Star. She was preceded in death by her husband, Lilbon Debo, who died August 31, 1969.

Funeral services for Mrs. Debo were held Wednesday, February 26, at 2:00 p.m. at the Clements Chapel with Rev. "Buddy" Johnston officiating, assisted by Rev. T. A. Fowler. Interment followed at the Burnet Cemetery under the direction of Clements Funeral Home.

Survivors include two sons, Clyde Debo and Bert Debo, both of Burnet; two brothers, Watson Kirk of San Angelo, and Barton Kirk of Fort Worth; three grandchildren; and four great-grandchildren.

Pallbearers were Bill Foster, D. V. (Jennie) Hammond, S. H. "Pete" Elliott, John Kroger, L. D. Allbritton, and Howard Counts.

Lilbon and Hattie Debo were the parents of two sons, both of whom were born in Burnet County:

a. WILLIAM CLYDE, who was born July 18, 1903, and died July 16, 2002, two days short of ninety-nine years. He attended the Hairston Creek rural school and graduated from Burnet High School in 1923. He rode a donkey to the Hairston school and a pony and bicycle to the Burnet school from Hairston in 1917 and 1918 before the family moved into town; and he played left end on the Bulldog football teams of 1922 and 1923. Clyde attended business college in Tyler, and then was employed by W. R. (Bill) Orr in the wholesale business in Llano. In Llano he met Lucille Atchison, daughter of William Thomas (Willie) Atchison and the former Jessie Elizabeth Decker, and Clyde and Lucille were married in the Christian Church in Llano on June 7, 1930. (Lucille was born April 26, 1906, died May 14, 1985, of a heart attack, and is buried in the Llano Cemetery.) In the midst of the Great Depression and after the birth of their first son, Darrell, in 1931, they moved to Fort Worth where Clyde found employment at the federal building. The Debos moved from Fort Worth to Burnet in the fall of 1936 where Clyde and his brother Bert purchased the restaurant from their father. (The Debo's Coffee Shop was in operation till 1944 when it was closed due to war shortages and health problems.) Lucille and son had stayed in Llano with her parents until a new house was completed for the family on Highway 281 in Burnet. While staying with the Atchisons in Llano another son, Jack, was born and the family moved into the new home in Burnet in December. Clyde was an accountant for Victoria Gravel Company and later for a number of Burnet businesses after retiring from the restaurant business. Lucille taught piano lessons privately and at the school for many years and also substituted in the Burnet schools as well. She had attended TCU in Fort Worth and taught at schools in Evergreen (Llano County), Jarrell, Llano, and Burnet. After Lucille's death, Clyde was married to Dorothy Schultz, on May 15, 1993, but they divorced February 21, 1994. Clyde died July 16, 2002, in a Burnet hospital, two days before his 99th birthday, and was buried beside Lucille in the Llano Cemetery. His obituary follows:

WILLIAM CLYDE DEBO

William Clyde Debo, 98, a lifetime resident of Burnet County, departed this life Tuesday, July 16, 2002 – two days prior to his 99th birthday. He was born July 18, 1903, in the Spring Creek community of Burnet County, to Lilbon (Lib) Debo and wife, the former Hattie Kirk.

He attended the rural school at Hairston Creek before graduating from Burnet High School in 1923 (he was the last surviving member of that class). Clyde was the oldest surviving Burnet Bulldog football player, competing as an end on the teams of 1922 and 1923.

He was married June 7, 1930, in Llano, to the former Lucille Atchison, who preceded him in death May 14, 1985. Also preceding him in death were his parents, Mr. and Mrs. L. Debo; a brother, Bert Debo; and daughter-in-law, Mrs. Jack Debo.

For a number of years, on the east side of the Burnet square, Debo operated Debo's Coffee Chop, which he and his brother, Bert, had purchased from their father in 1936. World War II rationing and shortages plus health problems caused its closure in 1944. For the remainder of his life until retirement, he was a prominent and well-known public accountant in the Burnet area, having attended a business college in Tyler during his younger days.

He had been a member of Valley Lodge AF&AM #175 in Burnet for 78 years, and received his 75-year award three years ago. He was a 32nd degree Mason and a Shriner, having received many Masonic honors and awards too numerous to list. He was a member of O.E.S. Chapter #425 in Burnet. He was also an elder in the First Christian Church of Burnet for many years, and active in civic affairs, having served as president and secretary of the school board for a number of years. During his tenure the rural schools were consolidated with the Burnet ISD.

He is survived by two sons, Darrell Debo of Burnet, and Jack Debo of Fort Worth; a grandson, Terry Debo and wife, Debbie, of Grapevine; a granddaughter, Sherri Debo, of Fort Worth; two nieces, Margaret Ann Hornsby of Burnet and Sarah Thompson of Llano; and a host of acquaintances and friends.

Funeral services will be at 10:00 a.m. in the Edgar Funeral Home Chapel in Burnet, Friday, July 19, 2002, with Ernest Spiekermann officiating. Burial will follow in the Llano Cemetery in Llano, Texas.

Pallbearers will be Jerry Graves, Bill Dailey, Bob Dickens, Roy Oakley, Buck Jones, and Donald Fawcett. Honorary pallbearers are all of his Masonic brothers in the various lodges in the area.

Arrangements by Edgar Funeral Home, Burnet, Texas.

Clyde and Lucille Debo were the parents of two sons, both born in Llano:

    a. BILLY DARRELL, who was born Sept. 15, 1931, and lives in Burnet. (For further information see data on the author of this volume.)

    b. JACK LEE, who was born Oct. 29, 1936, and died Dec. 13, 2004 in Fort Worth. He graduated from Burnet High School in 1955 and attended TCU. He retired from Champlin Oil co. after many years employment there. He married Jesse Elizabeth Whaley, Jan 17, 1959, in Rockwall, Texas, who was born Sept. 5, 1932, and retired from teaching in the Fort Worth schools. Jesse died July 15, 2001, of a heart attack while on vacation in Woodland Park, Colorado. Jesse and Jack had two children: TERRY LEE, born Feb. 23, 1959, who lives in Southlake, is a graduate of TCU, an accountant, and was married July 28, 1984, to Deborah Elaine (Debbie) Barnett, born Oct. 24, 1956, who is also a TCU graduate; and SHERRI LYNN, born July 22, 1962, who is a graduate of Texas Wesleyan College and North Texas University, and is employed in the Fort Worth school system.

2. LEWIS BERTON, who was born Oct. 5, 1911, died March 21, 1989, and is buried in Post Mountain Cemetery, Burnet. He graduated from Burnet High in 1930. After operating the

restaurant with brother Clyde, he entered the insurance business in Burnet and won many trips and awards for sales volume. He first married Sue Melton, and was later divorced. He was married Aug. 4, 1946, by J.P. Manley to Gladys Godwin, who was born Sept. 7, 1906 and died December 23, 1998. Gladys was a florist for a number of years and also taught in the Burnet schools. Bert and Gladys had one child, a daughter:

a. MARGARET ANN, born Sept. 10, 1947, who attended Sam Houston State University at Huntsville, lives in Burnet, and was married Jan. 25, 1967, to William James (Jimbo) Hornsby, born Sept. 18, 1947. They have six children: JAMES BERTON, born Dec. 29, 1967; MELISSA ANN, born Aug. 19, 1971; REBECCA LYNN, born May 13, 1981; LEAH MICHELL, born Mar. 24, 1983; DANIEL AARON, born Dec. 19, 1984; and JOHNATHAN LEWIS, born Mar. 3, 1987.

d. Eppa Debo[1]

Eppa Debo, fourth child and second son of Cornelius and Mary Debo, was born on the old Debo home place January 5, 1881, and was named for Gen. (Col.) Eppa Hunton of Virginia under whom Cornelius had served during the War Between the States. Commonly called "Eppie," he was reared and attended the rural school in the Spring Creek community of Burnet County. He, along with his older brother Lilbon, became responsible for the farming and providing for the family after their father's health failed and he was unable to work.

Eppa developed a sterling character and trustworthiness that was well known in the community. He received quite some teasing from his brothers and sisters after a Methodist preacher named Theophilus Lee, during a summer revival meeting in the Spring Creek community, used Eppa as an example during one of his sermons as one to be followed because of his moral uprightness. The preacher said, "If someone would tell a scan'alous lie on brother Eppa Debo, no one would believe it because everyone would know it wasn't so." The kids in the family thereafter went about repeating what the preacher said about telling a "scan'alous lie on brother Eppa Debo," to the dismay of Eppa!

After the other members of the family had left home and established families of their own, Eppa's mother and younger sister Julia continued to live with him at the home place until his marriage. He,

Lillie Scott Debo; Frank Debo; Eppa Debo; Jewel Debo

at the age of thirty-eight, on Nov. 8, 1919, was married by George G. Smith to Minnie Jewel Burns, born February 19, 2002, daughter of Baxter Euens Burns and the former Nellie May Newton. After the marriage, Mary Debo and Julia moved to Burnet and lived with the Lindsey Fisher family until after Julia's marriage. Eppa continued to farm and raise stock on the home place, while Jewel raised turkeys as well as chickens, and sold eggs and butter to Burnet merchants. After the death of Mary Debo in 1944, the home place was sold and the proceeds divided among the many heirs. Eppa and Jewel bought the Gill R. Reed place northeast of Burnet in the Oak Hill neighborhood, and they lived there until his death, after which Jewel sold the place and moved into a house on South Main Street in Burnet across the street from the Clyde Debo family.

Eppa lived to the ripe age of ninety-three, and died February 16, 1974. He was a member of the Methodist Church in Burnet for eighty years. Jewel survived him twenty-one years, passing from this life on December 2, 1995, at age 93. They had no children. Eppa's obituary appeared in the local paper, as follows:

EPPA DEBO[1]

Mr. Eppa Debo, 93, of Burnet, died Saturday, February 16, 1974, in the Burnet hospital. He was born in the Spring Creek community in Burnet County on January 5, 1881, and was the son of Cornelius Debo and the former Mary Ruth Schooley, pioneers of the county. He was a member of the First United Methodist Church of Burnet, and had been a member of that congregation for 80 years. He was the last surviving son of the late Mr. and Mrs. C. Debo

Services for Mr. Debo were held Sunday, February 17, at the Clements Funeral Chapel with Darrell Debo and Methodist ministers T. A. Fowler and A. S. Neely officiating. Interment followed at the Burnet Cemetery under direction of Clements Funeral Home.

Survivors include his wife, Jewel Burns Debo of Burnet; four sisters, Mrs. Jennie Fisher of Houston, Mrs. Sallie Simpson of Clyde, Mrs. Nell Johnston of Burnet, and Mrs. Julia Wolf of Austin; and numerous nieces and nephews.

Pallbearers were Clay Debo, Otis Fisher, Clarence McFarland, Dorr McFarland, Stanton Johnston, W. H. "Koon" Johnston, Bert Debo, and James C. Norred, nephews of Mr. Debo.

e. Frank Debo[1]

Frank Debo, seventh child and fifth son of Cornelius and Mary Debo, was born on the old Debo home place February 24, 1887, and was named for one of Mary's brothers, Frank Schooley. He attended the rural Spring Creek school along with his brothers and sisters.

One Christmas season Frank saddled his horse and rode over the mountain east of the Debo place to the Fraziers to attend a seasonal party. Upon returning home that night he unsaddled his horse and placed his saddle on the yard fence before coming into the house to go to bed. After he had fallen asleep some of his brothers slipped out of the house and placed his saddle on an old ugly-faced cow named Oley, one of whose horns turned downward, who was grazing nearby. When the household awoke the next morning, there stood old Oley outside the yard fence all saddled and ready for business, bawling at the top of her lungs! Frank's siblings had a great time teasing him about having "one too many" at the Frazier party and instead of unsaddling his horse and placing his saddle on the fence he had put it on old Oley! Some of the folks reported that Mary Debo, upon see-ing the prank pulled on Frank and with Oley duly saddled standing before her, shook quite vigorously with laughter. (I, as a child, never remember Grandma Debo ever laughing out loud; rather she would just shake when amused at something.)

Frank, after reaching manhood in the early 1900s, went to Califor-nia with a cousin, Charlie Windsor, "to get rich" and they worked at a lumber yard awhile. The riches were not soon forthcoming and Frank left California for Wyoming, and spent some time there with his uncle and aunt, Sam and Mollie Schooley, at Sunrise. (The Sam Schooley family had moved there from Texas in 1907, following Mrs. Schooley's parents, Asa J. and Evaline Covington, who had settled there in 1897. Sam was reportedly a fine fiddle player, according to my grandfather, and Frank learned to play the fiddle from his Uncle Sam. Frank taught me a waltz he had learned while there, and since he didn't know the name we termed it the "Wyoming Waltz," for he had learned it there.) Following are the contents of a postcard from Sunrise, Wyoming, Frank wrote his sister Nell in Burnet in 1910:

Hello girl!

Christmas gift. Haven't got time to write you a letter as I am just starting to town. You must take one extra one for me Xmas and you think things will be brought to a close Xmas. Well I am plumb willing you should see what I have got out here. Maby I will show you some time see.

(On the front of the card is a picture of the town of Sunrise, and underneath Frank wrote,"How do you like our town?" The card was addressed to "Miss Nell Debo, Burnet, Texas," and was mailed Dec. 14, 1910.)[2]

After returning home to Texas, Frank was married on December 18, 1915, to Bertha Irene Baker, the ceremony being performed by Robert T. Howell, a minister in the church of Christ of which the Baker family were members. Bertha, the daughter of Newton Isaac Baker and the former Ardelia Glimp, of the Council Creek and Morgan Creek neigh-borhoods of Burnet County, was born July 22, 1894, and died Septem-ber 3, 1952, after battling cancer for several years. Frank and Bertha bought property off the Old San Saba road and settled in the Pebble Mound community of the county where they lived the remainder of their days. Frank farmed and ranched all his life, and Bertha – did as

Frank and Bertha Baker Debo

many wives of that day and age – raised chickens and sold butter and eggs to merchants in Burnet. She was a very frugal person.

After Bertha's death, Frank lived alone on the place for a number of years. On January 9, 1961, he was married to a widow, Lillie Elizabeth Scott, born August 15, 1895, and died June 27, 1972, who owned and operated a motel in Burnet. The ceremony was performed in Bertram by his great-nephew, Darrell Debo, at his home, who was minister of the Bertram church of Christ at the time. Frank lived in Burnet at the motel until his death, although he kept his place in the country and saw after his interests there. Following is his obituary from the Burnet paper:

FRANK DEBO SERVICES
HELD SUNDAY, MAY 3

Mr. Frank Debo, a lifetime resident of Burnet County, died at Shepperd Memorial Hospital on May 2 1964.

Mr. Debo was born in Burnet County on March 24, 1887, and was a member of the Methodist Church here.

Funeral services were conducted by Minister Robert Turner and Rev. S. S. Davis at Clements Funeral home at 3 p.m. May 3, 1964.

Burial was in the Burnet Cemetery under the direction of the Clements Funeral Home. Pallbearers were Clyde Debo, Bert Debo, Bill Debo, Howard Johnston, Thomas Johnston, Barney Baker, Hollis Baker, and Roger Scott.

Survivors besides his wife, Mrs. Lillie Debo of Burnet, include a son, Hubert Clay Debo, San Antonio; four sisters, Mrs. Jennie Fisher, Houston, Mrs. Sallie Simpson, Clyde, Mrs. Tom Johnston, Burnet, and Mrs. Julia Landtroop, Austin. Also surviving are three brothers, L. Debo, Eppa Debo, and Hardy Debo, all of Burnet; and two grandchildren Hubert Frank Debo and Miss Mary Debo, San Antonio.

Frank and Bertha Debo had one son:
1. HUBERT CLAY, who was born Oct. 22, 1916, in Burnet County. He served in the U.S. Air Force during World War II. On April 19, 1943, he was married to Rita Belle Mabry, who was born Nov. 9, 1919, and died Aug. 15, 2012. After retirement from the Air Force, Clay and Rita lived for a time in San Antonio before returning to Burnet County to live on his homeplace in the Pebble Mound community. Clay died July 11, 1993, and was buried in San Antonio. They had two children.
   a. HUBERT FRANK, who was born March 22, 1949, and lives in Bossier City, Louisiana. He was married May 27, 1972, to Mickie Sue Wilder, who was born July 27, 1950. They have two daughters; Lourin Marie, born Aug.9, 1980; and Emily Jane, born Nov. 17, 1983.
   b. MARY CAMERON, who was born Jan. 13, 1954, and teaches in the Burnet schools. She was married Nov. 17, 1973, to Barney Wilbert Kneese, who was born Sept 15, 1953, and is employed by LCRA. They have two sons: RUSSELL EDWARD, born Nov., 29, 1980; and BRYAN MATTHEW, born Nov. 13, 1987.

f. Sam Hardy Debo

Sam Hardy Debo, eighth child and sixth and youngest son of Cornelius and Mary Debo, was born on the Debo home place May 30, 1889, and was named for a Methodist preacher named Sam Hardy. He was reared and attended the rural school in the Spring Creek community, and was a farmer and rancher all of his life.

Hardy was married June 21, 1911, to Agnes Belle Daugherty, born November 7, 1892, the daughter of William Jasper Daugherty and the former Mary Catherine Fisher, who was a sister of Lindsey Fisher. The ceremony was performed by Robert T. Howell, minister in the church of Christ. Hardy and Belle lived for many years on the Corder place east of Burnet, and later moved to and lived near Bertram for some time before settling in Burnet in their declining years.

Farmer Hardy Debo - sitting on the back steps at the farm near Bertram, Texas.

On a vacation trip back to old Virginia, I visited the Appomattox Court House, scene of Lee's surrender to Grant in 1865. There in a little store I purchased a little clay pipe bowl and brought it back home and gave it to Uncle Hardy. He fitted that clay bowl with a stem and seemed to be as proud of it as he could be because it came from Appomattox in Virginia, the state from which his father had come.

Following declining health, Hardy died December 27, 1973, at the old Allen Clinic and Hospital in Burnet, and was buried in Burnet Cemetery. Belle survived him about six and a half years, departing this life June 25, 1980. Their obituaries from the local paper are as follows:

DEBO

BURNET---Hardy Debo, 84, of Burnet, died December 27, in a Burnet hospital.

Mr. Debo was born in Burnet County May 30, 1889, the son of Cornelius Debo and the former Mary Schooley. He was a lifelong resident of Burnet County and a 50-year member of Valley Lodge #175 A.F. & A.M.

Funeral services were held December 28 at the Clements Chapel. The Rev. T. A. Fowler officiating. Burial followed at Burnet Cemetery under the direction of Clements Funeral Home, with graveside Masonic services conducted by Valley Lodge #175 A. F. & A. M.

Members of the Valley Lodge served as pallbearers.

Survivors include his wife, Belle Debo of Burnet one son, Bill Debo of Nacogdoches; three daughters, Mrs. Iris Graves of Burnet, Mrs. (Peggy) Agnes Fulcher of Crane and Mrs. Clara Belle Lawson of Austin; one brother, Eppa Debo of Burnet; four sisters, Mrs. Jennie Fisher and Mrs. Nell Johnston, both of Burnet, Mrs. Sally Simpson of Clyde and Mrs. Julia Wolf of Austin; 14 grandchildren; 12 great-grandchildren and one great-great-grandson.

MRS. DEBO

Belle Debo, age 87, of Austin, formerly of Burnet, died Wednesday, June 25, in the nursing home in Austin, Mrs. Debo was born November 7, 1892, in Burnet County, the daughter of William J. Daugherty and the former Mary Fisher. She was a lifelong resident of Burnet County. She was preceded in death by her husband, Sam Hardy Debo, on December 27, 1973.

Funeral services were held Friday, June 27, at the Clements-Wilcox Chapel in Burnet with Darrell Debo officiating.

Survivors include one son, Bill Debo of Burnet; three daughters, Iris Graves of Burnet, Peggy Fulcher of Crane and Clara Belle Lawson of Austin; one brother, Claud Daugherty of Denison; twelve grandchildren; twelve great-grandchildren; seven great-great-grandchildren.

Grandsons of Mrs. Debo were named as pallbearers.

Hardy and Belle were the parents of one son and four daughters, all born in Burnet County:

1. IRIS ALMA, who was born Sept. 19, 1913, and died Jan. 23, 2000. She was married Dec. 17, 1932, to Acy Lee Graves, born Nov. 3, 1910, and died Dec. 13, 1975, son of John Preston (Press) Graves and the former Annie Mae Watson. Iris and Acy had three children:

   a. AGNES ANN, who was born Nov. 3, 1933, and lives in Burnet. She was married June 14, 1952, to Joseph R. D. Pare, born Oct. 28, 1928 and died May 14, 2015. They have three children: ANNETTE, born July 14, 1953, who married Daniel Reeves, born Dec. 10, 1951; CATHERINE JANE, born April 13, 1955, who married RUBEN GARZA; and RAY-

MOND NEAL, born Aug. 2, 1961, who married Nancy Finklea, born March 17, 1964.

b. JERRY VAUGHN, who was born Aug. 27, 1935, and died April 25, 2015. He was married Nov. 28, 1964, to Mary Lee Smith, born March 19, 1934. Mary Lee had three sons by previous marriages.

c. DONALD LEE, who was born Jan. 19, 1938, and lives in Marble Falls. He was married April 20, 1963, to Janet Rodgers, born May 10, 1937. They have three children: STEVEN MARK, born Feb. 16, 1964; CHERYL MICHELLE, born Aug. 10, 1967, who married Shawn McDuffie; and JANA LEA, born March 20, 1971.

2. WILLIAM CORNELIUS (Bill), born Dec. 21, 1917, and died Jan. 18, 1995. He was married Nov. 11, 1937, to Wilma Gray Garrett, born Jan. 15, 1919, and died Aug. 23, 2011. They had two children:

a. SAM PAFFORD, born Oct. 15, 1938, who was married Sept. 19, 1959, to Ann Vernelle Crider, born April 27, 1943. They had three children: DAVID WILLIAM, born Dec. 25, 1960, who first married Kimberly Finen in 1981 by whom he had two sons, ZACHARY SAMUEL (Zack), born Feb. 3, 1982, and MATTHEW NICHOLAS (Matt), born January 22, 1984. David later married Marina Gamez by whom he had another son, JOSHUA HARDY (Josh), born May 28, 1998. (NOTE: The three sons of David are the only males in the descendants of Cornelius Debo to carry on the Debo name in future generations.): TINA REGINA, born May 16, 1963, who married Gordon McClain Aug. 27, 1986; and AMY MARIE, born Aug. 12, 1970, who married Clifton Lindsey, but they were later divorced.

b. JUBY CATHERINE, born Sept 2, 1947. She was first married to Richard Campbell, later to Jim Whitten, and was married June 19, 1987, to Jim Stout, born July 17, 1946.

3. MARY CATHERINE (Susie), who was born Aug. 1, 1920, and died Dec. 20, 1952, in an auto accident. She was married Feb. 11, 1947, to Claude Earl Whitehead, born July 27, 1919.

4. AGNES ALVERA (Peggy), who was born Dec. 20, 1922, and died Oct. 27, 2006. She was married June 13, 1953, to Thomas Lee Fulcher, born Aug. 18, 1921, and died June 16, 1994. They

had four sons:

    a. EDWARD ROSS, BORN July 1, 1955, and died April 20, 2008.

    b. JESSIE JAMES, born Feb. 4, 1957, and died April 2, 1977.

    c. CHARLES RAY, born Feb. 4, 1957, and died Nov. 27, 1974.

    d. LEE ROY, born April 1, 1958.

5. CLARA BELLE, who was born Dec. 26, 1926, and died Jan. 27, 2015. She was married March 24, 1946, to Noel Gilbert Lawson, born Dec. 28, 1923, and died Sept. 18, 1998. They had five sons:

    a. WILLIAM PAUL (Bill), born Oct. 16, 1946, and married Patricia Ann Pemberton on Sept. 15, 1966.

    b. GILBERT ANDREW (Andy), born Aug. 3, 1949, and on Dec. 1, 1967, married Ruth Chustine.

    c. RICHARD LEON (Dicky) born May 25, 1953, and was married Cynthia Ann Weber, but was later divorced.

    d. JOEL DUANE, born July 16, 1958, and was married Aug. 13, 1988, to Mary Jane Ledesma.

    e. JON HARDY, born Feb. 22, 1961, and married Nov. 20, 1980, to Beatrice Martinez

g. Sallie Esterline Debo Simpson

Sallie Esterline Debo, ninth child and third daughter of Cornelius and Mary Ruth Debo, was born at the home place October 1, 1891, and was named for Cornelius' sister Sallie Debo Bowmer, and an acquaintance of the family, Lina Curry Jones. Sallie grew to adulthood and attended the rural school in the Spring Creek community with her brothers and sisters.

Sallie was married January 14, 1912, by Walter L. Brandon to Andes E. Simpson, who was born Decembr 26, 1885, and died July 8, 1955, in Winters, Texas. Andes was the son of Frank M. Simpson and the former Lucy Eulalia (Ula) Fisher, and was reared by his grandfather and grandmother, Alexander (Zan) and Sarah Jane Fry Fisher. He was a farmer and rancher all of his life. Andes' and Sallie's first two children were born in Burnet County.

The Fishers had moved to near Winters, and when Zan Fisher decided to retire from farming in 1916 he asked his grandson and his wife, Andes and Sallie, to move to Winters and take over his farm.

Eppa (Happy) was born while they lived there. A few years later the Zan Fishers, the Simpsons, and some of the Fisher children all moved back to Burnet County. While here Dorothy Sue and Robert Charles (Bobby) were born. About 1921 the Simpson family moved back to Winters where the remainder of the children were born.

The Simpsons were a part of the usual small town and community life in Winters. They were active in the Methodist church where Sallie taught the women's Sunday school class for many years until she moved to Clyde to reside with daughter Dorothy Sue in her later years. All the Simpson children, upon graduating from school and marrying, left Winters and established homes elsewhere. Sallie passed away November 13, 1982, in Clyde but was buried beside her husband in Winters.

The children of Sallie and Andes were:
1. ANDES EMMET, JR., who was born Oct. 1,1912, and died Aug. 27, 1957. He was married in 1934 to Irene Jennings, who was born in 1917 and died Oct. 15, 1941. Their children were: BILLY WAYNE, born June 7, 1936; PEGGY JEAN, born Aug. 20, 1938; and LINDA, born May 17, 1941. After Irene's death, Emmet married Rosa Lee Swafford Nov. 15, 1944, and their children were: ANDES E. III, born Nov. 22, 1946; SHARON, born March 9, 1948; CYNTHIA, born Dec. 27, 1950; RICHARD R., born Sept. 20, 1952; and BECKY, born Dec. 27, 1953.
2. MILDRED JULIA, who was born March 28, 1914, and lives in Elgin, Texas. She was married Nov. 17, 1933 to James Earl Mabry, who was born Dec. 25, 1908, and died Jan. 25, 2001. Their children are: JAMES EARL, JR. (Jimmy), born Feb. 11, 1937; HARVEY MILTON, born Sept. 19, 1938; ANDREA SUE, born Jan. 14, 1942; CLAYTON IRVIN, born October 7, 1944; and CHARLES DAVID, born Sept. 29, 1951.
3. EPPA ALEXANDER (Happy), who was born June 20, 1916, in Winters, and died Oct. 12, 1945. He was married to Edna Attnip, who was born April 4, 1915, and they lived in Winters. Their children were BETTY MARTHA, born Oct. 9, 1940, and JIMMY RALP, born Nov. 29, 1943.
4. DOROTHY SUE, who was born Oct. 5, 1918, in Burnet County and died March 28, 1992. She was married April 1, 1944, to Roy Goin, who was born Sept. 4, 1918, and died Feb.11, 1974. They lived in Clyde, Texas. Their children were: LEAH SUSAN,

born Feb. 19, 1945; and GARY RAYMOND, born Sept. 13, 1948.

5. ROBERT CHARLES; (Bobby), who was born March 22, 1921, in Burnet County and died March 19, 1971. He married Rosalie Ernst, who was born March 20, 1921, and they lived near Winters. Their children were: CHARLES EDMOND, born Aug. 19, 1940; DON LOUIS, born Sept. 11, 1945; HELEN FRANCES, born March 29, 1947; and KAREN JOY, born April 27, 1956.

6. IMOGENE (Genie), who was born Sept. 29, 1923, in Winters. She was married Oct. 30, 1943, to Bill Scoggins, born June 27, 1924, and they lived in California. Their children are: WILLIAM NATHAN (Nick), born July 13, 1946; and MICHAEL DARIUS (Mike), born Dec. 1, 1948.

7. DAYTON EDWARD, who was born Oct. 3, 1925, in Winters. He was first married to Dorothy Moser: and later to Arline_____. They live in Canada. The children are: DAYTON MICHAEL, born Nov. 3, 1949; JOHN JAY, born Dec. 29, 1955; and CARLA MARIE, born May 8, 1981.

8. GARY DEBO, who was born Dec. 8, 1928, in Winters and died Nov. 13, 1992. He was married in Jan. 1950 to Gerry Elioppolas (later changed to Elles). They later divorced, and Gary remarried. The children are: SALLY ANN, born Aug. 5, 1951; MARY NELL, born Jan. 11, 1953; GARY MATTHEW, born Dec. 1, 1954; and JOHNNA KATHRYN, born July 30, 1957.

9. RUTH ANN, who was born Sept 11, 1936, in Winters. She was married to Peter W. Back Aug. 7, 1955. He was born Jan. 19, 1932, and they live in Iowa. Their children are: PETER KIM, born April 25, 1957; SHERWIN BRUCE, born Jan. 12, 1960; JUDY ANN, born Feb. 3, 1961; and CHRISTOPHER LEE, born Feb. 11, 1962.

h. Cornelia Ruth Debo Johnston

Cornelia Ruth (Nell) Debo, tenth child and fourth daughter of Cornelius and Mary Ruth Debo, was born at the old home place February 21, 1894, and was named for her father and mother. She grew up and attended school in the Spring Creek community along with her brothers and sisters and contributed her share of work helping to provide for the large family.

Nell was married on November 24, 1915, to Thomas Benjamin

Johnston, who was born December 12, 1890, and died April 18, 1961, the ceremony being performed by Robert T. Howell, a minister of the church of Christ. Tom was the son of William Benjamin (Buck) Johnston and the former Susannah Catherine King. The Johnston family was some of the pioneer settlers in the Council Creek community of Burnet County, and Buck Johnston also had roots in Virginia, being born in Louisa County of that state.

Cornelia Ruth (Nell) Debo Johnston

Tom and Nell established their home on the old Johnston place in the Council Creek neighborhood. All their children were born there with the exception of the last two, who were born after they moved to the Oak Hill community in 1928. Tom was a farmer and rancher all of his life. Upon moving to the Oak Hill community the Johnston family lived for a while on a place where his half-brother and sister-in-law, Bill and Annie Johnston, had formerly lived. They later moved to the Levingston place in the same community, and the children attended school at the Oak Hill School prior to its consolidation with the Burnet schools. The Johnstons were members of the church of Christ in Burnet.

Age and failing health brought retirement from farming and Tom and Nell were living on the Long place in the Hamilton Valley neighborhood when Tom died. Tim's bachelor brother, Edwin Holland (Uncle Ed) Johnston, made his home with the Johnstons until his death in 1958. After Tom's death Nell moved into Burnet where she lived the remainder of her days. It was during these latter years that I spent many happy visits with her as she shared pictures, letters, and so many stories and events in the Debo family with me. Many of the pictures in this book were made from copies of the originals she had, and several of the letters included herein were supplied by her.

Of the many happy memories I have of the older members of the

Debo family (besides the family reunions), two involving Aunt Nell especially stand out. One day I took my grandfather and grandmother (Lib and Hattie) out to Nell's house when she was living north of Burnet on Highway 281 and Aunt Jennie Fisher was there visiting. We got out the old Debo pictures and as they identified who each was I would write the names on the backs of the pictures (and a few were not identified!). We all had a great time talking about each one and laughing and reminiscing about incidents of the past. On another occasion, I went by and picked up Uncle Hardy and Aunt Belle Debo, and then by to get Aunt Nell when she lived on Vandeveer St., and we went out to the old Debo place and out to old Cottonwood Spring. We stopped on top of the hill and walked carefully down to the spring where the ever-flowing water was issuing forth in its usual strength and beauty. Aunt Nell and I were determined to have a good drink of that spring water, and, looking around, we spied an old tin cup hanging on a nearby tree. We got our drink of that spring water, and was it sweet and good! But Hardy and Belle wouldn't drink; they were afraid the water was contaminated! But as an old woman said one time, "We (Aunt Nell and I) lived and done well!"

Nell departed this life just eight days short of her 89th birthday on February 13, 1983, and was buried besie Tom in the Odd Fellows Cemetery at Burnet. The following obituary appeared in the local paper:

JOHNSTON

Nell D. (Nannie) Johnston, age 88, of Burnet, passed away Sunday, Feb. 13, 1983, at Shepperd Hospital.

Mrs. Johnston was born Feb. 21, 1894, in Burnet County, the daughter of Cornelius Debo and the former Mary Ruth Schooley. Mrs. Johnston was a member of the Vandeveer Church of Christ. She was a lifelong resident of Burnet County.

Funeral services for Mrs. Johnston were held Tuesday, Feb. 15, at the Clements-Wilcox Chapel in Burnet with Brother Morris Kemper officiating. Interment followed at the Odd Fellows Cemetery under the direction of Clements-Wilcox Funeral Home.

Survivors include three sons, Thomas S. (Shorty) Johnston, Howard (Koon) Johnston, both of Burnet; Gene (Wart) Johnston of Fredericksburg; three daughters, Reba Lastly of Burnet, Betty Ogden of Austin, Ann Banta of San Antonio; one sister, Mrs. Victor (Juby) Wolf of Burnet; 18 grandchildren and 20 great-grandchildren.

She is preceded in death by two children: Ben Johnston in May 1938, and Mary Sue Shelburn, January 1959.

Grandsons served as pallbearers.

Tom and Nell had the following children:

1. REBA INEZ, who was born Sept. t, 1916, and died Nov. 28, 2002, in Llano. She was married Aug. 26, 1944, to Jimmy B. Lastly, who was born Sept. 2, 1919, and died July 8, 1990. He was the son of Marcus A. and Mary Magdalene (Maggie) Lastly and was a rancher and carpenter, Reba and B. had six children:
   a. JIMMY WAYNE, who was born Nov. 21, 1946. He was married Nov. 24, 1973, to Stella Melton, but they were later divorced. Their children are JAMES BENJAMIN, born Nov. 15, 1976, and JOHN MARK, born April 7, 1979.
   b. THOMAS ALBERT (Tommy), who was born Aug. 26, 1950, and was married Apr. 4, 1975, to Pat Lewis. Their children are THOMAS CHRISTOPHER, born Sept. 1, 1977; and MICHAEL LANDON STANDIFER, born Sept. 1, 1970.
   c. CONNIE MAXINE, who was born Oct. 24, 1952. She was first married Oct. 13, 1973, to Roy Lyda but they were divorced, and she later married James Wofford.
   d. EDDIE REX, who was born July 11, 1955, and was married to Amanda Daniel. Their children are SHELBY DANIELLE, and COLE B.
   e. EMMA JO, who was born July 14, 1956, and died July 22, 1978, in a tragic auto accident near Austin. She married Adrian Handley, who was born March 28, 1952, and they had one daughter, ADRENA JO, born July 17, 1978.
   f. WILLIAM JOHN (Johnny), who was born Nov. 30, 1960, who lives on the Lastly home place.
2. HELEN ELIZABETH (Betty), who was born July 25, 1918, and died April 2, 1997. She was married Dec. 26, 1968, to William A. (Bill) Ogden, who was born Oct. 5, 1915. They lived in Austin.
3. THOMAS STANTON (Shorty), who was born Sept. 17, 1920, and died June 21, 1993. He was married July 6, 1962, to Ona Roberds, who was born Oct. 1, 1919. Shorty served in the U.S. Marines during World War II. He was a contractor along with his brother, W. H. (Koon), and they lived in Burnet.
4. BENJAMIN CORNELIUS (Ben), who was born July 7, 1922,

and died May 5, 1938, while a student in Burnet High School.

5. WILLIAM HOWARD (Koon), who was born Sept. 13, 1924,
    and died March 25, 1988, in Kerrville. He was married Sept.
    26, 1947, to Jannette Eaton, born July 21, 1927, in Kempner,
    who was the daughter of Arthur and Elizabeth Howell Eaton.
    Koon served in the U. S. Army during World War II. He was a
    contractor and builder in partnership with his brother Shorty.
    Koon and Janette had two daughters:
    a. LINDA KAY, who was born Jan. 27, 1949, and was married
        March 27, 1970, to Robert Underwood, born Aug. 27, 1936.
        Their children are ROBERT GLYNN, born July 4, 1973;
        LARA KAY, born Aug. 30, 1975; AMANDA ELAINE, born
        May 9, 1978; and JANA BETH, born January 19, 1983.
    a. b. NANCY MARIE, who was born July 22, 1950, and was
        married Sept. 3, 1971, to Robert E. (Bob) Stacks, who was
        born April 11, 1944, and died March 13, 2011. Their children
        are SAMUEL SHANE, born Jan. 28, 1973, and SARA SUE,
        born Sept. 3, 1976.

6. MARY SUE, who was born July 13, 1927, and died Jan. 30, 1959,
    shortly after the birth of Meg. She was married Jan. 15, 1947, to
    Gerald Shelburn, who was born Dec. 10, 1927, the son of Edgar
    and Mattie Griffin Shelburn. Their children are:
    a. GWENDOLYN ELAINE (Gwen), born July 14, 1948.
    b. BARBARA SUSAN, born Oct. 4, 1950.
    c. MARGARET ANN (Meg), born Jan. 27, 1959.

7. WILTON HOLLAND (Gene), who was born June 25, 1929, and
    died Mar. 8, 2009, in Fredericksburg. He was married June 6,
    1959, to Glenda Glover, born March 18, 1938, the daughter of
    Ralph and Ima Glover of the Lake Victor community. Gene
    served in the U. S. armed services during the Korean conflict.
    He earned his degree from Abilene Christian College (now
    University), and served numerous congregations among the
    churches of Christ as a gospel preacher until his retirement.
    The children of Gene and Glenda are:
    a. LEAH NANNETTE, born Nov. 23, 1960.
    b. PHILLIP EDWIN, born Sept. 5, 1968.
    c. STEPHEN KENT, born March 27, 1971.

8. ANNIE RUTH (Ann), who was born Oct. 19, 1932, and died
    May 21, 2006, in San Antonio. She was married March 3, 1952,

to Darrell Lee Banta, who was born Oct. 19, 1928, in San Saba County, and died July 16, 1994. He was the son of Jesse Jefferson Banta and the former Marie Fry. Their children are:
a.   RONALD LEE, born Feb. 19, 1954.
b.   DEBORAH ANN, born Jan. 3, 1956.
c.   JEFFERY LYNN, born Sept. 26, 1958.
d.   REBECCA SUE, born Aug. 12, 1960.
e.   ROGER DEAN, born May 18, 1967.

i. Julia Southerland Debo Landtroop Wolf

Julia Southerland (Jubie) Debo Landtroop Wolf, twelfth child and youngest daughter of Cornelius and Mary Ruth Debo, was born at the old Debo home place on March 1, 1899, some four and a half months after the death of her father. She was named after her uncle Reed Debo's daughter Julia and a family acquaintance, Emaliza Southerland. She grew to adulthood and attended school in the Spring Creek community. Jubie lived at the home place with her mother and brother Eppa until Eppa was married in 1919 after which she and her mother moved into Burnet and lived with her sister and brother-in-law, the Lindsey Fishers.

On September 30, 1920, she was married by Methodist minister George G. Smith to Winter Andrew Landtroop, who was born February 18, 1894, and died April 2, 1949. The following announcement appeared in the October 7, 1920, *Burnet Bulletin*:

DEBO-LANDTROOP

Last Thursday, September 30th, at the Methodist parsonage, Rev. George G. Smith officiating, Miss Julia Debo and Mr. W. A. Landtroop were united in marriage.

The bride is a daughter of Mrs. Mary Debo, for many years a beloved and highly respected resident of the Spring Creek community. Miss Julia is a modest sensible young lady, loved and admired by all who know her. Mr. Landtroop has been a resident of this place for many years and has the respect and esteem of our entire citizenship. The Bulletin joins the numerous friends of this happy couple in extending congratulations, and wishing for them many years of future happiness.

Winter and Jubie lived awhile in Burnet, but moved to Cedar Park where they lived for a number of years. Mary Ruth Debo lived with them much of the time. Jubie lived in Austin after the death of her husband where she later met Victor Hugo Wolf, born September 5, 1896; died May 22, 1972, and they were married April 4, 1970. In later years (1989) she bought a home and moved back to Burnet. She sold the home afterward and returned to Austin for a time; however, failing health caused her to return to Burnet where she passed away in a nursing home August 31, 1997. Julia was a member of the Church of the Nazarene. She and Winter had no children.

The following obituary appeared in the *Burnet Bulletin*:

WOLF

Julia "Jubie" Debo Landtroop Wolf, 98, of Burnet died Sunday, Aug. 31, 1997. Funeral services were held Sept. 3 at Clements-Wilcox Funeral Chapel with Pastor E. A. Heye officiating. Burial was at Burnet City Cemetery under the direction of Clements-Wilcox Funeral Home of Burnet.

Pallbearers were John Lawson, David Debo, Rex Lastly, James Hornsby, Darrell Debo, and Sam Debo.

A native of Burnet County, she was born March 1, 1899, the daughter of Cornelius and Mary Ruth Schooley Debo. She resided in Burnet and married Winter Landtroop Sept. 30, 1920. They lived in Austin when he died April 2, 1949. She continued to live in Austin and met and married Victor Hugo Wolf April 4, 1970. They lived in Austin until his death May 22, 1972. She returned to Burnet in 1989 to be with her family.

Survivors include nieces and nephews, Clyde Debo, Iris Graves, Peggy Fulcher, Clara Lawson, Reba Lastly, Gene Johnston, Annie Ruth Banta, Ruth Fisher, Dorr McFarland, and many great-nieces and great-nephews.

Memorials may be made to the American Cancer Society.

Jubie was buried in the Burnet Cemetery beside her first husband, Winter Landtroop.

j. William Clay. John Henry, and Cora Lee Debo

William Clay Debo was the fifth child and third son of Cornelius and Mary Ruth Debo. He was born January 6, 1883, at the old home place and was named for his grandfather, William Sturgis Schooley, and his uncle, Henry Clay Bowmer. Clay, attended the Spring Creek School, and had the misfortune of an early death because of a tragic ac-

Adult children of Cornelius and Mary Debo (Back Row: Nell; Eppa; Julia; Frank) (Front Row: Sallie; Hardy; Jennie; Lilbon (Lib))

cident. On a Sunday afternoon he, along with some of his brothers and neighborhood boys, were out riding their ponies when Clay's horse shied and went under a low-hanging limb, which struck the young man on the head and knocked him to the ground unconscious. He never recovered and died on Monday, November 21, 1898. Thus, only a little over a month after burying her husband, Mary Debo interred her 15 year-old son in the family cemetery north of the home place. The following report appeared in the November 24, 1898, *Burnet Bulletin*:

SAD ACCIDENT

It does look like misfortunes never come singly. Called on to mourn the death of her husband a few weeks ago, Mrs. Debo now sits at the side of her dying boy, Clay, aged 13 years. Riding out Sunday with some other boys, in passing under a low hanging limb, the horse shied in the wrong direction which the rider wanted to go, when the limb struck the boy on the head, from which he has since been unconscious. The attending physician has little hopes of his recovery.

P. S. The poor boy died on Monday, it is supposed from his back being broken, from which he was paralyzed. A part of his side turned black. He complained of the back of his neck. The boys were running their horses at the time of the accident.

Rev. Bell conducted the burial services.

* * * * *

John Henry Debo, the sixth child and fourth son of Cornelius and Mary Ruth Debo, was born December 26, 1883, at the home place and attended the Spring Creek rural school. He was named after his Grandfather Debo and his uncle, Henry McClure. He developed spinal meningitis and died on Monday night, November 30, 1903, just about a month short of his nineteenth birthday and was buried beside his brother Clay in the family cemetery. The following account appeared in the December 3, 1903, *Burnet Bulletin*:

ANOTHER GONE

Again our quiet little community wept when the sad news was wafted from ear to ear, that our friend and loved one, Henry Debo, had passed from earth to Heaven.

He departed this life Monday night, Nov. 30, 1903. His remains were interred in the family cemetery, Tuesday afternoon, Dec. 1.

A large crowd of relatives and friends followed the remains to the last earthly resting place.

Rev. T. Lee conducted the burial services.

He was just entering manhood, and a life of usefulness lay before him. He will be greatly missed in Sunday School and other religious activities…(part of the clipping is missing) he usually led the ch….

Cora Lee Debo, the eleventh child and fifth daughter of Cornelius and Mary Ruth Debo, was born at the home place February 26, 1896, and was named for Cora McFarland and her Uncle Reed Debo's son, Lee Debo, of Boonville, Missouri. She was referred to in the family as "Little Lee." She became ill and died in the arms of a beloved neighbor woman on March 2, 1901, a few days past her fifth birthday. She was having difficulty breathing and as she expired the neighbor holding her said: "Sister Mary, she's gone." Little Lee was buried in the family cemetery with her father and two brothers who had preceded her. The following notice appeared in the *Burnet Bulletin*:

Mrs. Debo had the sad misfortune to lose her little daughter, Lee, last Sunday morning from congestion of the stomach. Her cup of sorrow is certainly full. Counting father and grandchildren (sic), this is the 6th death in the family in the last two years.

6. Sarah James (Sallie) Debo Bowmer[1]

Sarah James (Sallie) Debo, the seventh child and second daughter of John and Jane Debo, was born October 20, 1846, in Bedford County, Virginia, and grew to womanhood on the Debo place in south side Bedford County. After the War Between the States, her brothers had left home and gone to Missouri. Her brother, Cornelius had come back to Virginia in 1879 to bring brother Reed's family back to Missouri, and Sallie decided to go with them for a visit. After arriving in Howard County she met Henry Clay Bowmer and they were married September 25, 1870, at Reed Debo's home.

Clay Bowmer was born November 15, 1840, in Howard County, Missouri, the son of Peter Bowmer. He had gone to Texas in 1859, and when the War Between the States broke out in April 1861 he enlisted in the Confederate service at Georgetown, Texas, and was mustered into the 7th Texas Calvary, 3rd Regiment, of Gen. Sibley's Brigade on October 26, 1861, at San Antonio. After the war was over he returned to Missouri and met his future bride, Miss Sallie Debo.

In 1872 Clay and Sallie Bowmer with infant daughter Elsie, along with Sallie's brothers, Thomas and Cornelius (called Teeny by Sallie and her family) Debo, left Missouri for Texas [see account of this journey in the section on Cornelius Debo]. The

Henry Clay Bowmer and wife Sallie Debo Bowmer near their old home near Maxdale (Bell County) Texas.

Bowmers settled on the Lampasas River near Maxdale in Bell County – just a short distance from the northeastern line of Burnet County – and lived there until October 1905 when the family moved to Comanche, Indian Territory (now Oklahoma), where they lived the remainder of their days. All the children were born at the home near Maxdale except Elsie. The family was Methodist.

Clay Bowmer died January 25, 1920, in Comanche, Oklahoma, and was buried there:

H. C. BOWMER DEAD

Henry C, Bowmer was born in Howard County, Missouri, November 15th, 1840, moved to the state of Texas in the year 59. When war was declared he joined the Confederacy and served four years under General Green. After the war he returned to Missouri, remaining there two years; during which time, in 1869, he met and married Miss Sallie Debo. Later, with his bride, he returned to Texas where he lived until October 1905. Five children blessed this union, four of whom, with his aged wife, are still living.

In 1880, Mr. Bowmer was converted and united with the Methodist church. In 1905 he, with his family, moved from Texas to Comanche, Oklahoma, where he lived till the day of his death – Sunday, January 25th, 1920, when peacefully he folded the tent of his earthly pilgrimage and slipped away to encamp upon the hills of Eternal Life and Light forever.

Sallie lived more than sixteen years after his death, passing away September 6, 1936, at the home of her daughter, Elsie Cooke, in Montgomery, Louisiana. She was buried beside her husband in Comanche.

LAST RITES FOR COUNTY PIONEER

Mrs. Sallie Bowmer Passes in Home
Of Daughter in Louisiana:
Funeral Here Tuesday

Funeral services for Mrs. Sallie J. Bowmer, for many years a resident of Comanche, were held Wednesday morning at the First Methodist church with Rev. W. S. Collins, pastor of the Methodist church at Corum officiating and Beeson Grantham Funeral Home in charge of arrangements. Interment was in Fairlawn cemetery beside the body of her husband, who preceded her death sixteen years ago.

Mrs. Bowmer was almost ninety years of age and despite her age, she was active in church work and her household duties until ill health overcame her three years ago. Friday night she suffered a stroke of paralysis in the home of her daughter, Mrs. L. C. B. Cooke, in Montgomery, La., and her condition became gradually worse until her death Sunday evening. The body was brought by train to Comanche, when Beeson Grantham assumed charge.

Mrs. Bowmer was for years an active member of the Methodist Church here and attended services regularly as long as she was well enough to go. She had a wide circle of friends, especially among the pioneer families of the town.

Besides Mrs. Cooke, she is survived by two other daughters. They are Mrs. J. F. Towler of San Angelo, Texas and Mrs. Eva Hoover of Amarillo, Texas. All were here for the funeral. One son, Early Bowmer, passed away here several years ago. Mrs. Naomi Isom and Nebo Bowmer are her grandchildren.

Pall bearers included Emory Green, Wm. Binder, Ewalt Boone, Bob Patty, E. Q. Haltom, Chas. Gregston and Joe Burk.

Clay and Sallie Bowmer had the following five children:
1. ELSIE, who was born August 28, 1871, in Missouri and died March 3, 1973, in Monroe, Louisiana. She married J. C. Cooke. Soon after their marriage they moved to Louisiana and lived there the remainder of their lives. I visited Elsie in a nursing home in Monroe, Louisiana, in 1970 and had a memorable exchange of old family tales with her. I was never able to obtain a record of her children. I was acquainted with two of them, Rupert Cooke and Crystal Cooke Robinett, who attended our Debo family reunions in Burnet, Texas. Rupert lived in Gulfport, Mississippi, and Crystal lived for many years in Shreveport, Louisiana, until after the death of her husband when she moved to Oklahoma near a son.
2. EVALINA (Evie), who was born February 26, 1874, and died February 27, 1952. She married Jack Hoover.
3. PRUNELLA (Prunie), born February 26, 1878, and died June 16, 1969, in San Angelo. She was married to John F. Towler. Prunie and daughter, Mildred Moreland, attended the Debo reunions in Burnet, and she was always jolly and full of life, a

joy to be around.

4. ROBERT EARLIE, born July 7, 1883, and died September 13, 1935, in Comanche, Oklahoma. Earlie was killed by lightning as he was turning off a light switch. He was married circa 1903 or 1904 to Maggie Corina Moore, born August 28, 1885, in Copperas Cove, Texas, and died February 20, 1970, in Comanche, Oklahoma. She was the daughter of Walter Samuel Moore and Mittie L. Flowers. Earlie and Maggie had three children:

    a. ELGIN THEODORE, born November 14, 1904, in Maxdale, Bell County, Texas, and died in April 1976 at Lawton, Oklahoma.

    b. NAOMI RUTH, born June 11, 1912, in Oklahoma, and died December 23, 1998, at Comanche, Oklahoma. She married Leland Grady Isom.

    c. OPAL, born June 11, 1912, in Oklahoma.

5. WILLIAM EMMETT, born October 24, 1887, and committed suicide August 10, 1909, somewhere in West Texas.

7. Marie Eliza (Mollie) Debo McClure[1]

Marie Eliza (Mollie) Debo, the tenth child and youngest daughter of John and Jane Debo, was born December 28, 1854, in southside Bedford County, Virginia, at the Debo home place. She was reared in the usual rural home of that day, and attended the rural school with her siblings.

Mollie lived at home with her parents after her brothers and sisters had left home. She continued to live with her father after her mother died in 1873; and when John decided to leave Bedford County and go to Missouri where some of his children had settled, she went with him. Mollie came to Texas (I have never learned exactly when; possibly when her sister Sallie and brothers Cornelius and Thomas came.) where she met Henry Campbell McClure.

Henry McClure was born June 4, 1839, possibly in Cherokee County, Alabama, died September 18, 1918, and was buried at Coleman, Texas. He was the son of Robert McClure [born June 27, 1809, at Dalton (Murray County), Georgia, and died September 25, 1893, in Somerville (Morgan County), Alabama] and the former Martha (Patsy) Langley [born June 27, 1813, in Georgia and died in the 1870's in Alabama], daughter of Noah and Sarah Langley. Henry and Mollie were married January 14, 1877, at the home of her sister and brother-in-law, Sallie and Clay Bowmer, in Bell County, Texas near Maxdale.

The McClures made their home at Lampasas for a number of years before moving to Coleman where they lived out the remainder of their days. Their children were:

1. VIOLA, who was born Nov. 19, 1877, and died April 10, 1883, less than six years of age. She was buried at Lampasas. Her brother, Marvin McClure, on one of his trips to the Debo Reunion in Burnet, stopped at the cemetery in Lampasas on his way home to Coleman and tried to locate Viola's grave, but was unable to do so.
2. ALMA, who was born Nov. 7, 1879, died Feb. 17, 1947, and was buried at the McClure cemetery lot at Coleman. She never married.
3. FLORA, who was born June 29, 1882, died July 12, 1905, at age 23.
4. MARVIN, who was born Dec. 3, 1887, died Dec. 26, 1989, at the ripe age of 102. He was active in the Methodist church of Coleman and sang in the choir. For many years he annually made the journey from Coleman to Burnet for the Debo Reunion and enjoyed the visit with his cousins. Marvin never married.
5. CAMILLE (Cammie), who was born March 24, 1891, and died July 4, 1980, in a Dallas nursing home. She was married in Nov. 1938 to George William Riddell.
6. CLOYCE (Tot or Totsie), who was born October 17, 1893, and died June 3, 1989. She was married in June 1913 to Ben Strickland. They had one son, Burl, who is a mathematician, having taught math in Crane (Tex.) High School, and working at White Sand Missile Range in New Mexico until retirement in 1980. He moved back to Coleman in 1982. Cloyce and Ben Strickland were buried in Coleman. In 1975 on a vacation trip, I went through Coleman and while there had a happy amd memorable visit with Cloyce and Marvin. Cloyce and Camille attended one of our Debo Reunions held that year out at Lake Buchanan.

8. Martha, Prudence, Bettie Jane; and John Bruce Debo[1]

Martha Prudence Debo was the third child and oldest daughter of John and Jane Debo. She was born September 20, 1836, and died January 22, 1862, at the age of 25.

Bettie Jane Debo, eighth child and third daughter of John and Jane Debo, was born November 7, 1849, and died January 12, 1862, at age 12.

John Bruce Debo, ninth child and youngest son of John and Jane Debo, was born February 7, 1852, and died January 20, 1862, lacking 18 days being 10 years old.

These three children were all born at the home place in Bedford County, Virginia, and all of them died there within the span of ten days time and presumably were buried in the family cemetery. The Bedford County records say they died of typhus fever. It seems more than likely, however, that they died of typhoid fever since their deaths occurred in the wintry month of January, and some accounts I have read seem to indicate that a typhoid epidemic may have been raging in that section of Virginia at that time as others were dying of the malady. Whatever the actual cause of their death, can you imagine a father and mother losing three of their children within ten days time and the heartache and trauma that would be involved? And then the next year, to lose another son – Dabney – at the Battle of Gettysburg. The strength of the pioneers is indeed amazing compared to the weak-kneed moderns brought up on ease, comfort, and selfishness!

C. Elizabeth (Betsy) Debo Blankenship[1]

Mary Elizabeth (Betsy)Debo, third child and oldest daughter of Michael Debo, Sr., and Katharine Saunders Debo, was born circa 1801 in Bedford County, Virginia, on the Debo home place and died in March 1845. She was married February 16, 1816,[2] at fifteen years of age to Abraham Blankenship, Jr. Abraham was born 1759 and died March 8, 1845, and the former Susan Wyatt (Wiatt), born in 1758 and died after 1845. They were married in Chesterfield County, Virginia, in 1781 and moved to Bedford County 1784.

Known children of Elizabeth and Abraham are:
1. JOHN JAGO, was born Sept. 26, 1817, and died Nov. 4, 1862 in Franklin County. He was married April 16, 1838, in Bedford County to Christina Catharine Plymale who was born June 18, 1819, the daughter of Thomas Plymale. John J. and Christina Blankenship were buried in the Blankenship Cemetery about two miles east of Scruggs, Virginia, in Franklin County. According to the U.S. Census of 1860 for Bedford County, Virginia, the following children were listed.

a. FRANCES FLORA, was born Dec. 29, 1839 and died Jan. 26, 1916 in Bedford County.
b. JULINA, born Sept. 6, 1841; married Joseph Robertson, born also in 1841.
c. JOHN HENRY, born Sept. 28, 1843, and died May 17, 1909. He was married Dec. 1, 1870, to Ursula A. Saunders, who was born Feb. 18, 1850, and died Dec. 23, 1923. He was a Confederate veteran.
d. THOMAS G., born Apr. 7, 1845, and died Aug. 25, 1909 in Franklin County. He was married in 1859 in Franklin County to Missouri Williamson, born in 1845 and died in 1859.
e. ABRAM S., born Feb. 5, 1848, in Bedford County.
f. MISSOURI C., born Arp. 11, 1851, in Bedford County, and died in 1880 in Franklin County. She married John R. Maxey, born Sept. 19, 1853, in Franklin County.
g. VIRGINIA B., born June 18, 1852, in Bedford County. She married Jeremiah (Jerry) Whitworth, who was born in 1856 in Bedford County.
h. WILLIAM PIERCE, born Mar. 11, 1855, in Franklin County, and died Oct. 12, 1928, in Franklin County. He was married in 1875 to Samuel Elizabeth Scruggs, who was born in 1859 in Franklin County and died on Jan. 29, 1946 in Franklin County.
i. JAMES C., born Sept. 26, 1857, in Franklin County.
j. DANIEL PERRY, born Jan. 12, 1859, and died Jan. 2, 1933, in Roanoke. He was married Marc. 27, 1896 in Huddleston, VA, to Narcissia Plymale and was named for his mother Elizabeth's brother of the same name.
2. NANCY EMMELINE, was born circa 1818. She was married on December 22, 1840, in Bedford County to Wyatt W. Truman, who was born 1814\15. The U.S. Census of 1850 for the county lists no children.
3. MARTHA ANN, born circa 1825 and died November 14, 1880, of blackleg. She was married on May 20, 1856, to Andrew J. Carter, who was born circa 1825. The U.S. Census of 1870 for Bedford County lists the following children:
a. MAGGIE, born 1857.
b. COLUMBUS, born 1859.
c. SERELDA, born 1861

d. ELIZA, born 1863.

4. MICHAEL JEFFERSON (sometimes called Jeffey or Jeffrey), born circa 1826 and died in 1911. He was married on Dec. 21, 1847, in Bedford County to Sarah Ann Carter, born circa 1830, daughter of Sallie M. Carter. Their children, listed in the U.S. Census of 1870 for Bedford County, were:
   a. BETTY F., born 1851.
   b. SARAH V., born 1852.
   c. WILLIAM D., BORN 1854
   d. MARTHA J., born 1856.
   e. THOMAS J., born 1858.
   f. NANCY B., born 1860.
   g. JOHN G., born 1862.
   h. STANHOPE D., born 1865.
   i. IDELLA, born 1869.

5. JAMES CALOHILL, born circa 1828. He served in Co. G., 28th Virginia Regiment (the same unit the Debo brothers served in), during the War Between the States, enlisting on March 14, 1862. His Confederate records reveal him to be a farmer, and a private, with dark complexion, black hair, gray eyes. He was absent from his unit from June 5, 1862, to September 15, 1863, in the hospital with "debility." He was also in the hospital with dysentery from May 1864 to November of that year. He was captured at Burkeville April 6, 1865, and released at Pt. Lookout, Maryland June 1865. Callohill Blankenship was married on December 14, 1859, to America Elizabeth Fielder, born Apr. 20 1835. Their children were:
   a. ELIJAH M. ALEXANDER, born 1860. He was listed in the 1894-95 city directory of Lynchburg, Virginia.
   b. ELVIRA, born April 10, 1862.
   c. COLUMBUS B. (Lum), born Oct. 1867. He ran a store in the 1930s on Rt. 608 (it is now gone), and is buried at Stonewall, VA in Appomattox County.
   d. OSCAR EARLY, born May 9, 1870, and died March 5, 1914. He and brother Lum were ice fishing in February in James River and fell in. He died of pneumonia, and was buried in woods on a ridge near a small creek on Rt. 611, Box 125, in Appomattox County near Stonewall. Oscar was married January 23, 1901, in Campbell County, Virginia, to Susie Dodson, daughter of

Ellison C. and Laura L. Dodson.
  e. FANNIE, born in January 1871 and died June 15, 1871, of typhoid fever.
  f. JOHN, born in Dec. 1871.
  g. ALONZO B., born 1876.
  h. RUFUS B., born in April 1882.
  i. ANNIE, born in Aug. 1883; buried at Amherst, Virginia. Alonzo B., Rufus B., and Lillie P. Blankenship are all buried in the cemetery at Mr. Hermon Methodist Church on Rt. 43, west of Lynch Station, Virginia.

D. Sally Debo Blankenship[1]

Sally Debo was the fourth child and the second daughter of Michael Sr. and Katharine Saunders Debo, and was born circa 1803 on the Debo place in Bedford County, Virginia, and died in 1826 in Bedford County. She was married on January 26, 1818, to Lawson Blankenship, son of Abraham Sr. and Susan Wyatt Blankenship, and a brother of Abraham Blankenship, Jr.

Information on this family is even sparser than that on the Elizabeth Debo and Abraham Blankenship family. Known children of Sally and Lawson are:

  1. WILLIAM B., who married Elizabeth Murray on December 27, 1849, at Lafayette, Montgomery County, Virginia. He served in the 1st Virginia Infantry, Co. D., during the War Between the States.
  2. ARDENA, who married William H. Moses, son of William Moses, on March 21, 1843, in Montgomery County, Virginia.

It is presumed that the family moved from Bedford County to Montgomery County at some time after Lawson's second marriage. It is assumed that Sally died in 1826, since Lawson was married in Bedford County on January 22, 1827, to Luney Martin, daughter of John Martin.

Other sons of Lawson Blankenship included OTEY BLANKENSHIP, whose wife Susan filed a claim for his pay as a Confederate soldier in the 54th Virginia on April 25, 1864. He died in Marietta, Georgia. Other sons were SAMUEL L., WILLIAM M., HENRY CLAVIN, and DAVID M., all of whom served in the 54th Virginia during the War Between the States. David is buried in Salem, Virginia, and Henry Clavin at East Hill Cemetery in Salem.

E. Margaret Debo Saunders[1]

Margaret (Peggy) Debo, the fifth child and third daughter of Michael Debo, Sr., and Katharine Saunders Debo, was born circa 1805 on the Debo place in southern Bedford County, Virginia. She grew up in the usual rural society of that day and at age about nineteen was married on December 20, 1824, in her native county to John Rollins Saunders, who was born in 1801 in neighboring Campbell County, Virginia. It is uncertain just when the family moved south into adjoining Franklin County, probably soon after their marriage, for the last six of their children (Catherine, Littleberry, David Rush, Daniel, Joseph, and Margaret) plus sons John Quincy and Andrew Jackson were all born in Franklin County, while Stephen Preston, Alexander, and Michael Marion were all born in Bedford County.

John R. Saunders was a farmer and blacksmith, and after moving to Franklin County the family lived at Long Branch Township, Blackwater District, in the northern part of the county. After the birth of ten children and the death of Margaret sometime in 1844, John was married by Theo F. Webb on August 4, 1845, in Franklin County to Nancy Leftwich, who was the daughter of Sarah C. Leftwich and was born circa 1815/16 in Bedford County. John had six more children by her for a total of sixteen offspring. He died April 13, 1884, in Franklin County at age 83, forty years after the death of Margaret Debo Saunders, his first wife. Their burial site has not been ascertained.

The children of John R. and Margaret were:
1. JOHN QUINCY, born in March 14, 1825, on the headwaters of the Blackwater River. He was a farmer and was married by Abraham Nafe to Susan Nancy Webster, daughter of John R. and Deborah Webster, on July 17, 1851, in Franklin County. She was born either in 1834 or 1835 (census) or 1838(obituary) and died on January 1, 1903. Sometime after the birth of all their children, all of whom were born in Franklin County, they moved to Mexico, Missouri. John Quincy's death date is uncertain. He was named for John Quincy Adams, president of the United States at the time of his birth. Children of John Quincy and Susan Nancy were:
   a. JAMES DANIEL, born in 1852, and died in Franklin County August 8, 1933. He was married Dec. 26, 1878, in Bedford

County to Ellen D. Hurt, born in 1856 in Bedford County, daughter of Joel L. and Sarah Grigsby Hurt.

b. MARY CATHERINE, born January 20, 1854, and died Aug. 30, 1934. She was married on Nov. 2, 1881, in Franklin County to Jacob R. C. Webster, son of Adam and Susannah Akers Webster, who was born in 1852 in Franklin County and died May 2, 1904.

c. SARAH MARGARET, born October 12, 1856, and died Sept 4, 1900. She was married on Sept. 26, 1880, in Franklin County to Thomas Mills, son of Cornelius and Sarah Wray Mills, who was born in 1854/56 in Franklin County.

d. ELIZABETH V., born March 3, 1859 and died March 16, 1949, in Versailles, Missouri. She married John Ramer.

e. NATHANIEL G., born July 24, 1860, and died in infancy.

f. SUSAN, born in 1862.

g. JOHN WILLIAM, born December 9, 1865, and died March 13, 1920.

h. MARTHA JANE, born April 29, 1868.

2. ANDREW JACKSON, born in 1826, and died March 30, 1915, in Franklin County. He was married by Abraham Nafe January 6, 1851, in Franklin County to Ann Peters, daughter of David and Christine Brubaker Peters, who was born Sept. 18, 1823, in Franklin County and died there Sept. 5, 1893. They lived in Maggodee District, and were members of Bethlehem Brethren Church. Andrew J. was named for Andrew Jackson, the president of the United States at the time. The children of Andrew J. and Ann were:

a. HENRY W., born March 26, 1852, and died Jan. 17, 1854, of scarlet fever.

b. SARAH ELIZABETH, born Jan. 13, 1854, and died in September 1860.

c. MARY E., born Sept. 5, 1856, and died in the late 1860s.

d. MILTON JEFFERSON, born in 1858. He was married Aug. 9, 1883, in Franklin County to Emma E. Webster, daughter of Jesse B. and Tabitha Fisher Webster, who was born in 1866 and died July 17, 1890.

e. JOHN DAVID, born 1864/65.

f. EMMA, born 1867/1868.

3. STEPHEN PRESTON, born in 1828 in Bedford County; and

died October 2, 1939, Wayne County, West Virginia. He was married Nov. 11, 1852, in Franklin County by George W. Kelly to Louisa O. Helms, daughter of Thomas and Frances Saunders Helms, who was born in 1837 in Franklin County. They moved to Wayne County, West Virginia, sometime in the late 1860s. After the death of Louisa, Stephen P. was later married Jan. 25, 1883, in Wayne County to Lucinda Frances Piles, daughter of George W. and Elizabeth Piles, who was born Oct. 13, 1860, at Whites Creek, Wayne County, West Virginia. The children of Stephen P. and Louisa were:

a. SARAH FRANCES, born Aug. 12, 1853.
b. MARGARET A., born April 16, 1855, who was married May 5, 1873, in Wayne County to McFarlin Booten.
c. MARTHA J., born in 1857.
d. LOUISA C., born in Oct. 1858, and died Feb. 1, 1859.
e. HARRIET E., born Nov. 29, 1859.
f. ALICE, born circa 1860.
g. ALBERTA, born 1861/62, and was married to Jesse Scaggs on Dec. 12, 1884.
h. GEORGE THOMAS, born circa 1865. He was married Dec. 23, 1886, in Wayne County to Laura Jackson, and died Oct. 2, 1939, in the same county.
i. VICTORIA, born circa 1866. She was married Dec. 24, 1884, in Wayne County to Johnson Hensley.
j. CORA E., born circa 1867 in Lincoln County, West Virginia. She was married May 16, 1886, in Wayne County to Joseph Newman and died June 14, 1954 in the same county.
k. JOHN B., born circia 1869.
l. OLIVIA, born 1870/71.
m. ROSA BELL, born April 20, 1872, and died June 5, 1888, in Wayne County.
n. FRANCES O., born April 1874, and was married to George Cain.

Children of Stephen P. and Lucinda Frances (all born in Wayne County, West Virginia)

o. HENRY, born in Feb. 1884 and died June 26, 1955
p. JOSEPH E., born in Sept. 1886 and died March 20, 1891.
q. LAURA E., born in March 1888.
r. BAYMAN, born Jan. 5, 1890, and was married Feb. 10, 1917,

to Mary Allen.

   s. SHERMAN, born in 1892.

   t. CEBURN CECIL (twin), born March 17, 1896, and died Feb 8. 1966. He married Gladys Irene Adkins, and is buried in Ridgelawn Cemetery, Huntington, West Virginia.

   u. CHEPHIS (twin), born March 17, 1896, and died March 18, 1896.

   v. ALFONZO FORREST, born Jan. 29, 1898, and died Aug. 4, 1970. He was married July 26, 1928, to Nona Opal Church, and is also buried in Ridgelawn Cemetery.

   w. GARLAND, born Dec. 12, 1900; never married.

4. ALEXANDER, born in 1830 and must have died at an early age.

5. MICHAEL MARION, born Nov. 10, 1832, and died Feb. 16, 1859. He was married June 8., 1855, to Sarah Helms, born 1840, daughter of Thomas and Frances Helms. They lived on the Pigg River in eastern Franklin County, Virginia. At his death at age 26 due to "pneumonia fever," the inventory and appraisement of his personal estate was $673.79.

6. CATHERINE, born 1836. She was married July 20, 1854, in Bedford County, Virginia, to a widower, Wesley Morgan, who was born in 1811 and was the son of Mordecai and Elizabeth Nichols Morgan. Wesley died in 1859 in Bedford; he and Catherine had one known child, a son Morgan. Catherine was re-married circa 1860 to William G. Nichols.

7. LITTLEBERRY, born in 1836 and died Dec. 31, 1860, of diphtheria.

8. DAVID RUSH, born in 1838 and listed in the 1850 Census but not in the 1860 Census.

9. DANIEL, born in 1840 and died Dec. 21, 1860 of diphtheria.

10. JOSEPH, born in 1842, but not listed in the 1860 Census.

Children of John and Nancy were:

11. MARGARET (Peggy), born 1846. She was married July 19, 1866, in Franklin County to Joseph Sledd, born 1841, the son of William and Ann Sledd.

12. ZACHARIAH, born 1848 and died Jan. 10, 1861, of diphtheria.

13. SAMUEL S., born 1850, and was married Nov. 11, 1869, to Mary E. Slone, born 1853 to Samuel and Lydia Slone. Known children included OCTAVIA M., born Nov. 29, 1870, and SAM-

UEL N., born Oct. 15, 1879.

14. VICTORIA, born Aug. 19, 1852, and died Dec. 25, 1860, of diphtheria.

15. NATHANIEL, born 1854.

16. EDMUND, born 1859.

F. Valentine Debo

Valentine Debo, sixth child and third son of Michael Debo, Sr., and Katharine Saunders Debo, was born circa 1807 on the Debo place in southern Bedford County, Virginia. At age 25 he was married in his home county to Mary Ann Bishop on July 23, 1832.[1] Jonathan Bishop was surety for the marriage bond.

Nothing further has ever been found concerning this couple.

G. Daniel Perry Debo

Daniel Perry Debo, seventh child of Michael Debo, Sr., and Katharine Saunders Debo and their fourth son, was born circa 1809 at the Debo homeplace in southern Bedford County, Virginia, near Goose and Rockcastle creeks. There he was reared along with his siblings in the rural society of that day, and was never married. Shortly before his demise, in his will he described his physical condition as "being weak and debilitated in body but in full possession of a discriminating and disposing mind," which would lead one to believe that his impending death was caused by some physical malady, perhaps tuberculosis (or consumption, as it was then called) or some other common debilitant of the time. His will was dated December 11, 1849, and his death occurred shortly thereafter on January 3, 1850. He was buried in the family cemetery of his brother-in-law's family, the Hubbards, on Body Camp Creek in Bedford County.[1] Daniel had named his brother-in-law, Taliaferro G. Hubbard, who had married his sister Mary, as the executor of his will, and Hubbard soon followed him in death on May 7, 1850, and was buried in the same cemetery.[2]

Following is Daniel Perry's last will and testament:[3]

I Daniel P Debo of the County of Bedford and State of Virginia being weak and debilitated in body but in full possession of a discriminating and disposing mind, and being fully aware of the uncertainty of life as well as the certainty of Death do make this my last Will and Testament.

First – When I shall have filled the measure of my days upon

Earth, I bequeath my Soul to Almighty God, and cosign my body to its mother Earth from whence it came.

Second – It is my Will and desire that all my just debts be paid.

Third – Having purchased of my brother John Debo about the year Eighteen hundred and forty three or forty four his entire Interest in the Estate of my Father, Michael Debo Sr. I now give and bequeath the said Interest to Jane Debo (the wife of my brother John) during her natural life, and at her death it is my will and desire that the said Interest with the increase thereof if any shall be equally divided between all the children of said Jane Debo.

Fourth – It is my Will and desire that all other property of every kind whatsoever of which I may be possessed at the time of my decease shall be sold by my Executor and after my just debts shall have been paid, the balance of the proceeds shall be divided into three equal parts, one part of which I give and bequeath to Jane Debo (the Wife of John Debo) the same being given to her to be disposed of as she may think proper.

Fifth – I give and bequeath to Taliaferro G. Hubbard one third part of the proceeds of the property sold as above, the same being given to him and his heirs forever.

Sixth – I give and bequeath the other third part of the proceeds of the property sold as before named to Michael Debo Jr and to his heirs forever.

Seventh – It is my Will and desire that the Interest alluded to in the third Item of this my Will shall be so construed that Jane Debo (wife of my brother John Debo) shall have as a portion of the Interest alluded to, the tract of Land on which the said John Debo now resides, the same being rated at two hundred and fifty-four Dollars and twelve and a half cents.

Eighth – I hereby constitute and appoint my friend and brother-in-law Taliaferro G. Hubbard my Executor to this, my Will. In witness where of I have hereunto set my hand and affixed my seal this 11th day of December One thousand eight hundred and forty nine.

Daniel P. Debo (seal)

Signed and acknowledged
in the presence of
William A. Creasey
John T. Creasey
Thos. W. Robertson

At a Court held for Bedford County January 28, 1850, this last will and testament of Daniel P. Debo Decased produced in Court and proved by the oath of William A. Creasey and Thomas W. Robertson subscribing witnesses thereto and ordered to be recorded and on the motion of Taliaferro G. Hubbard the Executor in said will named who made oath and together with George Hubbard and William Lindsay his securities entered into and acknowledged bond in the penalty of fifteen hundred dollars conditioned according to law, certificate is granted him for obtaining a probate of said will in due form.

Teste   Jno. R. Steptoe C.B.C.

H. Mary Debo Hubbard[1]

Mary Debo, eighth child and fourth daughter of Michael Debo, Sr. and Katharine Saunders Debo, was born May 7, 1810, on the Debo homeplace in southern Bedford County, Virginia, and died October 8, 1857, and was buried in the Hubbard Cemetery on Body Camp Creek. At the age of 26 she was married by John Ayres to a widower, Taliaferro Graves Hubbard, also of Bedford County, on November 7 (10), 1836.[2] Hubbard was born September 25, 1800, and was the son of John and Elizabeth Hubbard, who settled in Bedford County in 1811 along Body Camp Creek in what is known as the Body Camp community. The Hubbard place was owned by T. G. Hubbard after the death of his parents as he had bought out the interests of his siblings. He died May 7, 1850, and was buried in the Hubbard family cemetery on the place.

Taliaferro (pronounced Tolliver) Hubbard was first married to Charlotte L. Hunter, daughter of A. W. Hunter, on April 26, 1827, by Frederick Kabler. She was born June 9, 1805, and died November 20, 1835. They had four children: (1) MARY SUSAN, born in 1828 and died November 20, 1835 (the same day her mother died); (2) STEPHEN, born October 28, 1829, and died in 1909; (3) JOHN FRANCIS, born May 10, 1831, and died June 23, 1893; (4) AUSTIN, born October 25, 1833, and died as a child.

The property sale of Mary and Taliaferro's estates areas follows:[3]

The following is a list of the Sales of property belonging to the Estate of Mary Hubbard deed made on the 16th day of Nov. 1857 by A. L. Thurman admr.

Property	Purchasers	Price
1 fine Bed B Stead & Furniture	Charles H. Rorer	27.00
1 Trundle Bed	Charles H. Rorer	3.00
1 Bed Quilt	Harstin A. Leftwich	1.25

1 Bed Blanket	Charles H. Rorer	1.50
1 Counterpane	Charles H. Rorer	2.00
10 Bushels Wheat	John H. Boyer	12.50
10 Bushels Wheat	Grandison Leftwich	12.60
Balance of wheat 1 ¼	Walter B. Dowdy	1.88
1 Lot of Irish potatoes 7 ½	Ellis R. Witt	3.37 ½
4 Boxes	John H. Boyer	1.00
1 Tub	A.L. Thurman	.06
126 head cabbage 2¢	Grandison Leftwich	2.56
160 head cabbage 1 3/8	E.C. Jacobs	2.20
10 Box corn @ 2.66	E.C. Jacobs	26.6
10 Box corn @ 2.68	E.C. Jacobs	26.8
10 Box corn @ 2.75	John B. Witt	27.50
10 Box corn @ 2.79	John B. Witt	27.90
10 Box corn @ 2.90	William J. Creasey	29.00
1 Lot Shucks $5	Walter B. Dowdy	5.00
1 Bay Horse	E.C. Jacobs	80.25
1 Stack Straw	E.C. Jacobs	1.80
1 Stack Straw	G. Leftwich	2.60
Chalf & Straw	E.C. Jacobs	1.30
1 Stack Oats	E.C. Jacobs	5.00
1 Stack Oats	Walter B. Dowdy	6.85
1 Dish & Wash pan	Charles H. Rorer	1.00
1 pr Pitchers	Charles H. Rorer	1.00
2 Com Pitchers	D.H. Mitchell	.15
1 Deep Dish	Geo. T. Metts	.12 ½
1 Dinner Dish	D.H. Mitchell	.31
2 Dinner Dish	A.L. Thurman	.06
Property	*Purchasers*	*Price*
1 Large Dish	J.J. Garrett	.25
4 Plates	A.L. Thurman	.06
6 Plates	A.L. Thurman	.37 ½
8 Plates white	James R. Metts	.40
1 Set cups & saucers	Walter B. Dowdy	.45
1 Set Broken	Walter B. Dowdy	.16
Slop Bowl pheal etc.	A.L. Thurman	.03
1 Set Tumblers	Walter B. Dowdy	.35
5 Bot & Contents	D.H. Mitchell	.30
Tea Pot & Sugar Dish	Charles H. Creasy	.12 ½
1 Dish & Tea pot	Walter B. Dowdy	.25
Slop Bowl & S Dish	Geo T. Metts	.25
1 Set Knives & forks	Walter B. Dowdy	1.30
1 Lot T Spoons	John B. Witt	.37 ½
1 set Knives & forks	John B. Witt	.40
1 Dozn Tea Spoons	John B. Witt	.30
1 molasses can	Charles H. Rorer	.20

1 mug	Charles H. Creasy	.12 ½
1 salt Stand	Steven Hubbard	.12 ½
1 cream pot	Walter B. Dowdy	.12 ½
1 Castor	Geo. T. Metts	.75
1 Large Coffee Pot	Walter B. Dowdy	.25
Coffee Pot & Bucket	James R. Metts	.06 ¼
1 Butter pot	Charles H. Creasy	.37 ½
1 Demijohn	Walter B. Dowdy	.50
1 large Tin Bucket	Chas. H. Rorer	.25
2 large Tin Bucket	A. L. Thurman	.15
Bucket & Strainer	James R. Metts	.20
1 Tin Bucket	C.H. Rorer	.12 ½
1 Tin Bucket	John B. Witt	.06 ¼
1 Stone Basin	Grandison Leftwich	.12 ½
2 Smoothing irons	C.H. Rorer	.45
1 Brass Kettle	G. Leftwich	1.72
1 Tea Kettle	Samuel Updike	.50
2 Candle Stick	James R. Metts	.17
1 Churn	Samuel Updike	.85
1 Water Bucket	William J Creasey	.25
1 Looking Glass	Geo. T. Metts	.37
1 Looking Glass	Geo. T. Metts	.50
1 pr. Sole Leather	B.H. Moulton	1.10
1 Side Saddle	Grandison Leftwich	7.30
1 pr. Window curtains	Joseph C. Drewry	.05
1 Lot Table Cloths	Walter B. Dowdy	.95
1 pr. Window curtains	C.H. Rorer	.50
1 Lot cotton	Geo. T. Metts	1.00
Property	*Purchasers*	*Price*
1 claw hammer	Saml McConaha	.12 ½
2 pr. Harnesses	James R. Metts	.50
1 pr. Candle moulds	E. C. Jacobs	.37 ½
1 coffee mill	Joseph St. Clair	.05
1 small jug	Wm. Fields	.15
1 Jar & Jug	Tinsley R. Williamson	.30
2 Stone Jars	E. C. Jacobs	.50
2 sack Bags	T. R. Williamson	.25
1 Sifter	D. H. Mitchell	.31
8 Fl. Barrels	Samuel McConaha	1.00
1 Lot vinegar	Geo. T. Metts	.46
Brick moulds	E. C. Jacobs	.08
2 Buckets	D. H. Mitchell	.20
1 Cooking Stove	B. H. Moulton	19.50
Pr. Gear & hip strap	Saml. McConaha	1.12 ½
Pr. Gear & hip strap	E. C. Jones	1.75
1 Blind Bridle	E. C. Jacobs	.42

1 Horse collar	E. C. Jacobs	.37 ½
1 Horse collar	A. P. Drewry	.50
1 Blade Stack	A. L. Thurman	1.75
1 Top Stack	A. L. Thurman	1.50
Flax seed & barrels	E. C. Jones	.55
1 lot flax	E. C. Jones	.51
1 Top Stack	Saml McConaha	1.90
1 Blade Stack no. 1	E. C. Jones	5.00
1 Top Stack	E. C. Jones	1.60
1 Top Stack	G. Leftwich	1.85
1 Blade Stack no. 2	E. C. Jones	5.00
1 Black Stack	E. C. Jones	3.50
2 Slays	D. H. Mitchell	1.00
Warping Bars etc.	W. I. Creasy	.70
Waggon tire	Saml. McConaha	.50
6 Bush wheat @ 7/6	E. C. Jacobs	7.50
9 Barrels corn Rent	E. C. Jacobs	<u>23.94</u>
		469.67 ½

I hereby certify that I kept the foregoing list of Sales and they are correct. Given under my hand this 25th day of January 1858.   Wm. P. Tinsley

In Bedford County Court Clerk's office February 22nd 1858. This List of Sales of the estate of Mary Hubbard decd was produced in said office and admitted to record.
Teste   A.A. Arthur C.B.C.

A list of Sales of Property belonging to the estate of Taliaferro G. Hubbard decd made on the 16th day of Nov. 1857 by A.L. Thurman, adm.

Property	Purchasers	Price
1 mason hammer	Charles H. Rorer	.16
1 lot old axes etc.	Saml. McConaha	.56
Ox Ring & Staple	John Debo	.16
1 Lot chains	Euel Arthur	.55
1 Lot old Irons	Saml. McConaha	.30
1 Wing @ Coulter	Saml. McConaha	.19
1 cro bar	Grandison Leftwich	.75
1 axe	Samuel McConaha	.26
1 G Stone crank	David H. Mitchell	.35
1 Log chain etc.	Saml. McConaha	.21
1 fan mill crank	Richard Maxey	.15
1 wheel bearer	E.C. Jones	.75
1 cutting knife & box	A.L. Minter	2.00
1 cutting knife	Saml. Updike	.62 ½
2 plains & Jointer	William B. Sims	.81

1 lot croze	Walter B. Dowdy	.25
1 frow	Thomas C. Goggin	.70
2 chisels	Walter B. Dowdy	.35
1 coulter & Stack	Walter B. Dowdy	.55
1 Shovel plough	Obediah Blanks	.32
1 Shovel plough	Obediah Blanks	1.00
1 mowing Scythe Etc.	Richard Maxey	.05
4 augers	Thos. Nunery	.52
1 Drawing knife	Walter B. Dowdy	.75
1 Drawing knife	William B. Sims	.30
1 Iron Square	William B. Sims	.25
1 Big plough & point	James R. Metts	1.37 ½
1 Double tree	A.L. Minter	.45
1 mattock	Walter B. Dowdy	.75
1 mattock	Walter B. Dowdy	1.50
1 Shovel mallet & hoe	John Debo	.06
1 Lot hoes	Walter B. Dowdy	.80
1 axel Tree	John S. Preston	.37 ½
1 hand saw	William Dowdy	.50
1 Basket of Irons	Saml McConahan	.70
1 pr. Stretchers	Grandison Leftwich	.65
3 Single Trees	Euel Arthur	.75
1 Scythe & cradle	Thomas Nunery	1.30
1 Harrow	A.L. Minter	.85
2 Blind & 1 riding bridle	Euel Arthur	.85
Chop Axe & churn	Nat Worley	.25
1 Lard Stand 7 ½ bushel	Walter B. Dowdy	.31 ¼
Property	*Purchasers*	*Price*
Pickling Barrell etc.	E.C. Jacobs	.05
Lard Stand & Basket	James C. Drury	.15
2 hogsheads	Walter B. Dowdy	1.45
1 Vinegar Cask	James C. Drury	.12 ½
1 Cot Wheel	Tinsley R. Williamson	2.90
5 Barrells	Richard Maxey	.10
1 Runlet	Geo. T. Metts	.40
1 Seive	Samuel McConaha	.11
Cake mould etc	David H. Mitchell	.45
1 pr. Cot cards	Richard Maxey	.25
Old kettle etc.	Richard Maxey	.35
1 pr Steelyards	Walter B. Dowdy	.75
1 Bread tray & sifter	D. H. Mitchell	.45
1 Stone basin	Richard Maxey	.20
1 Bread Tray	Robert Johnson	.25
Flax Hackel	Geo. T. Metts	1.00
1 Lantern	William D. Morgan	.33
Bridle & martgales	Ellis R. Witt	.01 ¼

Property	Purchasers		Price
1 Side Saddle	H.A. Leftwich		2.30
2 1st choist shoats	Grandison Leftwich		5.30
1 2nd choist shoats	John J. Garrett		15.90
2 1st choist Pork	Thomas Nunery	$8.25 ea	16.50
2 2nd choice Pork	James M. Phelps		15.00
3 3rd choice Pork	James M. Phelps		18.75
1 Sow	James C. Drury		10.06
1 Oven & Lid	D. H. Mitchell		1.45
Lid & Baker	Charles H. Rorer		1.50
1 Large Pot Iron etc	Wm. H. Newman		.50
1 small Oven	Stephen Hubbard		.30
1 Dinner Pot	Charles H. Rorer		.75
1 Small Pot	Charles H. Rorer		.85
1 large Oven & Lid	A.L. Minter		1.10
1 pr Hooks	Thomas S. Mitchum		.25
1 pr Hooks	D.H. Mitchell		.26
1 Tribbet	Steven Hubbard		.06 ¼
1 Tribbet	D.H. Mitchell		.26
Shovel & Tongs	Thomas Mitchum		.55
1 Frying Pan	John Creasy		.25
1 Pot Rack	T.R. Williamson		.85
Cross cut saw	C.H. Rorer		1.92
Loom & temples	Obediah Blanks		1.12 ½
1 Table	W.H. Creasy		.85
1 Press	D.H. Mitchell		10.00
1 Water Bucket	D.H. Mitchell		.50
1 Falling leaf Table	Daniel M. Morgan		8.75
Property	*Purchasers*		*Price*
1 Bed Bed Stead & furniture	Daniel Field		18.75
4 Split B Chairs	Joshua Drury	.55ea	2.20
5 Windsor Chairs	Grandison Leftwich		3.25
2 Small Chairs	George Metts		.50
1 large chair	George Metts		.65
2 Cloths Baskets	D.H. Mitchell		.45
1 Dish	Charles H. Creasy		1.80
1 Clock	James S. Kasey		3.25
1 Beauro	D.H. Mitchell		16.25
1 Lot Books	Thomas Shepherd		1.00
1 Shot Gun	Thomas A. Kasey		3.90
1 Bed Stead & furniture	D.H. Mitchell		18.60
1 Bed Stead & furniture	Geo. T. Metts		16.25
1 Square Table	William H. Newman		1.00
1 Wash Stand	A.L. Thurman		.12 ½
1 flax wheel	Wm. H. Newman		2.85
1 Bed Bed Stead & furn	Richard Maxey		17.15
1 large chest	C.H. Rorer		1.70

1 Small Trunk	Richard Maxey	.10
1 Bed Stead & furniture	James R. Metts	5.80
1 Trundle Bed & furniture	James R. Metts	2.30
1 pr fire dogs	Grandison Leftwich	1.55
1 pr fire dogs	Thos. Nunery	.80
Shovel & Tongs	Thos. Nunery	1.50
1 White counterpane	Charles H. Creasy	2.00
1 White counterpane	W.H. Newman	3.30
1 Yarn counterpane	W.H. Newman	5.80
1 pr Bed Blankets	Euel Arthur	2.50
1 White counterpane	Chas. H. Creasy	3.05
1 White counterpane	W.H. Newman	2.75
2 Bee Stands	E.C. Jacobs	1.88
1 Cow	Lewis Krantz	20.25
1 Cow	John H. Franklin	19.00
1 Cow	John F. Franklin	20.00
2 Calfs	Ben Scott	9.10
1 Waggon	J.J. Garrett	<u>63.50</u>
		427.07 ¾

I hereby certify that I kept the foregoing list of sales and that they are correct.
Given under my hand this 25 day of Jan 1858   Wm. P. Tinsley

The children of Taliaferro G. Hubbard and Mary Debo Hubbard were:

1. ELIZABETH SMITH, born Oct. 23, 1837, and married by Thomas C. Goggin Feb. 1855 to George T. Metts (sometimes spelled Metz in court records), son of John and Matilda Metts of Franklin County. Their children were:
   A. MOLLIE, who married J.C. Hunt and lived in Gretna, Virginia.
   B. Lottie, who married a Parker.
   C. ALICE, who married a Keesee.
   D. BEE, who married a McGhee.
   E. LILLIE, who married a Farmer and lived in Altavista, Virginia.
   F. OLA, who married a Crouch.
   G. CORA, who never married.
   H. CLARENCE
2. ANNIS PRESTON, born May 14, 1839, and died March 16, 1926. She was married by Thomas C. Goggin on Nov. 15, 1857, to Charles Henry Rorer of Pittsylvania County. He was the son of John David Rorer and the former Frances Custard, was born Jan. 1, 1830, and died October 17, 1918. Annis P. and Charles were cousins. Annis' grandfather, Michael Debo, Sr., and Charles' grandmother, Betsy Debo Rorer were brother and sister. The Rorers made their home in the Brights community of northwestern Pittsylvania County, reared their 11 children there, and are buried in the Somerset church cemetery. Annis P. Rorer corresponded with her cousins, Reed Debo in Missouri and Sallie Debo Bowmer in Texas, who had left Virginia after the War Between the States. The following letter was written to Sallie Debo Bowmer in Texas.[4]

Brights, Va.   1st Sunday   June the 7th 1896

My Dear old Cousin Sallie

I received yours of the 30th of May last Thursday. Was glad to hear from you and learn you are doing well and also in good health, my health is not so good as it was last year. I have been troubled with neuralgia, and my kidneys are affected and I need medicine that I am not able to buy, if I had three bottles of Warner's Kidney & liver cure it would set me all right again, but money is so scarce and we have so much family they need all we can get. I will just have to do without it, let the result be as it may, I never would have got off the bed when I was down so long had I not taken Warner's medicine but I should give my Maker more praise than anything else he was the divine help. Sallie you know we have a good home, and there is no mortgage on it, and we have stock a plenty & plenty to eat, and anything that is very necessary and our chaps go in foremost society fixed well enough, but to get any money we can't, it is just aggravating. Chas sold 4000 pounds of Tobacco for the pitiful sum of $46. Just about enough to pay his Tax & Fertilizer bill, we had some corn to trade or we would been left, I can't see how the farmer is to make it if there is not an amendment soon, Chas lets the boys take the team and do any hauling they can to get any money for but people that has money had rather die than to pay them that works for them. The negroes would starve if it won't for public works, the farmers ain't able to hire them, some few have got them a piece of land, and doing well, I think the way they are linched in the South it is strange they don't behave. I have one line to boast in. I have as good Husband and as good Children as any woman could have, they are not as Educated as some are but they are all right in every other respect, Rosie is from home now, she is helping the commissioner write up his books. He is Sams fatherinlaw. The old man & Sam, two daughters & one son constitute the family. Sam has to ride & take the list. They live 15 mile from here in the neighborhood of Chalk-level. I haven't heard from Katty in a long time. I will try to go down that way as soon as they get done plowing. Rena is living down that way now. Martin rented land from the Pannels close where Berton died. Give my love to Dabney. I would be so glad to see him, tell him I say stay there with you and not go back to that old heatheny Mexico. I want him to send me his picture so I can see how he has changed. Poor boy I use to see so much trouble about him when he was the only one of uncle Johns family left. All of Bets and Ruths family are well so far as I know. We got a letter from Graves girls last week. They at Dans, Mrs. Parker has never married any more, she is a good woman, Tommy Goggin died last summer. There is some flux raging about here. The measles has died out it never does take here, but that's all right. You must

excuse my nervous writing, and write as often as convenient
to your cousin.

Annis P Rorer

Also included herewith is a letter from Annis Rorer to Reed P.
Debo in Missouri.[5]

Brights, Va. Sept. 22, 1902

Mr. R. P. Debo
Dear Cousin

It has been some time since we past any letters. I know I
wrote first and asked you to write before my letter got cold and
you said it freezed before you received it but I don't think this
will freeze, although we have had some frost but not to injure
anything. We have had a bad crop year this time from the beginning. Too dry. Wheat was nearly a perfect failure. Some few
never carried a scithe in their field. We only made 4 ½ bushel.
They sowed 18 bushell, and two tons of guana but we had old
wheat enough to last till Xmas. Have bought seed wheat. Corn &
tobacco very inferior, but by planting near the creek we've had
vegetables tolerable plentifull.

Well I must first tell you we are all living yet, all my children
& brothers and sisters were living the last I heard from them for
which I feel very thankfull to my Maker. The 3rd Sunday in July
Chas. had a spell of vertigo, the Dr. called it. He was standing
here in the door and he said how my head swims, and I was
writing and I raised my eyes to look at him and he had clinched
the door facing, but he was breaking his hold and all doubling
up and out the door he went with his head on the ground and
his feet on the top step, apparently dead. Was unconscious about
two hour. It was about 10 a.m. All gone to S. School but him &
me. I got to the door quick as I could, took hold of one foot &
shook it and called him but he knew no more about it than you
did. A colored man lives over at the spring. One of his chaps was
here in the yard and I told him to run tell his Pa to come, and
him & wife came and lifted him in the house on the floor. We put
pillows under his head and bathed his head in cold water and
his face & pulse in camphire, and I wet his lips & tongue in wine
and very soon discovered he was living. You can realize my feelings at that time. I feared he was parelized but when he got so he
could talk I knew he was not parelized. He was sick 2 weeks, but
thank God he is at work now.

Doubtless you've heard of Dick Metts death. There is so many Turners out there. Bet has been staying with Tilda ever since he died, but her & Tish Fitz came down and spent a week last month. I sure do like Tish. She is just as peart and good company as if she wasn't but 30 & she is 60. She is a different woman to old Tilda. Tom has built him a new house. Says she don't live in old Capt. Deems house now. Mary Ann Metts, Martin died last spring and John Metts lost his wife last winter. No one is living with Cass now but a black woman. Blanch Craghead is at Frank's. I don't know what made her leave Cass but you know no one can please a 60 year old maid. Haven't you found one yet you think you can please, but you have plenty housekeeping if they aint married and gone.

We have John & Berta Perry & Tiny with us yet. Don't know what we would do without them if they was to marry. Maggie and her chaps came and spent 3 weeks with me in August. She lives in Danville & Dany in Lynchburg. He came and stayed two weeks while Maggie was here. I do enjoy visits from my children, for I seldom go to see them. I will quit; it is getting so dark.

Sept. 27. It is raining this morn. All are well. As regards Rosa being in So. Dak., she is doing well. Got a nice Christian young man. He is of a good family. Don't use any whisky or tobacco. They are both members of a Baptist Church, she is a member of a ladys aid society and both members of the Modern Brotherhood of America with life policy of 2000 dollars each. The trouble of it is she became in love with a drinking young chap and got into trouble with him, that she knowed be throwed up to her if she staid here and she joined the corresponding club and got 8 or 10 pictures but didn't like but the one she married. They wrote to each other 12 months, made an honest contract and he sent her money to pay her expenses out there. Said he would meet her at the train, and he did. She said she saw him on the platform before the train stopped. He carried her to a hotel. They had two hours conversation. Perfectly satisfied with each other and he got license & parson & married.

Write to me as soon as you get this. I want to hear from you. You may bet I have seen a lot of trouble, but God has helped me to bear it all. Pray that he will still be my friend. Chas joins me in love to you & all of yours.

From your old cousin
Annis

The children of Charles and Annis Rorer are:
  A. MARY FANNIE, born Nov. 5, 1858; married W. Thomas Thompson
  B. SALLIE KATE, born Oct. 9, 1860, and died in infancy.
  C. HENRY J., born Oct. 13, 1863, and died in infancy.
  D. ARRENA JAMES, born April 23, 1866; married Rufus Martin.
  E. THEO OTTIE, born Dec. 25, 1867, and died in infancy.
  F. MAGGIE ELIZABETH, born Aug. 25, 1870; married Alexander Keesee.
  G. JOHN GRAVES, born Feb. 19, 1873; married Fannie Bell.
  H. ROSA DICKENSON, born Nov. 23, 1874; married Miles Putnam.
  I. DAVID TILDON, born Nov. 9, 1876; died Oct. 28, 1952; married Cora Davis, born April 16, 1874, and died May 2, 1944.
  J. BERTA PERRY, born Jan. 14, 1880; married Gilmore Haley
  K. TINY RAMSEY, born March 4, 1885.
3. KATHERINE RUTH, born April 21, 1842, and died July 12, 1924. She was married in 1865 to Vincent Crawford Goad, born Dec. 25, 1842, and died April 29, 1923. Their children were:
  A. ELLA GRAVES, born Jan. 22, 1866; married Jan. 9, 1889, to William J. Crowder, born Aug. 26, 1858.
  B. DANIEL CRAWFORD, born Sept. 22, 1869; never married.
  C. ROBERT ALEXANDER, born June 11, 1873; married first to Miss Worsham, and second to Virginia Bondurant.
4. CHARLOTTE SHELTON, born May 14, 1844, and died Dec. 19, 1907. She was married January 7, 1869, to Richard Fox Lindsay, born Oct. 29, 1838, and died May 10, 1909; son of Solomon and Sarah Lindsay. They moved to and lived in Marshall, Texas. Their children were:
  A. MARY ELIZABETH, born Nov. 30, 1869, and died Sept. 9, 1870.
  B. SOLOMON GRAVES, born July 22, 1871; married Mattie William French.
  C. SAMUEL LUTHER, born June 22, 1874; married Beulah Izorah Williams.
  D. WALTER HUFF, born June 2, 1877; married Willie Mae Atkinson.

E. JOSEPHINE JANE, born April 22, 1881; married first to William Bentley, and after his death John Harrington.

F. HELEN LEE, born Sept. 26, 1885; married Walter Ford, who died Jan. 29, 1910.

5. TALIAFERRO GRAVES, born Sept. 3. 1846, and died Jan. 3, 1936. On April 27, 1861 (at age 14 but gave his age as 18), he enlisted at Chestnut Fork, Bedford County, Virginia, as a private in Co. G, 28th Virginia Infantry (known as the Patty Lane Rifles), commanded by Capt. Augustus L. Minter and Richard Wright. After serving in the battles of Manassas, Williamsburg, Seven Pines, the Seven Days around Richmond, and Sharpsburg, he was taken prisoner at Gettysburg at the "stone wall" in Pickett's charge. He was imprisoned at Ft. Delaware, Delaware, and Point Lookout, Maryland, but was released on February 25, 1864, and returned to his unit. He remained until captured again April 6, 1865, at High Bridge, Virginia, three days before Gen. Lee surrendered at Appomattox. After the war he returned to Bedford County, and was married November 7, 1867, to Fannie L. Saunders, born February 16, 1853, and died January 20, 1921, in Liberal, Kansas, who was the daughter of James C. and Mary Saunders. He loaded up a covered wagon pulled by mules in 1886 and moved his family to Haskell County, Kansas, and located on a homestead four miles north and six miles west of the old Santa Fe Trail. In 1893 he bought a ranch in Stevens County, residing on it awhile, but moving to Liberal, Kansas, in 1906. While there he was police judge for many years and served as bailiff for the district court of Seward County.

Children of Taliaferro and Fannie Hubbard, all born in Bedford County, Virginia, were:

A. ROBERT JAMES, born April 13, 1869; married Addie Tanderley, Dec. 4, 1890. He was a teacher for a number of years, having taught in three states. He also wrote articles for papers and magazines.

B. LYNWOOD C., born Jan. 30, 1871, died June 1, 1930; married Viola Milburn.

C. TRISTAM WORTH, born Feb. 22, 1873; married Blanche Stout, and was a policeman.

D. EDDIE GRAVES, died in infancy.

E. SAMUEL T., born Dec. 29, 1877; married Addie Neatherley.

F. MARY P. (twin), born Feb. 20, 1880, and died Dec. 21, 1920. She was married April 24, 1900, to Ira L. Milbour.

G. MARTHA D. (twin), born Feb. 20, 1880; married to Frederick Y. Cott Nov. 23, 1898.

6. DANIEL PERRY, born July 14, 1849. He was first married by R. E. Lee February 15, 1870, to Virginia Frances Rorer of Pittsylvania County, Virginia. He was later married October 18, 1892, to Nancy C. Thompson. There were no children by the second wife, however, the children of Daniel P. and Virginia F. Hubbard were:

A. CHARLES STEVENS, born Jan. 21, 1871.

B. CEPHALUS LA'HUGH (Fal), born March 24, 1873.

C. ANNICE WALKER, born Jan. 2, 1877.

I. Michael Debo, Jr.[1]

We are all the children of many sires, and every drop of blood in us in its burn betrays its ancestor.
Ralph Waldo Emerson

Michael Debo, Jr., the ninth child and fifth son of Michael Debo, Sr., and Katherine Saunders Debo, was born in 1811 on the Debo homeplace on Goose Creek in southern Bedford County, Virginia. He was reared in the rural society of his day, and was appointed a lieutenant in the U.S. Army in 1835. According to his son's obituary, it is stated that Michael served in the cavalry during the war with Mexico. All research I have attempted to prove these statements, however, has proven fruitless.

Michael was married in Bedford County November 15, 1836,[2] by William Leftwich to Wilmoth Waldron Leftwich, daughter of Joel Leftwich and Sarah C. Adams Leftwich. She was born in 1819 and one source says she died March 22, 1894. The family Bible of Mrs. Ruby Price DeBoe, however, contains the following: "Wilmoth Leftwich DeBoe died March the 3rd 1891. She probably died of cancer of the stomach. She was ill several months. She was so patient and humble. So kind to all. How I have missed my mother. She cannot, probably, come to me, but I can go to her." Michael had preceded her in death on August 19, 1883, of consumption.

The will of Michael Debo, Jr., dated July 14, 1883, is as follows:[3]

Wilmoth W. Leftwich Debo   Michael Debo, Jr.

I Michael Debo, of the county of Bedford and State of Virginia, this the 14th day of July in the year of our Lord one thousand eight hundred and eighty three, recognizing the uncertainty of life and the certainty of death, being in feeble bodily health, but in the possession of my usual state of mind, desire to make the following disposition of my earthly effects, both real & personal.

1st I desire that all my just debts and funeral expenses be paid including a balance, which I think upon a fair settlement I will be due A. Stevens.

2nd I bequeath to my daughter Mrs. Harriet T. Stevens of the State of Missourie the sum of twenty ($20) dollars and to my daughter Mrs. Ann K. Craghead also of the State of Missourie the sum of fifty ($50) dollars, they having already had about their portion of my estate.

3rd I desire the remainder of my property to remain in the hands of my beloved wife Wilmuth W. Debo and my three remaining children, Sarah C., Jno. F. and Joel D. Debo, to be managed as they may think best for the maintenance of their mother and themselves and have the privilege of disposing of any property for the benefit of the family, by the concurrence of all.

4th At the decease of my wife, I desire the property which may be on hand, to be equally divided between the three last named children, or such of them as may survive her, and if she should survive all three of them, I desire that she dispose of the property as she may think best.

5th I have sold Jerry Watson cold (stands for colored) a lot of land on Goose Creek the metes and bounds of which are known and understood by my son Jno. F. Debo, and when said Jerry Watson shall have paid the purchase (one hundred dollars) I desire that my wife & three children named make him a title to said land, and lastly,

I prefer that my wife remain unmarried, inasmuch as she might make a bad choice, and her hard earned property be wasted, and that the children remain with her as long as she or they may live, and, that, unless unavoidable, no executor or administrator be appointed, as I have confidence in their ability to carry out my behests, without the assistance or intervention of the law.

Given under my hand & seal this day and date afore mentioned.

Michael Debo (seal)

Witnesses:
W.L. Garrett
V.O. Smith

In Bedford County Court April 28th 1884.
This last will and testament of Michael Debo deceased bearing on the date of the 14th day of July 1883 was produced in court, proved, according to law by the oath of William L. Garrett one of the subscribing witnesses thereto, who testified that the said Michael Debo, signed and acknowledged the said will in the presence of him the said William L. Garrett and of V.O. Smith, the other subscribing witness thereto, and that the said subscribing witnesses signed the said will as witness in the presence of each other, and of the testator, and at his request, and that the testator was at the time of sound mind and disposing memory, it is ordered that said will be recorded as the true last will and testament of Michael Debo deceased.

Teste   Ro. S. Quarles, C.B.C.

The children of Michael and Wilmoth Debo, all born in Bedford County, were:

1. HARRIET TOMPKINS, born Jan. 9, 1838, and died June 27, 1919.[4] She was married Feb. 18, 1858, to Alfred Solomon Stevens, born April 6, 1837, and died May 15, 1905. Stevens served in the 28th Virginia Regiment of Pickett's Division, Army of Northern Virginia, along with many of the Debo brothers. After the war Harriet and Al Stevens moved to Mexico, Missouri, and are buried there in Elmwood Cemetery. Their children were:

   A. THOMAS JEFFERSON, born Jan. 5 (25), 1860 (1862), in Bedford County, Virginia; died Sept. 24, 1918, at Mexico, Audrain County, Misouri. He was married Nov. 3, 1886, to Alice Lee Hall, born Jan. 10, 1867, and died in 1941. Their children were:[5]

      1) ELLA, born Oct. 10, 1887, Audrain County, Missouri, died Sept. 28, 1905, Mexico, Audrain County, Missouri.

      2) MAMIE ALMA, born Nov. 13, 1890, died 1970. She married Thomas E. Dunavant, born 1880, died 1966; they had two sons, Leslie and Paul Ray.

      3) MARY L., born 1893, died 1951, Audrain County, Missouri.

      4) CLARA B., born June 18, 1894, died June 26, 1969. She married Albert L. Kettrey, born April 25, 1894, and died Feb. 11, 1967. They had a son, Albert Eugene, born Oct. 18, 1927, died April 8, 1969.

      5) EUNICE BLANCHE, born 1896, died 1992.

      6) GEORGIA ANN, born Feb. 12, 1899, died April 22, 1986. She married William Alonzo Debo, born June 27, 1895, died April 19, 1961. They had a son, William Bruce.

      7) EUGENE RALPH, born Sept. 7, 1901, died Nov. 8, 1980, in Mexico, MO. He was married Aug. 30, 1924, to Reta Rose Meadows, born Feb. 9, 1906, died April 10, 1994. Their children were Juanita R., Wyma Jewell, Ralph Eugene (Little Gene), born May 19, 1931, and died May 19, 1931, and Reta Wyema.

      8) THOMAS J., born in 1904, died 1974.

      9) ELIZABETH, born in 1909, died 1990.

   B. ALFRED MICHAEL, born Dec. 22, 1863. In Bedford County, Virginia.

C. DANIEL LEAFET, born March 3, 1866, in Bedford County, Virginia.

D. WILMOTH VIRGINIA, born June 17, 1868, in Callaway County, Missouri, died July 1, 1941. She married William D. Thomas, and they had a daughter Pearl Evelyn, born 1891, died 1978.

E. EDWARD CHARLES, born Oct. 5, 1870.

F. ANNIE AUGUSTA, born Nov. 19, 1872.

G. MINNIE MEAD (twin), born Feb. 9, 1875.

H. MYRTLE B. (twin), BORN Feb. 9, 1875.

I. KATIE EVINA, born March 7, 1877.

J. NANCY MAUDE, born Nov. 10, 1881, died May 24, 1974.

2. ANNIE K. (possibly Katharine), born in Dec. 1840 and died in 1901 in Fulton, Missouri. She was married by D.M. Grandfield on Sept. 14, 1869, in Bedford County, Virginia, to Nickolas Robinson Craghead, who was born Apr. 10, 1838, and died June 5, 1912. They also moved to Missouri and are buried in Mt. Carmel Cemetery, two miles southwest of Fulton on Highway 54. Known children of the Cragheads are:

A. WADE H., born in May 1871 in Missouri.

B. KATIE F. (Cattie), born in May 1873 in Missouri. She was married Oct. 22, 1922, to T.T. Mosley.

C. WILLIAM MICHAEL (Mike), born in Aug. 1875. He was married Nov. 28, 1900, to Rosa Pearl Yake (born in 1880). They had a daughter, Edith E., born in 1901.

D. INFANT DAUGHTER, born in 1878

E. ANNIE F., born in Dec. 1884.

3. SARAH KATHERINE (Cassie), born Feb. 17, 1842, Died Jan. 6, 1918,[6] and was buried in the family cemetery in southern Bedford County, Virginia, on the homeplace. She was the last to live in the old house on the Debo place. The following obituary appeared in the *Bedford Bulletin*, Jan. 10, 1918:

Miss Cassie Debo

Following an illness of only a few days of pneumonia, Miss Cassie Debo, aged about 70 years (actually 76. D.D.) passed away at her home on the south side of the county, near Hayden's Bridge, Sunday afternoon. She had lived all of her life in that community, where she had many warm friends who heard of her death with extreme regret. She is survived by one brother, Mr. Frank

Debo, of Bedford County, and two sisters, who live in Missouri, and many other relatives in the county. The funeral service was conducted at the home Monday afternoon and burial was in the home cemetery.

In the family Bible Ruby (Mrs. Frank) Debo wrote: "Sister Kate DeBoe died Jan. 6, 1918, of pneumonia. I stayed with her throughout her illness of a week. She was about 76 years old. I miss you, Kate."

Included here is a letter from Cassie to her cousin, Sallie Debo Bowmer, in Texas at the last of the year 1870:[7]

Fancy Grove
Bedford Co.
Dec. 29/70

My Dear Cousin

It is needless to offer an apology for my long delay. I received your very interesting and most welcome letter some time ago, but was head and ears into preparations for Christmas, and scarcely had time to breathe much less write a letter. This being the 4th day of Xmas I find myself alone for the first day since the Holidays set in with nothing to do but reply to you, which is quite a pleasure. Oh: CHRISTMAS GIFT and you have got to pay it and let me tell you what it must be before I further go yours and Cousins Clays Photographs. Now I know you can't refuse me, so I shall expect the gift in your next letter.

Well Sallie I will tell you how I have been spending the holiday so far. Sunday morning early a spry little fellow came over and stayed till Monday morning just the kind of fellow I love to sit up to and court a little, what I didn't fail to do. Monday evening the Misses Creaseys and Wildmans came over and stayd till Tuesday evening. They brought two Beaux along. You bet we spent the time finely. I haven't been to a single Party yet havnt even heard of one. I'm invited to a Sociable at Mr. Hurts Friday Evening. Anticipate a nice time.

By the way I expect to see George Shelton their. Did you know he was in Va.? He has been to see me since he returned. He is looking quite well, spake of you often. He says he has come after a wife. Emma and I are going back with him (Mabie). Ho; Did you know Ira Weeks was married, one of your old sparks. He married a lady in Kentucky and is now in Mo. Boarding at All's.

Sallie there has been so many little sterred up weddings about here this fall it is rearly disgusting to speak of them. I prefere being an old maid until it is less common.

Tell Cousin Clay I will acknowledge I exaggerated if he will let me off without an explanation about you know what.

I have not seen any of Uncle Johns folks since the Reception at Mr. Turners. Mollie was their. Oh: I had such a good time at Toms and Jinnies Infare. Sallie I wish I could tell you how funny Tom acted that night. He knows (in his own mind) no one else ever was married. Emma S. and I were all the Girls over this way that were their. You may bet we had our fun. We went for that purpose. Mud and Ellen staid a night at Uncle Johns a short time ago. They were all well.

Sallie we have had some of the coldest weather for the last week I ever felt. There is snow on the ground now and I am so cold, although I'm in the Office sitting on the Stove. I can scarcely write atall. Hope you can make out what I've tried to write. Please don't let any one see it.

Hope you will not mind my delay and will write very soon. Your letters are so interesting. Please write soon and remember the Xmas gift and I will pay you back some day.

With much love to you both I am as ever your true friend
and Cousin Cassie

4. WILLIAM L., born in 1845, died in a Richmond, Virginia, hospital of "disease" April 25, 1862, in the Confederate service. He was a private in Co. G., 28th Virginia Infantry Regiment, and was described as 5'6 ½" with florid complexion, red hair, hazel eyes, and a farmer. He enlisted on March 10, 1862, in Bedford County under Capt. A.L. Minter for the duration of the war.[8]

5. MONTEREY W., born Nov. 7, 1847, and died Nov. 15, 1863, of diphtheria.

6. McHENRY F., born Oct. 23, 1849, and died Oct. 29, 1863, of diphtheria.

7. MICHAEL S.C., born Oct. 31, 1851, and died Nov. 7, 1863, of diphtheria.

8. JOHN FRANKLIN PRICE, born Feb. 19, 1853, and died "as day was breaking" on Oct. 7, 1939. He was married at Callaway, Virginia, December 10, 1884, to Ruby Charitie Price, who was born August 4, 1863, in Franklin County and died February 10, 1945, in Bedford County. Both John Franklin (Frank) and Ruby

Charitie DeBoe are buried in Longwood Cemetery, Bedford, Virginia.[9] (This family chose to spell the family name DeBoe or deBoe.) The following obituary of Frank DeBoe appeared in the *Bedford Bulletin* October 12, 1939:

John Franklin Debo

Funeral services were held Sunday afternoon for John Franklin Price DeBoe in the Carder Mortuary Chapel. Burial was in the family plot, Longwood Cemetery, Bedford. Pallbearers were Haywood Nance, H.C. Hicks, Robert Q. Owen, Clyde Bays, Lawrence Patterson, and Winston Patterson. He died at daybreak Saturday morning following a short illness. He leaves the wife, Mrs. Ruby Price DeBoe, of Bedford County; one daughter, Mrs. Samuel L. Leterman of Charlottesville, and a son, Dr. Michael Price DeBoe, of Miami, Florida.

Born on Feb. 9, 1852 on his ancestral Goose Creek plantation, Bedford County, John Franklin DeBoe was the son of Michael DeBoe, Lieutenant U.S. Army, cavalry services during the Mexican War, and of Wilmoth Waldron Leftwich, daughter of Joel and Sarah Adams Leftwich, distinguished and early families of Virginia.

He was the grandson of Doctor Michael DeBoe (spelled Debo), [this should be Philip Debo. D.D.] who served as physician in the Continental Army of the American Revolution, and was with Washington during the winter at Valley Forge.

Known as one of the finest planters of Bedford County, he learned the soil and its ways during the hard pressed reconstruction days of his youth. He observed and loved nature with the gifted eye and understanding heart of a naturalist. His friends loved him for his forthright integrity, his high sense of honor, and his warm, genuine hospitality.

The following, written by his son, was found in the family Bible and is here included:

I WOULD HAVE SAID THIS, IF THERE HAD BEEN NO OTHER ADDRESS AT MY FATHER'S GRAVE ON THE AFTERNOON OF OCTOBER 8, 1939

He died at daybreak when the first silver morning light began to filter through the oak trees and maples outside his doorway, as if he had stepped into a new life at morning.

It was the hour he always loved to get up.

Religious philosophy never played an important role in his life. Yet he trod the narrow pathway of human existence doing the best he could with his light on life, as every living organism has done since the earliest dawn of creation.

The sum total of a man's life consists in the acts done in the body. And every act is committed because the incentives to do that act are greater than the deterrents. These incentives and deterrents come from our own minds and our own environments, neither of which we created, and over which we have but little influence.

"We all hope to meet again the loved and the lost. In every human heart there grows this sacred flower. Immortality is the word hope whispers to love. The miracle of thought we cannot understand, but let us believe that over the cradle nature bends and smiles, and lovingly over the dead in benediction holds her outstretched hand."

Michael Price de Boe, M.D.
Sunday night, October 8, 1939

Ruby C. DeBoe's obituary appeared in the *Bedford Bulletin* February 15, 1945, as follows:

Prominent County Woman Dies at Home

Mrs. Ruby Charitie Price deBoe, widow of John Franklin Leftwich [this is wrong; it should be Price] deBoe, died of a heart attack Saturday morning, February 10, at home on her plantation, Bedford County. Funeral services were conducted by Dr. J.H. Grey at the chapel of the Carder funeral home, 3:00 o'clock Tuesday afternoon. Interment was in the family plot in Longwood cemetery.

Pallbearers were T.H. Nance, W.L. Lyle, G.E. Heller, Clyde Bays, Lawrence Patterson, and J.K. Walker.

She is survived by her son, Dr. Michael Price deBoe, of Miami, Florida, and Mrs. Samuel L. Leterman, Charlottesville, Virginia.

Mrs. DeBoe's short stories were published in several of the leading magazines, and her poems in a number of anthologies. Her poem, "Snowbound," won the national prize of 100 in the Crown Anthology of Verse, and her poem "Solitude," won distinction.

She was born August 4, 1862, in Franklin County, Virginia,

daughter of Reuben Price and Jane Leftwich Price, heir to the thousand acres of her father's Rich Run Plantation at a time when those lands lay stricken and idle with few of the negro retainers left to work them. But she played with their children along Rich Run stream, and they called her "sunshine."

She was educated by private tutors and at a young ladies' boarding school in Rocky Mount.

On her maternal side she was a descendant of Augustine Leftwich, one of the first settlers of Virginia derived from the Anglo Saxon Leftwichs of Leftwich Hall at the time of Edward the Confessor. On her paternal side she was the great-granddaughter of Charities deFleurs, of New Orleans, first cousin of Napoleon Bonaparte.

On her Bedford plantation which she has managed alone since her husband's death in 1939, she worked with devotion as her part in the war effort. She held the loyalty (...this line is missing in the account...). One of them with tearfilled eyes said, "The colored folks are writing an obituary for Mis' Ruby. They have lost their best friend."

Her love of Virginia, her people, and her land inspired her whole life. In her unhurried kindliness, with gentle voice, she befriended those she knew. Her gentle hospitality embraced all who entered her home. And she was loved. Her death marks the passing of a lovely lady of Virginia.

An interesting article appeared in the January 2, 1958, issue of *The Bedford Democrat* written by the late Kenneth E. Crouch. It concerns the possibility of the poinsettia Christmas flower and the famous pirate, Jean Lafitte, having a connection with the Debo family, and is herewith presented in full.

"Bedford Link Found to Flower of Christmas, the Poinsettia"

Viewers of the Jim Bowie television show Friday night, Dec. 20, saw a very impressive Christmas story, closely associated with the beloved Christmas flower, the poinsettia, and a man who had descendants living in Bedford County.

The story of the heroic Texas scout Jim Bowie involved the famous pirate Jean Lafitte and Gen. Antonio L. de Santa Anna in a story similar to the Nativity in Bethlehem.

The Bedford connection was that the pirate Lafitte was an ancestor of the DeBoe family, who lived for many years on Route 24 opposite Body Camp, the store operated by Mr. and Mrs. Clyde W. Bays.

The story began on Christmas Eve, 1829, when Santa Anna was at war in Mexico. He had kidnapped Dr. Joel R. Poinsett, the American minister to Mexico, and held him at his hacienda.

Rescue Minister

Lafitte was at the Gonzales Inn where Bowie met him and persuaded him to cooperate in rescuing the American minister and carrying him to safety aboard his ship.

As they were leaving the inn a young man and his wife arrived seeking room to stay but the inn was full and gay with Christmas preparations. The young man's home had been burned when he refused to join Santa Anna's forces and with his wife, who was expecting, they were placed in the stable at the inn.

Bowie and Lafitte finally rescued Dr. Poinsett from Santa Anna's home and brought him to the inn. Poinsett was educated as a physician in Scotland but had never practiced medicine, being a diplomat and botanist. He was persuaded to assist with the young woman and delivered the couple's son in the inn.

Like Bethlehem

When the excitement was over the innkeeper remarked of the birth years ago when three wise men came; he noted that three men were present that night. Bowie replied that the first Wise Men brought gifts so he gave the new father his horse; Dr. Poinsett said he had no gift but the father replied he gave life which was the most blessed gift; and Lafitte brought forth a bag of money as a gift.

Mr. and Mrs. J.N. Meador now live at the DeBoe home at Body Camp. Last year Mr. and Mrs. Warren L. Burnette bought from Mrs. Mizpah Otto DeBoe of Coral Gables, Fla., the remainder of the DeBoe home where their home, "Frankburn," is located. In the sale, recorded Nov. 12, 1956, Mrs. DeBoe retained as a memorial to her husband, Dr. Michael Price DeBoe, who died June 28, 1955, a 100 by 100 foot section in the center of which is a huge old walnut tree. Lumbermen have offered her several hundred dollars for this fine tree but she retained it as a memorial to her late husband, who was a prominent physician in Miami, Fla.

Bedford Connections

Dr. DeBoe was a descendant of the Leftwich family, who were prominent in Bedford and Franklin Counties. A son of John Franklin and Ruby Charitie Price DeBoe , his mother and father were first cousins. On his maternal side he was a great-great-grandson of Charitie de Fleurs, a cousin of the Emperor Napoleon Bonaparte. Dr. DeBoe was a graduate of the Medical College of Virginia in Richmond, began his practice at his home at Body Camp and visited there each summer.

Lafitte was the leader of a band of pirates which operated from Barartaria, La. In 1818 he fought in the defense of New Orleans, La., against the British. Col. James Bowie was among the 180 Texans killed at the battle of the Alamo in San Antonio, Texas, on March 6, 1836, when 4,000 Mexicans under Gen. Santa Anna stormed The Alamo in Texas' war for independence. The American dagger-like knife known as the Bowie knife is named for the Texan hero. The part of Bowie in the television series is played by Scott Forbes.

At the inn, Dr. Poinsett, who was very interested in flowers, was looking at the wild Mexican flower which had no name. He suggested naming it for a collegemate in Scotland, but Lafitte picked up a pot of the colorful flower and suggested it be named the poinsettia in honor of Dr. Poinesett.

Upon his return to his Charleston, S.C., home, Dr. Poinsett brought some of the plants and it has since become a colorful part of America's Christmas.

The Mexican Legend

To the people of Mexico the poinsettia is the flower of the Holy Night. The legend has it that on a certain Christmas Eve long ago a little girl was going to church, not with quick steps nor in a happy mood like the other children, but slowly with tears. She was sad because she had no gift for the Holy Child. As she drew nearer the church dejection increased and at last she knelt on the ground in prayer.

As she offered her childlike prayer she felt comforted and as she rose from her knees she saw springing up at her feet the most gorgeous blooms. This was the poinsettia. Her prayers had been answered and she plucked the branches of this plant, went on to church where she laid them as her gift to the Christ-child on the altar of the little sanctuary.

It is also interesting to note that on the front page of the "The Legend of the Poinsettia" is a scribbled note written by Mrs. Mizpath O. deBoe denying any connection whatsoever between the DeBoes and Lafitte. She said, "The deBoes (DeBoes) are no more kin to Lafitte than they are to Genghis Khan." Signed, M.O. de-Boe

Nevertheless, it makes a good story!

The two children of Frank and Ruby DeBoe, both born on the ancestral Goose Creek plantation of the family in southern Bedford County, were:

1. MICHAEL PRICE, born Nov. 29, 1885, and died June 28, 1955,[10] in Miami, Fla., following a heart attack. He was married by E.A. Harrison on April 22. 1919,[11] in Key West, Fla., to Mizpah Otto, member of a prominent Key West family, who was born there June 18, 1892, and died in Miami May 4, 1979. They had no children, and were buried in the Otto family plot in Key West. Educated in the rural schools of his Bedford County, Va., neighborhood, Michael P. deBoe later began train-

Dr. Michael Price de Boe
(Noted Ophthalmologist)

ing as a physician in the University College of Medicine (now known as the Medical College of Virginia) in Richmond from which he graduated in 1908. Upon his graduation he was given the old medical scales used by his great-great-grandfather, Philip Debo, by his father's first cousin, Annis P. Hubbard Rorer, whose mother was Mary Debo Hubbard. Michael began his medical practice in the Body Camp area of Bedford County. He served in the U.S. Navy during World War I and was commanding officer of the medical department at the Key West (Fla.) Naval Base. He became a widely known eye specialist after moving to Miami in 1924, and was greatly respected in the ophthalmological field by his peers. His obituary is as follows as it appeared in *The Miami Herald*, June 29, 1955:

Dr. de Boe Dies;
Noted Specialist

Dr. Michael Price de Boe, 69, of 1510 Pizzaro Ave., Coral Gables, widely known eye specialist, died Tuesday at Veterans Administration Hospital following a heart attack.

Dr. de Boe moved to Miami in 1924 after four years of practice in Key West, and became a leader in his profession. He was dean of the eye, ear, nose and throat specialists and was emeritus chief of staff for that field of medicine at Jackson Memorial Hospital. He was recently named an honorary life member of the Dade County Medical Association.

A senior fellow of the American College of Surgeons and the American Academy of Ophthalmology and Otolaryngology, Dr. de Boe was known as a writer on scientific topics. His contributions to medical eye history were quoted in the Duke-Elder textbook on ophthalmology, an outstanding honor.

During World War I, Dr. de Boe served as commanding officer of the medical department at the Key West Naval Base. He was a member of the Florida and American Medical Associations, the Masons, and the Coral Gables American Legion Post.

Dr. de Boe is survived by his wife, Mizpah Otto de Boe.

Services will be held at 5 p.m. Thursday at the residence, under the direction of Van Orsdel Coral Gables mortuary. Burial will be in the Otto family plot at Key West.

2. WILMOTH FLORA (Willie), born July 9, 1889,[12] and died of congestive heart failure on Aug. 1, 1950, in Charlottesville, Va. She was married by W.O. Talbert on June 3, 1918,[13] in Salem, Va., to Samuel Lee Leterman, son of Simon and Hannah Leterman, who was born Oct. 3, 1872, in Charlottesville, and died there June 1, 1951,[14] of cancer. They were both buried in Hebrew Cemetery, Charlottesville, and had no children. Willie was a graduate of the Cooperative Female Institute and New London Academy and Teachers College, and attended the University of Virginia and Columbia Conservatory of Music. Her

obituary follows:

Flora Wilmoth de Boe Leterman died August first in University Hospital, Charlottesville, Virginia of a heart condition. Daughter of the late John Franklin de Boe and his wife, Ruby Price de Boe, prominent family of the south side of Bedford County, she was born July 9th, 1889 on the ancestral Goose Creek plantation of her grandfather, Michael de Boe. She was a graduate of New London Academy and Teachers College, University of Virginia. She was known and loved by her friends as Willie. She is survived by her husband, S.L. Leterman of Charlottesville, and one brother, Dr. Michael Price de Boe of Miami, Florida. Interment was August third in Charlottesville.

9. JOEL D., born November 5, 1855, and died July 27, 1883, "of a fever."
10. ELLEN ROSE, born January 1858, and died in 1875.
11. WILMOTH E., born January 3, 1859; death date in unknown, but before 1883.
12. ELLA R., born in 1863, and died December 7, 1882, of typhoid fever.

J. Samuel Debo

Samuel Debo, tenth and youngest child of Michael and Katharine Saunders Debo and their sixth son, was born in 1813 at the Debo homeplace in southern Bedford County, Virginia. He was reared there with his siblings, and at the age of 29 was married on September 26, 1842, to Lucy Saunders, daughter of John Saunders, who was from neighboring Franklin County, was born there in 1818 and died in May 1850. John Saunders was a nephew of Samuel's mother, Katharine Saunders Debo, being the son of William David Saunders, a younger brother of Katharine. Samuel and Lucy made their home in Franklin County during the short time of their some year-and-a-half marriage where he was a tobacco farmer. Samuel died in April 1844, and Lucy six years later in May 1850.

Following is the will of Samuel Debo dated February 22, 1844:

I Samuel Debo of the County of Franklin and State of Virginia do make this my last Will and Testament In the Name following to wit, in the first place I wish and desire that all my Just Debts be paid, and particularly in the first Instance a Certain Debt due from myself, and Mesheck Griffith as Security in a Certain bond

184

due John A. Smith and assigned to Luke Woods. It is my request that the said debt be paid out of the Sale of my Crop of Tobacco now on hand as soon as it be got into Market. I wish and desire that the present Crop now. Commenced with myself and Lawson Hood go on Agreeable to our Contract, and after the Crop is made I desire the said Crop to be sold with my Stock of Cattle horse & hogs and all my Farming Utensials and Likewise all my Interest in my Fathers Estate both real & personal I give and bequeath to Beloved Wife Lucy and if any after her Decease I wish and desire that my Infant Child by the name of Sophia Ann Inherit the same. It is Likewise my wish and desire that all the household furniture in my possession which came by my wife be given to her again and Lastly my desire is that Mesheck Griffith act as my Executor of all my Estate in the County of Franklin and that John Saunders act as Executor of all my Estate in the County of Bedford. In Witness I have set my hand and seal this 22nd day of February 1844.   Samuel Debo (seal)

Witness
Henry Casper
Lawson Hood (his mark)
Lucy Griffith (her mark)

The lone child of Samuel and Lucy's union was a daughter:
1. SOPHIA ANN, born in November 1843 in Franklin County. The 1850 Census for Bedford County, Virginia, lists her as living in the home of Margaret Fields and seven years of age. The census was taken during September of that year, about four months after the death of her mother in May. Sophia Ann was married at age 16 on Nov. 9, 1859, to James Thomas Mitchell, who was born in May 1835 in Bedford County. Their children, all born in Bedford County were as follows:
    A. ROBERT LEE, born in 1861
    B. SARAH JANE (Sallie), born in 1864.
    C. JOHN WARD, born 18 Feb. 1868, and died 4 Jan 1952 in Roanoke, VA, with burial in Lynchburg, VA. He was married to Mary Austin Howell.
    D. LANDON C., born in 1875. He was married to Molly Bet Plymale 14 Dec. 1898, Huddleston, VA.
    E. JIMMIE, who married a Nichols
    F. Unknown name.

Chapter V:
Other Virginia Debos
In Pittsylvania County

There is no pride like the pride of ancestry!
— Disraeli

[When Philip Debo (2) brought his family from Pennsylvania down the Shenandoah Valley of Virginia in the Harmon Cook (Koch) migration in 1788, the family settled in the northwestern section of Pittsylvania County, Virginia, along Frying Pan and Potter's creeks near the Pigg River, along with Rohrers (Rorers), Criders, Saunders, et al. With the passing of time, however, the children of Philip did not remain there but scattered to other localities and areas. The preceding chapter has dealt with the family of Michael Debo, Sr., oldest son, who purchased land and moved over into neighboring Bedford County. This chapter will tell (sometimes in a limited way because of lack of data) about those who stayed behind in Pittsylvania County.]

Betsy Debo, oldest daughter of Philip (2) and possibly a twin to Michael, married into the Rohrer (name spelling was changed to Rorer) family and lived the rest of her life there. The author has happily been able to gather more information on her and the Rorer family than all the others who remained in this county, and it is herewith included. (More data on the Rorer family will be found in an appendix of this work.)

Christina, who married into the Crider family as did her sister Polly, is also dealt with here in a more limited way while Polly, who moved to western Kentucky will appear in the following chapter on the Kentucky Deboes.

Although the information is somewhat skimpy on son Abraham, he also appears here as one who lived the remainder of his days in Pittsylvania County. Philip Debo's son, Philip (3), who also moved to western Kentucky in 1830, will be covered there also, as will most of his children who went with him. Two of Philip's (3) sons, Benjamin and Joseph, however, remained behind in Virginia and will appear here in this chapter. These two lines have been exceedingly difficult to trace, but the author includes such data as has been possible to gather although the "tie-ins" of the lineage are many times uncertain.

Sally Debo, another daughter of Philip (2), married in Pittsylvania County but went with the others to Kentucky, and will be considered in that chapter also. Another daughter of Philip (2), Catharine, born in 1783 and died in 1874 in Putnam County, West Virginia, will also be included in this chapter.]

A. *Betsy Debo Rorer*

BETSY DEBO[1] (her name was probably Elizabeth, but it always appears as Betsy in the records), oldest daughter of Philip Debo (2), was born in 1769 Lancaster (Lebanon) County, Pennsylvania, and was married to David Rorer January 21, 1793,[2] in Pittsylvania County, Virginia. Bondsman for the marriage bond was John White and named as her father was Philip Debo.

David Rohrer was the son of John Rohrer and Barbara Weidman (who was the daughter of Abraham Weidman) Rohrer, who came to Pittsylvania County in 1788 with sons David and Abraham and daughter Polly. John Rohrer died October 10, 1805, and Barbara died in 1810 after living in her new home for only twenty-two years.

The original spelling of the family name was "Rohrer." After coming to Pittsylvania County, Virginia, the "h" was dropped and the name became Rorer. After the David Alexander Rorer family moved to Patrick County, Virginia, his descendants added an extra "r" and it was written "Rorrer."

It is not known just when Betsy's husband David died, but Betsy lived a long life, especially for that day and time, of 81 years. In the 1850 Census for Pittsylvania County, she was listed as the head of a family but no children – hence, a widow. She lived near William Cryder (Crider), Catherine Cook, and Obediah Hogan, and was 81 years old, having been born in Pennsylvania – she was illiterate. In an interview February 22, 1966,[3] the late John Alexander Rorer, a professor at the University of Virginia and a great-great-grandson of David and Betsy Debo Rorer, learned from Frank Jackson that "Betsy Rorer was the mother of John D.(avid) Rorer and lived during her late life on the John D. Rorer's homeplace in a small house near the big house. She died circa 1851 there and is buried (probably in an unmarked grave) in the John D. Rorer cemetery near Brights, Virginia and Somerset church."

The 1820 Census shows David Rorer as head of a family with one male between 26 and 45 years of age (himself); and one female (26-45), Betsy; two males under 10; and one female under 10. David and Betsy had three children, David Alexander, Mary (Polly), and John David.

1. DAVID ALEXANDER, was born Aug. 1, 1791, in Pittsylvania County, Virginia, was married by Joseph Hatchett March 3, 1814, to Nancy Ann W. Brown, and died Aug. 25, 1880. This family left Pittsylvania County, moved to Patrick County sometime between 1827 and 1835, and lived near what is now Woolwine, Virginia, at Buffalo Ridge. David did some farming, manufactured hats from beaver fur, and supposedly operated a store. He and Nancy Ann were buried in the family graveyard on the farm. Their children were:

A. JOHN, born in 1815, and married Jane Handy in 1836.

B. MIKE, who married Elizabeth (Susan) Ingram in 1841.

C. WILLIAM, who married Catherine Bowling in 1858.

D. THOMAS DUDLEY, born June 12, 1822, died Nov. 27, 1914, who married Arminda (Mindy) Davis in 1844.

E. DAVID C., who married Sarah Barbour and died in 1871.

F. ABRAHAM ALEXANDER, who married Pernina Smith Shelton and moved to Lanesville, Floyd County, Kentucky, where children were born. He died on a trip to Cincinnati in 1872.

G. SALLY, who married Tom Lawless.

H. MARY, who married John Morrison in 1842.

I. JUDY, who married Booker Adkins.

2. MARY (Polly), was born circa 1793, and was married also in Pittsylvania County, Virginia, September 12, 1807, to Elijah Towler, son of Joseph, and died June 30, 1833. Their children were:

A. ELIZABETH, born Sept. 19, 1808, and was married Dec. 18, 1828, in Bedford County to Shadrack Shockley, who was born Nov. 3, 1808.

B. FRANCES A., born June 7, 1811, and was married Jan. 2, 1837, in Pittsylvania County to Enos O. Robertson.

C. BENJAMIN FRANKLIN, born March 16, 1814, and died in May 1893 at Callands, Virginia. He was married Dec. 30, 1846, in Pittsylvania County to Mary Matilda (Tee) Harris, who was born Feb. 17, 1828, at Strawberry Virginia, and died Feb. 17, 1873, at Callands. They had five children.

3. JOHN DAVID, born circa 1795 and died in 1850. He was married in 1814 to Frances Custard, who was born July 3, 1798, and died June 9, 1880. In her late life, Betsy lived near the David Rorer family and was buried in the family cemetery on their place. John David and Frances had the following fourteen children:

A. DAVID J., born in 1814, became a physician, and lived in Georgia.

B. ELIZABETH, born in 1818, was married to William G. Bailey in 1840.

C. SARAH W., born in 1820, was married to James Keatts, Jr. in 1846.

D. ANNE DELILAH, born in 1822, was married to George Edwards.

E. DANIEL B., born in 1824

F. JOHN QUINCY, born in 1826 and died in 1899. He was married in 1854 to Sallie Baugh Hensley, who was born in 1837 and died in 1897. They had nine children.

G. REBECCA J., born in 1828, was married in 1850 to Charles Edwards.

H. CHARLES HENRY, born Jan. 1. 1830, and died Oct. 27, 1918. He was married Nov. 15, 1857, by Thomas C. Goggin to Annis Preston Hubbard, who was born May 14, 1839, and died March 16, 1926. They had eleven children. Annis P. Hubbard's mother was Mary Debo, daughter of Michael Debo, Sr., who was a brother of Betsy Debo Rorer. Charles and Annis are buried in the cemetery at Somerset chuch near Brights Virginia. (See the Mary Debo Hubbard section in the preceding chapter for their children.)

I.   MARY C. (Polly), born in 1832, was married to Terry Glenn.
J.   ARMISTEAD D.A., born Sept. 21, 1834, died Nov. 27, 1914, and is buried in the Somerset church cemetery near Brights, Virginia.
K.   WILLIAM A., born in 1835.
L.   SAMUEL T., born in 1840
M.   VIRGINIA FRANCES, born in 1841, was married Feb. 15, 1870, by Robert E. Lee to Daniel Perry Hubbard, who was born July 14, 1849. Daniel Perry was a brother of Annis P. Hubbard, who married Virginia Frances' brother, Charles H. Rorer. The Hubbards' mother was Mary Debo Hubbard, daughter of Michael Debo, Sr., brother of Betsy Debo Rorer.
N.   LUCIE E., born in 1842, was married to Alex Powell.

B. Christina Deboe Crider

CHRISTINA DEBO, daughter of Philip (2),was probably born circa 1774 or 1775 in Lancaster County, Pennsylvania, died sometime after 1850, and was buried at an unknown place in Pittsylvania County, Virginia. She was married January 1, 1796, in Pittsylvania County to Andrew Crider, who was born in 1775 in Philadelphia County, Pennsylvania, and died in 1856 in Pittsylvania County, Virginia. Andrew was the son of Daniel and Catherine Berger Crider of Lancaster County, who moved with the Harmon Cook expedition to Pittsylvania County, Virginia in the late 1780's.

The children of Christina and Andrew, all born in Pittsylvania County, Virginia, were:

1.   ELIZABETH, born circa 1797 and was married December 29, 1823, in Pittsylvania County to Wyatt Wallace, who was born circa 1795. They lived in Pittsylvania County, he was a farmer, and their marriage is recorded in Dalton's Register. Their children were:
A.   JAMES, born in 1824.
B.   MARY A., born circa 1825, who was married in the county Feb. 7, 1846, to Matthew McCrickard, who was born circa 1814 and was a miller. Their marriage is recorded in the Dalton's Register. Their children were: JOHN, born 1849; SAMUEL, born 1851; WILLIAM, born in 1853; THOMAS, born 1855; and DACTON H., born in 1856.
C.   JOHN M., born in 1833.
D.   WILLIAM WYATT, born in 1836. Private William W. Wallace was

in Co. I, 21st Virginia Infantry during the War Between the States, and was killed in action at Cedar Run, VA.

2. NANCY, born circa 1801, was married in Oct. 1823 in the county to William Tosh, son of George Jacob Tosh and the former Catherine Stevens. They moved to Caldwell County, KY, where she died in 1857 and was buried in the Tosh Cemetery of that county. William died circa 1858 in Caldwell County and was also buried in the Tosh Cemetery. Their children were:
   A. JOHN HENRY, born in 1824
   B. SAMUEL F., born in 1826, who died before Dec. 11, 1865.
   C. MARY JANE (Polly Jane)
   D. DANIEL
   E. NANCY
   F. ANDREW JASPER, born in 1838.
   G. MARTHA ANN
   H. PITTS, born in 1846.
   I. GEORGE W., born Oct. 17, 1831, in Pittsylvania County, VA, and died Dec. 27, 1909. He was married to Elizabeth Quill, who was born in Caldwell County, KY. They had a son, JAMES T., who was born in 1869 and married Flora Jane Canada, born in 1875.

3. SARAH (Sally), born circa 1804, who was married Jan. 29, 1833, in Pittsylvania County, VA, to Henry Towler, born Dec. 6, 1801, in Pittsylvania County and died circa 1845 in the same county. Their children were:
   A. JOHN, born in 1834.
   B. NANCY, born in 1836.
   C. MARY, born in 1837.
   D. JOSEPH, born in 1839.
   E. FRANCES, born in 1840.
   F. SAMUEL, born in 1842.
   G. CHRISTINA, born in 1844.
   H. HENRY, born in 1845

Sally was later married Feb. 22, 1847, in Pittsylvania County to Thomas Brumfield, born circa 1805, and they had one son, ANDREW, born in 1848.

4. CATHERINE (Caty), born circa 1816 and died circa 1890. She was married Jan. 20, 1840, in Pittsylvania County to Lewis Bobbitt, son of Thomas Bobbitt. He was born in 1816 in Pittsylvania County and died in 1863 in Jackson County, Ohio. Their children were:
   A. MARY A., born in 1842 in Campbell County, KY, died March 3, 1926 in Greene County, Ohio, and was buried Mar. 7, 1927, in Bowersville, Greene County, Ohio. Her husband's name is unknown.
   B. SAMUEL, born in 1843 in Pittsylvania County, VA, settled in

Missouri, and whose wife's name is unknown.

C. THOMAS, born in 1844 in Pittsylvania County.

D. GEORGE EDWARD, born in Mar. 1845 in Pittsylvania County.

E. ELIZABETH, born in 1846 in Pittsylvania County.

F. LEWIS, JR., born in Oct. 1849 in Jackson County, Ohio, died Feb. 5, 1930 in Highland, Highland County, Ohio, and was buried Feb. 8, 1930, in New Vienna, Clinton County, Ohio. He was married circa 1871 in Clinton County, Ohio, to Sarah Belle Stephens, who was born Apr. 11, 1848, in Williamsburg, Clermont County, Ohio, died Dec. 5, 1924, in Highland, Highland County, Ohio, and was buried Dec. 8, 1924, in the same place as her husband. She was the daughter of V.T. Stephens and the former Mary Ann Smith.

G. MARTHA, born in 1850 in Jackson County, Ohio.

H. JOHN H., born in 1853 in Jackson County, Ohio, and died Dec. 25, 1871 in Green Township, Clinton County, Ohio.

I. JAMES HARVEY, born in 1853 in Jackson County, Ohio.

J. AMINDA, born in 1856 in Jackson County, Ohio, and died in 1870.

K. JOSEPH, born in 1858 in Jackson County, Ohio, and died in Lancaster, Ohio, with burial in Elmwood Cemetery.

L. DAVID, born in 1860 in Jackson County, Ohio, and died March 13, 1913, in Lancaster, Ohio, with burial in Elmwood Cemetery. The name of his first wife is unknown. She was born in Missouri and died before 1889; they had one son. David's second wife was Mary Barnicle, born in 1866, and died Dec. 13, 1952, in Lancaster, Fairfield County, Ohio, with burial in the same cemetery as David.

5. GILLEY, born in 1813, who was married July 24, 1839, in Pittsylvania County to William McCrickard, born also in 1813. They had two children: SAMUEL, born in 1840; and MARTHA, born in 1842.

6. MARY (Polly): born in 1819, who was married Aug. 29, 1848, in Pittsylvania County to Samuel C. McCrickard, born in 1823.

7. SAMUEL., born before 1820 and died Oct. 22, 1826, in Pittsylvania County.

C. Abraham Debo

Abraham Debo was the second son of Philip (2) and was born in Lancaster County (Lebanon) County, Pennsylvania, in 1775. He migrated with the rest of the family down the Shenandoah Valley into Pittsylvania County, Virginia, about 1788 at about age 13. He was married in the same county November 14, 1797, to Sarah (Sally) Smith, daughter of William and Lucy Smith and a sister of Eleanor (Nellie) Smith, his brother Philip's wife. Little has been learned of this family, except they stayed in Virginia when several of the others went to western Kentucky. Abraham died in May 1850 and was buried in the county. It has not been ascertained when Sally died or where they were buried. Their children were:

1. JAMES, who was born circa 1798 or 1799 and died October 10, 1830.
2. ALLEN, who was born circa 1801 and died in 1821. He was married Nov. 21, 1820, to Jincey Love, who died in 1829.
3. ELIZABETH (Betsy), who married Christopher Wright Dec. 2. 1822. (He was the son of Thomas Wright, and was born circa 1799). Betsy was born May 6, 1802, and died between 1846 and 1850. The children of Christopher and Betsy were:
   A. ALLEN, born circa 1824.
   B. JOHN, born circa 1826.
   C. SARAH ANN, born Oct. 25, 1828, in Pittsylvania County, and died March 20, 1853, in the same county. She married John Ziegler Ramsey, who was born May 9, 1828, and died March 22, 1906, at Hebron, Grayson County, TX.
   D. JOSEPH, born circa 1831.
   E. POLLY, born circa 1834.
   F. CHRISTOPHER, born circa 1837.
   G. LUCINDA, born circa 1839.
   H. WILLIAM, born circa 1841.
   I. ABRAM, born circa 1843.
   J. TABITHA, born circa 1846.
4. JANE, who was born circa 1805 and married Oglesby Young Sept. 29, 1826.
5. LUCINDA, who was born circa 1807 and married a Butcher.
6. PHILIP, who was born circa 1809 and married Peggy Dalton Dec. 16, 1833, who was a sister to Locky and Polly Dalton, who married Benjamin and Joseph Debo and were all daughters of Winston Dalton.

D. Benjamin Debo

When Philip Deboe (3), along with most of his children, left Pittsylvania County, Virginia, in October 1830 "for the western country" (Kentucky), two of his sons – Benjamin and Joseph – remained behind. Benjamin had married Locky Dalton early in that year (March 10, 1830) and his brother Joseph and one of Abraham's son, Philip, would soon wed one of the Dalton sisters, who were daughters of Winston and Sarah Pullen Dalton, neighbors in Pittsylvania County. Philip married Peggy Dalton Dec. 14, 1833, and Joseph married Polly Dalton Nov. 21, 1835. After the death of Benjamin, Locky was listed in the 1850 Census as a widow pauper, and later married Richard Hoskins, born circa 1815.

BENJAMIN, son of Philip (3) and Eleanor (Nellie) Smith, was born circa 1806 in Pittsylvania County, and died there by early 1850 (he's not in the 1850

Census). His marriage to Locky Dalton produced the following children, all of whom lived their lives in the same county.

1. MARY ANN, born March 12, 1831, and died sometime after 1880 (she is listed in the 1880 Census). She was married circa 1846 to William Parker, born circa 1825 and died before 1870, and they had the following children.
    A. MARY JANE, born in January 1847.
    B. ELIJAH, born in 1854.
    C. PEMELIA, born in 1856.
    D. WILLIAM C., born in 1858.
    E. JOHN C., born in 1861.
    F. FRANCES, born sometime between 1861 and 1869.
2. WYATT, born July 4, 1833, and died Dec. 17, 1839, at age six. Name for his uncle, Wyatt Dalton.
3. MARGARET (Peggy), born Aug. 11, 1835, and still alive in 1880. In that Census she was living and evidently caring for ANNIE B., born in 1859; BENJAMIN L., born in 1866; and Bob Risan H. (R.H.), born in 1874.
4. MELISSA, born March 3, 1843, who married Joel W. Brooks May 17, 1866. He was born circa 1816.
5. JOSIAH, born in 1843. (He may possibly have been the 16-year-old Joseph listed in the 1860 Census as a factory laborer living in the John Hughey Home. Joseph enlisted in the 57th Virginia Regiment CSA during the War Between the States and was listed as missing, presumed dead.)
6. SMITH, born in 1844 and died Aug. 10, 1860, of a fever.
7. CENA ANN (sometimes listed as LENA), born in 1846. She (age 13) was living in the home of Richard and Locky Hoskins in the 1860 Census.
8. SEBUS (SEBE), born in 1850. In the 1880 Census he was listed as working in a sawmill.

E. Joseph Deboe

JOSEPH DEBOE, fifth child and third son of Philip (3) and Eleanor (Nellie) Smith Deboe, was born circa 1808 in Pittsylvania County, Virginia, and died sometime before 1850 (he is not listed in the 1850 Census). Joseph was married Nov. 21, 1835, in the same county to Polly Dalton, daughter of Winston and Sarah Pullen Dalton. Polly was a sister to Locky and Peggy Dalton, both of whom married Deboes. Accurate data – in fact, almost any data at all – has been impossible to obtain on this family. The only U.S. Census in which they are listed in that of 1840, in which Joseph and Polly are named along with two females under five. It has not been ascertained who these girls were, whether they died, or what became of them.

The Joseph Deboe, mentioned in the preceding section (D) of this chapter, may be the son of Joseph since Josiah and Joseph were born at about the same time (1843/44). The 1860 Census (taken the year before the War Between the States began) listed Joseph as being 16 years old, a factory laborer, and living in the home of John Hughey. The Deboes and the Hugheys were connected in that Catherine Deboe married Coleman Hughey. Joseph enlisted in the 57th Virginia Regiment after the war began (he would have been about 17 at the time) and was killed during the war. Claude J. DeBoe in a letter (a copy of which is in possession of the author) dated March 30, 1967, said: "About '61 [1861] I had a great-uncle by the name of Joseph DeBoe who was killed in battle and we lost all connection after that." Claude's grandfather was purported to be WILLIS WESTBROOK DEBO (according to Joseph L. DeBoe's marriage license) [Book 2, Pittsylvania County Marriage Records]. I have never found any mention of Willis W. Debo in any record, census, etc. I am assuming that Willis W. Debo was born sometime after 1840 and before 1850, and had a wife named America [surname unknown], according to the marriage license of Joseph L. The Joseph who died in the war may have been a brother to Willis.

If Willis W. Debo was indeed the father of Joseph L. DeBoe (father of Claude), then he had at least two other sons in addition to Joseph L. (maybe Willis or Westbrook), and DINK F. James W. was born in March 1859, died in April 1944, and was married in 1905 to Mary V. [surname unknown], who was born in 1864. JOSEPH L. was born in Dec. 1864, died in Oct. 1956, and was married Dec. 31, 1885, to Sallie Susan Mattox, born in 1865. She was the daughter of John C. and Tena Mattox. Dink F. (no other information or data on him) had a son, DINK F., JR., born in Feb. 1875, died in 1944, and was married June 29, 1898, to Rosa L. Davis, born in May 1881, the daughter of William J. and Mary Lee Davis. Dink Jr. and Rosa had a daughter, Hattie M., born in March 1899, who was later married to Mr. Cook and was mentioned as Hattie Cook in the will of Dink Jr. Rosa was later married on Dec. 28, 1905, to John H. Hoskins, and Hattie was living in the home at the time of the 1920 Census, along with a Herman, born in 1912, and James, born in 1914.

1. JAMES W., born circa 1859; married Mary V., born circa 1864. They adopted a son

A. MOSES LINWOOD DEBOE, born Aug. 26, 1896, and died in Aug. 1974. He was married circa 1918 to Dora V., born in 1897. Their children were:

1. Mary H., born in 1919
2. James Thomas, born in 1920.
3. Moses Linwood, Jr., born in 1922.
4. Lena Rivers, born in 1924.
5. Edgar Wilson, born in 1926.
6. Neal Carter, born in 1928.
7. Juanita, born after 1930.

2. JOSEPH L., born in Dec. 1864, died in 1954, and was married Dec. 31, 1885 [Book 2, Pittsylvania County Marriages], to Sally Susan Mattox, born in March 1865, who was the daughter of John C. and Tena Mattox. Joseph was a farmer and reared his family in the Piney Fork community of Pittsylvania County. The children of Joseph L. and Sally were:

A. CHARLES A., born June 11, 1883, died in April 1969, and was married circa 1910 to Minerva Ora ?, born Feb. 3, 1889, and died in Dec. 1983. Their children were:
   1. Edna, born in 1911
   2. Geneva, born in 1913.
   3. Erect (unreadable), born in 1915.
   4. Raleigh, born in 1917.

B. MARY J., born in March 1885, who married a Mr. Shelton.

C. ALBERT JAMES, born July 11, 1887, died in June 1972, and married circa 1908 to Nannie Owen, who was born in 1893 and died in 1957. Their children were:
   1. Mona E., born in 1910 and married James Moon.
   2. Perrow W., born May 4, 1911, and died in March 1972.
   3. Louise, born in 1913, who married a Mr. Steele.
   4. Bernice, born in 1915, who married Henry R. Ferguson.
   5. Margaret S., born in 1919, who married A.C. Smith.

D. CLAUDE J., born Nov. 12, 1889, died April 1970, and was married circa 1920 to Effie Beatrice Motley, who was born Feb. 23, 1891, and died in Dec. 1985. They had a daughter, Frances V., born in 1921, who married a Mr. Caldwell.

E. CHRISTINA, born July 23, 1893, died in 1978; married Douglas Barker.

F. LILLIE BELL, born Sept. 1, 1896, who first married a Payne by whom she had a son, Raleigh. She later married Murray Rice.

G. ETHEL, born in 1902; married William M. Watts

F. Catherine Debo Hedrick

CATHERINE DEBO, daughter of Philip Debo (2), was the last of Philip's children who was born in Lancaster County, Pennsylvania. She was born April 15, 1783, and was about five or six years old when the Debos migrated to Virginia, settling in Pittsylvania County about 1788. She was married on July 16, 1813, in that county to Philip Hedrick, son of Philip and Louvice Hedrick, who was born April 7, 1783. He died, presumably in Pittsylvania County, West Virginia. The children of Catherine and Philip, all probably born in Pittsylvania County, Virginia, were:
   1. WILLIAM ALEXANDER, born Dec. 14, 1814, who was married in 1843 to Elizabeth Jane Asbury.

2. GEORGE WASHINGTON, born Nov. 25, 1815, and died Aug. 28, 1900. He was married June 15, 1837, to Catherine Higginbotham.
3. JOHN WILLIAM, born in 1818, who married Martha A. McGrew, born in 1819.
4. JACOB, born March 2, 1819, and died April 12, 1866. He was married in December 1843 to Mary Ann Higginbotham, who was born in 1824 and died in 1879.
5. MARY ANN, born Oct. 21, 1820, and died Nov. 5, 1864. She was married to Samuel McGrew.
6. HENRY D., born Feb. 28, 1822 and died Jan. 10, 1896. He was married circa 1845 to his first wife, Rebecca Fielder, who died, and was married Dec. 6, 1857, to his second wife, Martha Ann West.
7. DANIEL, born in June 1825 and died June 4, 1864.
8. DAVID, born in1828.
9. BENJAMIN ADAM, born in 1830, who was married Aug. 8, 1854, to Margaret F. Fielder.
10. SALLY, who was either married to Benjamin Melton or a Mr. Pearce.

Chapter VI
Kentucky Deboes
I
Philip Deboe (3)

Philip Deboe (3), son of Philip Deboe (2), was born circa 1777 in Lancaster County, Pennsylvania, and was married on January 21, 1799,[1] to Eleanor (Nellie) Smith, daughter of William and Lucy Smith, in Pittsylvania County, Virginia. He, along with some of his children and other families, left October 28, 1830, for "the western country"[2] (Kentucky) where he settled in Caldwell County. He died October 19, 1835.

The children of Philip and Nellie, all born in Pittsylvania County, Virginia were:

A. NANCY, born September 26, 1799, and died March 1, 1865. She married Jacob (Jake) Crayne February 21, 1820. Jake Crayne was the son of Conrad Crain, and was born in 1797 in Virginia and died January 3, 1881. He and Nancy were buried in the Dollar Cemetery in Caldwell County, Kentucky. They came to Kentucky in 1830 with Nancy's father, brothers and sisters, and other friends and relatives, and were charter members of the Piney Creek Baptist Church, to whom they deeded five and one-half acres of land for a building. Their children listed in the "Dalton Register" all born in Virginia before they came to Kentucky were:

1. DAVID S., born March 31, 1821, killed August 11, 1864, during the War Between the States, and was buried in Dollar Cemetery. He took the name Green after coming to Kentucky because of the wrong spelling or the mispronunciation of his name, and his descendants went by that name also, although they were blood kin to the Craynes. He was married Jan. 4, 1847, to Clarinda Crayne, probably a first cousin, who was born circa 1834 in Illinois. They had five

children.

2. ELLINA or ELLENDER (Ella), born Nov. 26, 1822, and died in March 1905 (one source says 1910). She was married Feb. 10, 1842, in Livingston County, KY, to Wilson W. Dollar, born May 9, 1821, in Orange County, North Carolina and died March 19, 1870, in Caldwell County, KY. They had two sons.

3. JACOB, born July 6, 1825, and died prior to 1830 in Pittsylvania County, VA.

4. JACOB JOURDAN, born May 31, 1827, and died in Illinois. On March. 5, 1852, in Crittenden County, KY, he was married to Lucy Harris, born circa 1837 in Caldwell County, and probably died in Illinois. They had five children.

5. MARGARET ANN (Peggy), born Nov. 10, 1829, and died in May 1907 in Caldwell County. On Feb. 11, 1852, she was married to Wiley Jones Dollar, born circa 1823 in Orange County, North Carolina, and died in Nov. 1899 in Caldwell County, KY. They had six children.

Children born after coming to Kentucky were:

6. MARY J., born circa 1832 and died 2 Mar 1858, in Crittenden County with burial in Rushing Cemetery. On Feb. 27, 1857, in Crittenden County she was married to James Willis (Willie) Rushing, born July 27, 1836, in Rutherford, TN and died Oct. 1, 1896, in Crittenden County, KY with burial in the same cemetery along with an infant son, who was born and died Feb. 28, 1896.

7. MARSHALL N. (Marsh), born May 6, 1836, died Feb. 26, 1897, and was buried in Piney Fork Cemetery. On Jan. 4, 1860, in Caldwell County he was married to Frances P. Morse, born June 8, 1839, and died Apr. 4, 1904, with burial in the same cemetery. They had eight children.

8. JOSEPH ABRAHAM (Joe), born Feb. 9, 1838, died June 26, 1929, and was buried in Piney Fork Cemetery. He was a veteran of the War Between the States. In circa 1865 he was married to Pernecia Jane (Janie) Deboe, his first cousin, daughter of Abram and Mary Jane Smith Deboe. They were buried in Sugar Grove Cemetery. Joe and Janie had thirteen children. He later was married on Sep. 24, 1890, in Crittenden County to Arpha/Orpha (Guess) Cannon, but

they were later divorced. She was born Sep. 19, 1838, and died Dec. 16, 1924.

9. JAMES MANSFIELD (Jim), born circa 1842, died in 1918 in Ridgeway, Hamilton County, Illinois, with burial at Mt. Oval Cemetery in that county. He was married in Illinois to Elizabeth Shaw, who died Dec. 2, 1888, in Ridgeway. They had six children. By a second wife, whose name is unknown, he had two children. His third wife was Laura Ambers(?), by whom he had four children.

10. MARTHA A., born March 15, 1844, and died Nov. 11, 1921, in Crittenden County. On Mar. 3, 1863, in the same county she married James Bradley, born Oct. 28, 1830, and died Apr. 18, 1906, with burial in Piney Fork Cemetery. They had nine children. On Mar. 18, 1908, she was married to John Henry Thomason, born Mar. 20, 1839, in Crittenden County, and died Dec. 20, 1916, with burial in Piney Fork Cemetery of Crittenden County.

B. PHILIP (4), born October 12, 1802, died June 3, 1864, in Fredonia, KY, and was buried in the Dollar Cemetery, Caldwell County. He was married on December 17, 1827, to Rebecca Custard, who was born circa 1808 in Virginia and died circa 1834 in Livingston or Crittenden County, Kentucky. He was on Oct. 19, 1836, married to Jacynthia (Cynthia) Smith in Livingston County, KY, who was born on 16 June 1807 in Tennessee, and died May 3, 1893 in Kentucky with burial in Dollar Cemetery, Caldwell County. The children of Philip and Rebecca were:

1. JAMES WILLIAM, born 29 Apr 1829, in Pittsylvania County, Virginia, and died after 1900 in Livingston County, Kentucky. He was married March 1, 1860 in Livingston County, Kentucky, to Rodice Ann (Dicy) Heater, born circa 1840 in Kentucky. Their children, all born in Kentucky, were:
   a. SARAH, born circa 1865.
   b. ELISHA P., born circa 1868, who married Addie Heater.
   c. ADDIE, born circa 1870.
   d. MOLLIE, born circa 1873.
   e. MINNIE, born circa 1878.
   f. JOSEPH C., born in Oct. 1881.

2. JOHN CRAYTON, born May 15, 1830, in Pittsylvania County, Virginia and died Aug. 26, 1908 in Crittenden

County, Kentucky. He was married April 10, 1851, to Charlotte Amanda Cole, who was born Sept. 9, 1832, and died in the same county April 15, 1914. Both were buried in the Crayne Cemetery.

a. THOMAS, born circa 1852.

b. JAMES PHILLIP, born circa 1856 in Crittenden County, KY, and died in Crayne, KY. He was married Nov. 30, 1884, in Crittenden County to Mary Thomas Hammond, born Jan. 26, 1865, and died Feb. 5, 1961, Amarillo, Potter County, TX.

c. WILLIAM R., born circa 1858 in Crayne, KY, and died before 1880. He was married Dec. 26, 1878, to Margaret L. Leeper, born in Aug. 1863 in KY and died after 1930.

d. JOSEPH HENRY, born Mar. 13, 1860 in Crayne, KY, died July 25, 1932, in Crayne, Crittenden County, KY. He was married to Martha Ann Bebout March 5, 1883.

e. ABARHAM C., born circa 1862, in Crayne, Crittenden County, KY.

f. WASHINGTON FRANK, born circa 1863.

g. CHARLES A. (Charlie), born circa 1864.

h. JOHN EDWARD (Ed), born circa 1869.

i. ADA A., born circa 1873 in Crayne, KY, died in Crayne in 1937, and was buried there. She married William Binkley.

3. 3. BENJAMIN THOMAS, born June 4, 1831, in Kentucky. He was married Oct. 17, 1854, to Mary F. Cannon, born circa 1836.

4. 4. FRANCES ANN, born Dec. 30, 1833, died Nov. 15, 1863, with burial in Dollar Cemetery in Caldwell County. She was married in 1849 in Pop County, Ill. To Willoughby Hudgeons Guess, who was born May 4, 1831, in Orange County, North Carolina, and died Mar. 28, 1924, in Crittenden County with burial in Maple View Cemetery, Marion, KY. They had six children.

Children of Philip and Jacynthia, all born in Kentucky, were:

5. NANCY ELLEN, born Sept. 28, 1838, and died Jan. 27, 1914, Crayne, Kentucky. She was married Jan. 10, 1855, to James Grant Ordway, born Feb. 24, 1833, and died May 10, 1882, at Crayne, Kentucky. They had six children.

6. JOSEPH A. (Joe), born in Oct. 25, 1839, in Crittenden County, Kentucky, and died Jan. 18, 1896, in Livingston County. He was married on March 22, 1865, to Sarah Jane (Sallie) Freeman, who was born Nov. 6, 1843, and died Mar. 12, 1923, in Caldwell County with burial in Pinkneyville Cemetery, Livingston County, KY.

    a. ELIZABETH BELLE, born June 4, 1866, and died July 23, 1943 in Caldwell County. She was married circa 1902 to Morris Kirby, born circa 1865 in England and died circa 1920 in Michigan.

    b. MATHEW PHILIP, born July 6, 1869, and died April 11, 1947, in Livingston County with burial in Salem Cemetery. He was married Nov. 18, 1896, to Julia Florence Ryan, born Feb. 18, 1871, and died Jan. 27, 1960, in Livingston County with burial in the same cemetery.

    c. LUCY JOHNSON, born April 1, 1870, and died Dec. 23, 1871, with burial in the Fredonia Cemetery.

    d. THOMAS ASBERRY (Tom), born June 12, 1872 in Caldwell County and died March 15, 1938 with burial in Pinkneyville Cemetery, Livingston County. He married Mabel Moreland, who was born June 20, 1885, and died Jan. 5, 1956.

    e. ROBERT EDGAR, born Oct. 5, 1876, in Caldwell County, and died Dec. 30, 1917, in Livingston County; burial in Pinkneyville Cemetery.

    f. JOSEPH HENRY, born Mar. 22, 1878, in Caldwell County, and died Aug. 2, 1909, in Livingston County with burial in Pinkneyville Cemetery.

    g. NELLIE GRACE, born Feb. 14, 1881, in Caldwell County, and died Dec. 18, 1915 in Livingston County; burial in Pinkneyville Cemetery. She was married Jan. 28, 1900, in Crittenden County to Joseph Edward (Ed) Guess, born July 7, 1877, in Caldwell County and died May 25, 1955 in Livingston County.

    h. CARRIE J., born Mar. 14, 1883, in Caldwell County and died Aug. 15, 1951, Caldwell County. She was married May 13, 1903, in Caldwell County to Thomas Yewell (Tom) Ordway, who was born Aug. 4, 1875, in Caldwell County and died Oct. 28, 1938, in Caldwell County with a burial in Fredonia Cemetery.

    i.   CHARLES MARION (Charlie),born Nov. 22, 1885, in Caldwell County and died Sep. 23, 1901, in Livingston County with burial in Pinkneyville Cemetery.

7. ABRAHAM COLUMBUS (Abe), born Feb. 10, 1840, and died May 24, 1919, in Fredonia, Kentucky. He married Mary Ellen Freeman (born May 8, 1847, in Fredonia, and died Aug. 3, 1899). She was a sister of Sallie Freeman, who married Joseph A. Deboe, Abe's brother. Abe was mustered in as a private in Co. D., 20th Regiment, Kentucky Infantry, USA, January 6, 1862, for three years service, and was mustered out on July 17, 1865, in Louisville, KY, at age 19, according to his war records. Abe was later married Nov. 23, 1902 in Crittenden County to Malissa A. Freeman, who was born circa 1861 in Illinois. Abe and Mary Ellen's children were:

    a.   JOEL P. (Joe), born in 1869 in Crittenden County. He was married to Cordelia Myers circa 1893, She was born in Nov. 1872.

    b.   MATTHEW R. (Buddy), born May 7, 1872, and died Dec. 30, 1953, in Caldwell County. On Nov. 17, 18895, he was married to Maude Jacobs, who was born Sep. 1, 1876, and died June 3, 1961.

    c.   JAMES A., born Dec. 5, 1874, in Crittenden County, died July 9, 1911, in Hickman County with burial in Clinton, KY.

    d.   ALBERT MAXWELL, born Mar. 15, 1877, in Crittenden County. He was married to Florence Tabor, who was born Feb. 21, 1877, in Crittenden County, and died Dec. 2, 1900, in Crayne, Crittenden County, with burial there. Albert was later married on Mar. 29, 1903, in Crittenden County to Mrs. Allie Wheeler, who was born Apr. 1, 1883, and died Mar. 28, 1960, with burial in Mexico Baptist Church Cemetery, Crittenden County.

    e.   JESSIE FRANKLIN, born Dec. 7, 1880, in Crittenden County, and died Mar. 11, 1957, with burial in Crayne Cemetery. On Sep. 8, 1903, in Crittenden County, he was married to Flora Ordway, who was born Jan. 7, 1883, in Crayne, and died May 28, 1949, with burial in

Crayne Cemetery.

f.   NANNIE, born Mar. 5, 1882, and died Oct. 1, 1908, in Crittenden County with burial in Crayne Cemetery. On Jan. 13, 1903, in Kelsey, Caldwell County, she was married to Robert E.L. Traylor, born Nov. 23, 1876, in Crittenden County and died Dec. 17, 1961, in Tulare, California.

g.   WILLIAM SHERDIE, born in 1884 in Crittenden County. On Mar. 4, 1907, in Crittenden County he was married to Iva Phillips, born circa 1886.

h.   DOLLIE A., born Nov. 4, 1884.

i.   RUBY, born in 1887.

8. JESSE WATKINS, born in March 4, 1841, and died Dec. 28, 1903. He was married on Nov. 24, 1883, to Eliza Rebecca Pickens, born circa 1866 and died circa 1880 at Marion, Kentucky. They had one daughter, Era Deboe.

9. DAVID WASHINGTON (Wash), born May 15, 1842, and died Jan. 13, 1921, Crayne, Kentucky. He was married Nov. 1, 1866, to Nancy Susan Jennings, who was born Nov. 21, 1847, in Caldwell County and died May 13, 1935, at Crayne.

a.   PHILLIP WASHINGTON, born Oct. 4, 1867, in Crayne, and died in 1868.

b.   VIRGINIA ELIZABETH/EMMAZELLA (Jennie), born Jan. 25, 1869, in Crittenden County, died July 29, 1936, at Crayne. On Nov. 8, 1886, she was married to William R. (Willie) Brown, born in 1868 and died Dec. 25, 1927 in Caldwell County with burial in Crayne Cemetery.

c.   ROBERT FRANKLIN, born July 8, 1871, died May 13, 1947, in Union County with burial in Crayne Cemetery. On Jan. 20, 1896 he was married to Minnie F. Hall, born circa 1868 and died July 11, 1939, in Union County.

d.   SARAH ELLEN (Ellie), born Sep. 7, 1873 in Crittenden County and died Sep. 13, 1953, in Livingston County with burial in Macedonia Cemetery, Lyon County, KY. On Dec. 6, 1891, she was married to Milton Edward Thomason, born May 18, 1870, in Crittenden County and died Sep. 16, 1931, in Lyon County with burial in Macedonia Cemetery.

e.   DOLLY ANN, born Oct. 18, 1875, in Crayne and died in

1876 at Crayne with burial in Crittenden County.

f.　JOHN ALBERT, born May 19, 1878, in Crayne and died April 28, 1940, in Crittenden County with burial at Crayne. On Feb. 18, 1902, he was married to Carrie M. Young, born in 1881 in Crittenden County and died in Sep. 1904 in Crittenden County with burial in Paris Cemetery. John Albert was later married in Sep. 1904 to Ollie Blanche Braswell, who died in 1958 in Jackson, Michigan. Still later, John Albert was married in 1928 to Martha Annie King, who was born in 1880 and died Feb. 19, 1960, in Crittenden County with burial at Crayne.

g.　NONA LYNN, born July 5, 1880, in Crayne and died May 14, 1953, in Caldwell County with burial at Crayne.

h.　RUFUS (Rufe) MAXWELL (Max), born Oct. 6, 1882, in Crittenden County and died Mar. 14, 1912, with burial at Crayne. On Jan. 6, 1909, in Vanderburgh County, Indiana, he was married to Mary Lelia Sweets, born Dec. 28, 1879, in Union County, KY.

i.　ALMA LOUISE, born Feb. 2, 1885, at Crayne and died in 1961 with burial in Cedar Hill Cemetery, Princeton, KY. Circa 1905 she was married to John William Morgan, born in 1880 and died in 1951 with burial at Cedar Hill.

j.　LILLIS MAE (Lillie), born June 10 1887, at Crayne and died in 1966 with burial in IOOF Cemetery, at Clay in Webster County, KY. Before 1908 she was married to J. Spurling McCord, born in 1887 and died Sep. 27, 1941, in Webster County, KY with burial in the same cemetery.

10. PHILIP HOWARD (Phil), born May 10,1844, and died in 1917. He was married Dec. 18, 1867, to Mary Kirk Moss, born circa 1847. They were buried in Maple View Cemetery, Marion, KY.

a.　CORA, born in Crittenden County.

b.　JULIA, born in Crittenden County.

c.　NANNIE, born Sep. 1, 1876, in Crittenden County and died Aug. 14, 1947, in Hopkinsville, Christian County, KY with burial in Maple View Cemetery, Marion. On

Oct. 10, 1900, she was married to James B. Allen, born in 1874 and died Dec. 22, 1938, in Webster County with burial at Maple View.

- d. WILLIAM A. (Will), born in Dec. 1878 in Crittenden County. On July 11, 1903, he was married to Annie B. Carnahan. Burial in Blackford Cemetery.
- e. HUGH, born in Apr. 1882 in Crittenden County.
- f. MARY, born in 1885 in Crittenden County and died in 1950 with burial at Blackford Cemetery.
- g. EFFIE A., born in Dec. 1886 in Crittenden County and died in 1935 with burial at Maple View, Marion.
- h. EUDOXIE, born in Apr. 1889 in Crittenden County and married a Sheeks.
- i. MENDOZEN, born in 1890 in Crittenden County, died in 1948 with burial in Maple View, Marion, KY.

11. ALEXANDER ASBURY (Berry), born in March 31, 1846, and died June 22, 1935. He was married June 11, 1880, to Mary Elizabeth Pickens, born circa 1854 and died circa 1880.

12. DICEY JANE, born June 8, 1847, and died in April 6, 1917, with burial at Crayne. She was married Nov. 30, 1866, to Jesse M. McCaslin, born Aug. 31, 1841, in Caldwell County and died Oct. I, 1929. They had 11 children, and he was a Union soldier during the War Between the States, as were several of Jane's brothers.

13. SARAH AMANDA (Sally), born in 1852, and died in 1892 in Davidson County, Tennessee. She was married Aug. 9, 1875, to Samuel Albert Link, born July 10, 1848, in Wilson County, Tennessee, and died Feb. 12, 1909, in Cheatham County, Tennessee. They had four children.

C. ELLENDER, born October 17, 1803, and died March 14,1893. She was married July 20, 1825, in Pittsylvania County, Virginia, to James S. Woodall, born circa 1800 and died sometime after March 1842. The Woodalls came to Kentucky in the 1830 migration of the Deboes, Craynes, and others. They went on into Illinois for a time but returned to western Kentucky in 1840. The first three children were born in Pittsylvania County, VA. Most of the children lived and died in Crittenden County, KY. The children of Ellender and James Woodall were:

1. ANDERSON (Andy), born Oct. 19, 1826, in Virginia, and died Oct. 11, 1915, in Kentucky. He was married Oct. 23, 1851, to Jemira Ann (Myra) Hill, born Nov. 15, 1830, and died Oct. 13, 1907, who was the daughter of Robert and Kezia Smith Hill. They were buried in Hill Cemetery, Crittenden County, and had 14 children.
2. JAMES S., born March 31, 1828, and died Aug. 29, 1899. He was married Sep. 29, 1853, to Mary Jane Thomason, born in Aug. 1836 in Gallatin County, IL and died after 1900, the daughter of Richard and Letitia Gossett Thomason. They were buried in Piney Fork Cemetery and had 10 children.
3. MARY ANN, born Feb. 1, 1830, and died young before 1850 in Crittenden County.
4. NANCY, born June 24, 1833, in Green County, Illinois, and died circa 1895. She was first married May 11, 1853, to Hezekiah Tabor and after his death married Dec. 22, 1862, to John N. Mabry, son of Francis A. and Rebecca Oliver Mabry, born in Georgia and died in 1895. They were buried in Crayne Cemetery, Crittenden County. Nancy had five children by her two husbands.
5. JOHN, born Aug. 1, 1835, in Green County, IL, and married his first cousin, Vilenia Jerine/Jenne Hill, born circa 1842 in Crittenden County, KY. They had 13 children.
6. ELIZABETH, born May 10, 1837, in Green County, IL and died between 1865 and 1870. She was married Jan. 7, 1857, in Crittenden County, KY to Lemiah Newton Hill, born about 1834, son of Robert and Kezia Hill. They had four children.
7. SAMUEL ALLEN, born Jan. 3, 1840, in Green County, IL, and died July 24, 1912, in Lyon County, KY. He first married Dec. 7, 1862, a first cousin, Sarah Ellen Hill, who was born circa 1844 and died Oct. 4, 1866. He then married Dec. 5, 1866, Letitia Americus McNeeley, born Jan. 11, 1847. He had three children by Sarah Ellen, and twelve by Letitia.
8. PLEASANT H. (or JAMES PLEASANT), born Jan. 6, 1842, and died Dec. 19, 1863, in Russellville, KY, during the War Between the States.
D. BENJAMIN (Stayed in Pittsylvania County, Virginia. See Chapter V.)

E. JOSEPH (Stayed in Pittsylvania County, Virginia. See Chapter V.)

F. MARY (Polly), born March 7, 1811, died October 9, 1864, and was buried in Dollar Cemetery, Caldwell County, Kentucky. She was married in that county May 16, 1834, to Conrad (pronounced Coonrad) Crayne, who was born May 11, 1809, in Pittsylvania County, Virginia, and died in February 1899 with burial in Paris Cemetery, Crittenden County, Kentucky. He was the son of Conrad Crain and a brother of Jacob Crain (Crayne). After Polly's death in 1864, Conrad was married to Martha Hunt on March 18, 1868. Conrad and Polly had ten children:

1. JOSEPH C., born March 16, 1834, in Caldwell County, KY, and died in 1837.
2. JAMES W., born Sept. 15, 1836, in Caldwell County, KY, and died in 1837.
3. PERLINA ELLEN, born Oct. 9, 1838, in Crayne, Crittenden County, and died Nov. 20, 1930. She was married by Abram Deboe May 19, 1859, in Crittenden County to William Franklin Paris, born Dec. 27, 1838, in Smith County, TN. They had ten children.
4. BENJAMIN THOMAS, born Aug. 7, 1840, and died 26 July 1882. He was married Sept. 27, 1865, in Caldwell County to Ellender Emmeline Cole, who was born Jan. 1, 1848, in Caldwell County, and died May 3, 1906, in Yakima, WA.
5. JANE E., born Sept 6, 1842, and died in Oct. 26, 1928. She was married Dec. 2, 1866, in Crittenden County to Liguarian M. Hill, who was born May 24, 1835, and died July 19, 1871. After Hill's death, she was married April 8, 1874, in Crittenden County to Smith Patterson Hamby, born circa 1808 in White County, TN and died Oct. 21, 1888, in Crittenden County. Jane had three children by Hill and one by Hamby.
6. JOHN H., born Nov. 27, 1844, and died in 1921. He was married Oct. 21, 1868, to Mary Ella Cole, born circa 1843, and they had four children.
7. MARY ANN., born Dec. 11, 1846. She was married May 31, 1869, in Crittenden County to Henry Thomas (Tom) Jacobs, born Oct. 1, 1840, in Crayne, KY, and died Jan. 30, 1908.
8. PERNECIA (or PERNESA) CLABURN, born May 16, 1848,

died in Yakima Valley, WA. She was married Apr. 27, 1869, to Milton Johnson Jacobs, born Feb. 26, 1846, in Crayne, KY, and died in 1911 in Yakima Valley, WA.

9. MARTHA G. (Mattie), born May 18, 1851, and died Aug. 14,1875, in Crittenden County. She was married Aug. 28, 1872, in Crittenden County to James Robert (Jim) Woodall, born Jan. 1, 1852, in Crittenden County, and died Apr. 20, 1937. They had two children.

10. WILLIS CHAMPION (Champ), born Nov. 27, 1852, and died Feb. 16, 1931. He was married Dec. 27, 1879, to Ada Belle Ordway, who was born Oct. 21, 1861, and died July 21, 1946, in Caldwell County, KY. They had six children, two of whom died in infancy.

G. JOHN, born in 1814, died circa 1900 in Sangamon County, IL, and was married Feb. 25, 1839, in Caldwell County, Kentucky, to Maria Burton Smith, born July 1822 in Kentucky, the daughter of Garland and Harriett Smith. Their six children (all born in Crittenden County) were:

1. MARY JANE, born in 1844.
2. HARRIET ELLEN, born in Feb. 1845.
3. WILLIAM H., born in 1847.
4. JOSEPH F., born in 1849.
5. JAMES C., born in 1854.
6. ANNA (ANNIE), born in Sep. 1858 in Sangamon County, IL.

H. ABRAM, born Nov. 17, 1817, died in 1889 at Fredonia Kentucky, and was buried in Deboe Cemetery, near Farmersville, Caldwell County. He was married on Jan. 29, 1842, in Crittenden County, Kentucky, by Joel E. Grace to Mary Jane Smith, who was born May 12, 1826, died April 4, 1864. and was buried in Dollar Cemetery, Caldwell County. She was the daughter of Garland and Harriet Smith. After the death of Mary Jane in 1864, Abram was later married on Jan. 1, 1868, to Elvira Creekmur in Hopkins County, Kentucky. She was born in May 1840 and died after 1910 in Caldwell County.

Abram was a farmer, a Baptist preacher, a charter member of the Piney Creek church in Crittenden County when it was organized in 1844, and was the preacher for the congregation when the building was built. Politically, he was an old-line Whig prior to the War Between the States, and espoused the Union cause when the war broke out. He later became a Republican, and was a person of "strong convictions and unfaltering courage, maintaining a firm stand on matters political, religious, and otherwise."

Children of Abram and Mary Jane (born in Crittenden County) were:

1. JAMES MONROE, born Sept. 1, 1843, died Feb. 3, 1897, and was buried in Piney Fork Cemetery. He was married Oct. 24, 1878, to Margurette Marginia Wilson, who was born Oct. 24, 1878, Crittenden County, and died Nov. 29, 1933, in the same county with burial in the same cemetery as her husband. They had no children.

2. PERNECIA JANE (Janie), born June 5, 1844, died Dec. 3, 1889, in Crittenden County, and was buried in Sugar Grove Cemetery. She married a cousin, Joseph Abraham (Joe) Crayne, born Feb. 9, 1838, in Crittenden County, and died June 26, 1929, and they had fourteen children. Crayne was the son of Jacob Crayne and Nancy Deboe Crayne.

3. LOUISE/LOUISA ANN (Lue), born in April 1847, and died after 1920, possibly in Illinois. She was married in 1867 to Thomas G. Shinall, who was born in Aug. 1847 in KY and died after 1920 possibly in Illinois. They had eleven children.

4. WILLIAM JOSEPH (Joe), born June 30, 1849, died June 15, 1927, and was buried in Maple View Cemetery, Marion, Kentucky. He was married in 1886 to Victoria Larkin, who was born in 1848 in Mt. Vernon, Indiana, and died in 1936 in Crittenden County. Joe attended Crittenden County's schools, Bethlehem Academy in Caldwell County, and thereafter taught in common schools in his home and adjoining counties. He worked his way through Ewing College in Illinois and the Medical University in Louisville by teaching part-time. Receiving his medical degree in 1881, he carried on a successful practice as a Crittenden County physician and surgeon. Poor health, however, caused him to give up medicine, and he turned to law and politics, being admitted to the

bar in 1889. Deboe was elected to and served as county school superintendent from 1889 to 1893, but was unsuccessful in a 1892 bid for U.S. congressman from the First District of Kentucky. He served in the Kentucky Senate, however, from 1893 to 1897. On March 4, 1897, he was chosen by the Kentucky Legislature to represent the state in the U.S. Senate, the first Republican to do so. Senator Deboe served in the Senate until March 3, 1903, but declined to stand for reelection because of ill health. Returning to Marion, his hometown, he resumed his law practice and remained active in politics. On March 28, 1923, he began his last public service, acting as postmaster of Marion, to which he was official lyappointed June 6, 1924. He served until May 23, 1927, when the developing cancer with which he was afflicted forced his resignation, and he died at his home in Marion on June 14, 1927.

Children of Senator Joe and Victoria Deboe were:

a. MARY LARKIN, born in 1890 and died in 1923. She married Virgil L. Christian, Jr., of Union County, Kentucky, and they had three children: Martha L., Mary W., and Virgil Jr. The son became a professor of economics at the University of Kentucky in Lexington.

b. WILLIAM JOSEPH, JR., who died at age six.

5. SAMUEL B., born in Aug. 1850, died July 2, 1950, in Christian County, and was buried in the Deboe Cemetery in Caldwell County. He married Pemecy L. (Niecie) Keeney Nov. 5, 1874. She was born in Oct. 1853 in Caldwell County and died May 1, 1935, with burial in the same cemetery as her husband.

a. LAURA V., born in March 1876 in Caldwell County, died in 1944, and was buried in Deboe Cemetery, Caldwell County.

b. LOLA E., born in Jan. 1878 and died Feb. 7, 1957, and was buried in Cedar Hill Cemetery, Princeton, KY. She was married Oct. 25, 1906 in Caldwell County to Allie Prentice McNeely, born in Jan. 1867, died June 22, 1960, and buried in the same cemetery.

c. AMY F., born in Aug. 1880, died in 1924, and buried in

210

Deboe Cemetery.

    d. HARVEY, born in Dec. 1882.

    e. LUTHER L., born in Jan. 1886, died Jan. 13, 1980, and buried in Asher Cemetery, Caldwell County. He married Eula S. ???, who was born in 1887, died Nov. 27, 1946, and buried in the same cemetery.

    f. CHESTER ELLIS (Judge), born July 9, 1889, died Aug. 13, 1978, in Detroit, Michigan, and was buried in Deboe Cemetery. He was married Dec. 26, 1922, to Johnnie May Ray, born circa 1898, died Dec. 26, 1922.

    g. ONA, born in Oct. 1892, died Jan. 26, 1964, and buried in Cedar Hill Cemetery was married Nov. 12, 1919, to Carl Strong, born in 1893 and died Dec. 25, 1955, Caldwell County.

6. JOHN S., born April 16, 1853, in Crittenden County, and died after 1900, probably in Dallas, Texas.

7. THOMAS H., born Sep. 3, 1855.

8. NANCY ELIZABETH, born Feb. 22, 1859, died Oct. 3, 1933, and was buried in Maple View Cemetery, Marion. She was married Nov. 18, 1880, in Caldwell County to John Daniel Smith, born Mar. 30, 1861, and died February 12, 1940, in Crittenden County with burial in the same cemetery. They had no children.

9. MARTHA ELLEN, born Mar. 22, 1860, in Crittenden County, died June 30, 1947, at Marion with burial in Crayne Cemetery. She was married July 26, 1882, in Princeton to Davis Ewing Crider, born July 25, 1855, in Crittenden County, died Feb. 8, 1924, and buried in the same cemetery. They had ten children.

J. Children of Abram and Elvira Creekmur Deboe were:

10. SARAH A., born Apr. 19, 1868, died Mar.5, 1911, in Caldwell County, and buried at Perry Cemetery, Caldwell County. She was married Nov. 10, 1887, to Joseph W. (Buddy) Board, born May 30, 1866, and died Jan. 12, 1936, in the same county. They had four children.

11. MARY ALICE (Mollie), born in Nov. 1869, died in 1943 in Caldwell County, and Buried in Donaldson Missionary Baptist Cemetery, Caldwell County. She was married Nov. 10, 1887, in Caldwell County to Moses McNary (Mack M)

Stallins, born in 1856 and died in 1927, buried in the same county. They had one daughter.

12. DAVID GRANT (Dee), born Sep. 17,1871, in Caldwell County, died Jan. 4,1940, with burial in Perry Cemetery, Caldwell County. He was married July 9, 1890, to Dorothy Dora Belle (Dora) Board, born July 17, 1871, in Caldwell County, died Mar. 3, 1957, with burial in the same cemetery. They had the following eight children: Carrie M., born circa 1893; Annie Ethel, born in 1895, died 1924; Carlos Clinton, born in 1899, died 1967; Bertha, born 1902; Lora Novella, born 1903 and died in 1987; Johnny Warden, born in 1906 and died in 1947; Abram Augusta (Buster), born circa 1908 and died in 1965; and Virginia, born after 1910.

13. NORA BELLE, born in May 1874 in Caldwell County, died Nov. 2, 1937, with burial in the Deboe Cemetery, Caldwell County. She was married Oct. 25, 1894, in Caldwell County to Francis M. (Frank) Sheridan, born Mar. 1, 1864, died June 18, 1938, and buried in the same cemetery. They had five children.

14. VIRGINIA F. (Jennie), born in Mar. 6, 1876, died Dec.15, 1964, in Caldwell County, and buried in Donaldson Missionary Baptist Cemetery, Caldwell County. She was married Jan. 23, 1912, in Caldwell County to Edgar L. McNeely, born Aug. 28, 1879, and died Dec. 25, 1962, with burial in the same cemetery.

15. CORA, born circa 1878.

16. EDWARD M, born Nov. 28, 1879, died Apr. 12, 1946, in Caldwell County, with burial in Cedar Hill Cemetery. He was married circa 1909 to Sammy Felkner, and they had two sons: Howard (Burse?), born in 1910, died in 1967; and Harvey.

17. CARRIE, who died sometime after 1880 as an infant in Caldwell County.

I. ELIZA, born Aug. 1, 1820, and died Aug. 13, 1899. She was buried in the Hill family cemetery. Eliza was married circa 1839 to Robert Hill, Jr., who was born Aug. 6, 1806, and died May 13, 1884. Robert was the son of Robert Sr. and Sarah Slaton Hill. He first was married to Kezia Smith, daughter of Eleazor Smith and they had three children. After his marriage to Eliza

Deboe, they had ten children. Robert owned much land and a number of slaves, many of whom remained with him after they were freed. His homestead was three miles east of Crayne, Kentucky. The children of his first marriage all lived out their lives in Crittenden County, but a large number of the others moved to Washington State in the early 1900s. The children of Eliza and Robert were:

1. HASDON C. (Bulgar), born in circa 1840, died in 1917, and was married to Mary Jacobs.
2. VILENIA JERINE/JENNE, born in 1842 and was married to John Woodall, a first cousin, who was born Aug. 1, 1835, in Green County, Illinois.
3. SARAH ELLEN, born in 1844, died Oct. 4, 1866, and was married Dec. 8, 1862, to Samuel Allen Woodall, who was born Jan. 3, 1840, in Green County, Illinois and died July 24, 1912, in Lyon County, KY.
4. ROBERT HIATUS, born Feb. 27, 1845, died Feb. 21, 1916, and was married Nov. 19, 1868, to Harriet E. Farmer, who was born Nov. 2, 1848, in Tennessee and died Mar. 1, 1916, in Crittenden County, KY.
5. ANDREW SEXILE, born circa 1848, died in 1894, and was married to Sarah Adeline Travis Jan. 6, 1875.
6. MANDENA, born circa 1849, who died young.
7. WILLIAM ATTISON, born in 1852, and married Julia Parmely.
8. ARTIMISSA, born circa 1854, and was married Jan. 2, 1875, to James A. Parmely.
9. MARGARET MORELLA, born Aug. 23, 1858, died in 1918, and was married to L. M. Farmer on June 6, 1874.
10. ZILLA BELLE, born circa 1861, died in 1923, and was first married to Albert (Abb) Rushing and later to Henry Burr.

II
Mary (Polly) Debo Crider

Mary (Polly) Debo Crider, daughter of Philip Debo (2), was born in 1786 in Lancaster County, Pennsylvania, and died in November 1869 in Caldwell County, Kentucky. She was married by J. Hatchett on June 30, 1807, in Pittsylvania County, Virginia, to Samuel Crider, who was born April 21, 1783, in Philadelphia County, Pennsylvania, died April 24, 1843, in Crittenden County, Kentucky, and was buried in Piney Fork Cemetery in that county. Samuel was the son of Daniel Sr. and Catherine Berger Crider.

Early records show that Samuel and Polly, his young bride, arrived in western Kentucky as early as 1808, settling in what was then Livingston County. Samuel's brother Jacob and wife Mary Ritter Crider along with their family came to the same area at the same time. Shortly thereafter their brother Daniel Crider and family arrived after the taking of the 1810 Census. The area where the Crider brothers settled was in eastern Livingston County, but after April 1842 became a part of newly formed Crittenden County. Another Crider brother, Andrew, who married Polly's sister, Christina Debo, remained in Pittsylvania County, Virginia. At least one of their children, Nancy Crider Tosh, however, also settled later in the Crittenden County area of western Kentucky.

The children of Samuel and Polly Crider were:

A. DANIEL W, who was born circa 1808, probably in Livingston County, Kentucky, died April 25, 1839, in the same county, and possibly was buried in Piney Fork Cemetery in Crittenden County. (One family record indicates he was married August 24, 1826, to Elizabeth Reed, who was born in 1812. They were purported to have had two children: Solomon, born July 1, 1827; and Isabelle, born August 12, 1830. These children are not mentioned in either his will or in the estate settlement of his father, Samuel Crider.) Daniel was married by Samuel Glenn Oct. 4, 1832, in Caldwell County to Mary McElroy, who died before 1837, probably in Livingston County. Daniel and Mary had one daughter:

1. ARAMINTA (MINTY), born Aug. 22, 1833, died Jan. 16, 1852, in Crittenden County, and was buried in Piney Fork Cemetery. She was married Sept. 3, 1849, in Crittenden County to William Bennett Crider, a cousin, who was born April 10, 1828, in Livingston County, died Oct. 26, 1910 in Crittenden County, with burial at Piney Fork Cemetery. Minty died after the birth of a stillborn son, who was born that day.

Daniel was married by James Duvall on June 25, 1837, to Lilly Ann Bennett, who later was married to William Layton July 31, 1841, after Daniel's demise. Children of Daniel and Lilly Ann were:

2. ALLEN PEYTON, born circa 1838 and died before 1880, probably in 1876 in Lyons County. He was married on Jan. 21, 1860, in Crittenden County to Jane Edna Duvall, who was born circa 1843 and died after 1893.
3. MARY E., born in 1840, probably in Livingston County.

B. ORPHA (KATY), was born circa 1815 and died before 1843. She was married in Livingston County to Daniel Crider, Jr. (III), a first cousin, son of Daniel and Nancy Bennett Crider, who was born circa 1800 and died circa 1840. Children of Orpha and Daniel were:

1. NANCY CATHERINE, born between 1830 and 1840. She was married on 14 February 1848, in Crittenden County to John Aaron.
2. LUCINDA (LUCY), born in November 1833, and died in 1916 in Stigler, Haskell County, Oklahoma. She was married Oct. 23, 1849, by John Travis to William Thomason Pickering, born in 1822 and died after 1880.
3. SUSAN D., born between 1840 and 1842. She was married on April 27, 1858 to William S. Green, born in 1810 in North Carolina.

C. WILLIAM H., who was born in 1817, probably in Livingston County, and died in 1870, possibly in Johnson County, Illinois. He was first married April 9, 1837, in Livingston County to Matilda McElroy, who was born in 1812, probably Livingston County, and died between 1840 and 1842, Crittenden County.

1. Daughter Crider, born between 1835 and 1840, probably in Crittenden County, KY.
2. Son Crider, born between 1835 and 1840, probably in Crittenden County.
3. ALLEN P., born circa 1840 in Kentucky.
4. WILLIAM was married after Matilda's death a second time on Jan. 15, 1844, by John Travis to Sarah Carlton.
5. JOSEPHINE, born circa 1845 in Kentucky. She married John F. Gore, who was born in Illinois in 1840, and was later married to George W; Lambert. A third marriage was to John B. Harrison, born in 1848.
6. MARTHA A., born circa 1850 in Illinois.
D. FINIS (PHINEAS) EWING, who was born Dec. 1, 1818, in Livingston County and died Jan 21, 1881, in Moores Prairie Township, Jefferson County, Illinois. He was married by John Travis on Feb. 20, 1840, in Princeton, Caldwell County, Kentucky, to Sarah Towery, who was born in.1821 in Caldwell County and died in Jan. 1886 in Moores Prairie Township, Jefferson Township, Illinois. She was the daughter of Edward and Margaret McDowell Towery. Their children were:
1. MARGARET ANN (PEGGY), born Feb. 5, 1841, in Livingston County, KY, and died March 22, 1863, in Princeton, of childbirth. She was married on Feb. 14, 1870 in Caldwell County to James Bayliss Morse, who was born Sep. 3, 1843, in the same county, and died Dec. 30, 1915, in Mikesell Township, Kansas.
2. ELIZABETH JANE, born May 20,1844, in Caldwell County, and died Oct. 26, 1885, in Spring Garden, Jefferson County, Illinois, with burial in Union Cemetery, Ewing Township, Franklin County, Ill. She was married April 19, 1866, in Spring Garden to William Harrison McKenny, who was born May 3, 1846, in Union County, Kentucky, and died Aug. 11, 1906, in Franklin County, Ill. with burial in Union Cemetery.
3. GEORGE W., born March 30, 1847' Caldwell County, and died January 24, 1924, at Pearson, Cleburne County, Arkansas. He was married to Priscilla Neal, who was born in 1852 and died in 1928.
4. SAMUEL L., born circa 1848 in Caldwell County, and died

before 1870 (possibly in the War Between the States).

5. WILLIAM, born Nov. 1, 1852, in Caldwell County, and died Jan. 6, 1916. He first was married to Cora Fergus and later to Rado King.

6. LEWIS CASS, born Jan. 23, 1856, in Caldwell County, and died July 23, 1944. He married Zetta Border.

7. SARAH, born circa 1860 in Caldwell County, and died before 1870, probably in Kentucky.

8. MARY M., born Nov 20,1861, in Caldwell County, died May 13, 1953 in Atlanta, Logan County, Illinois, with burial in Union Cemetery, Franklin County, Ill. She was married to Edward Tucker, born in 1861 and died in 1941, with burial in the same cemetery.

E. MARY, born circa 1822 in Crittenden County, Kentucky, and died before 1860 in the same county. She was married on Feb. 12, 1840 in Livingston County to Joseph McDowell, who was born in 1821 and died before Dec. 1854 in Crittenden County. He was the son of John and Elizabeth Boyd McDowell. Children of Mary and Joseph McDowell were:

1. CYNTHIA E., born circa 1842 in Crittenden County, and died in 1909 in Caldwell County, with burial in Rowland Cemetery, Flat Rock, KY. She first was married to David Prowell Feb. 22, 1856, in Crittenden County, who was born circa 1834 in Smith County, Tennessee, and died between 1866 and 1870 in Crittenden County. She was later married on May 18, 1871, in Crittenden County to Asbury Traylor, born in 1837 and died in 1898 in Caldwell County with burial in Rowland Cemetery.

2. ALFRED, born circa 1844 in Crittenden County, Kentucky.

3. JULIA ANN, born Oct. 7, 1844, probably in Crittenden County, died Jan. 4, 1917, in Crtittenden County with burial in Sugar Grove Cemetery of that county. She was married on Jan. 6, 1867, in the same county by Mabron Marlow to John Seth Corley, born Feb. 8, 1847 in Smith County, Tennessee, and died Feb. 29, 1936, in Crittenden County.

4. JOSEPH MARION, born Feb. 3, 1850, in Crittenden County, and died July 3, 1924, in Caldwell County with burial in Piney Fork Cemetery of the same county. He was married on Jan. 29, 1871, in the same county to Sarah Elizabeth

(Bettie) Matthews, who was born in June 1849 in Kentucky, died March 24, 1928, in Enon, KY, with burial in Piney Fork Cemetery.

5. LOUISA JANE (ELIZA), born March 15, 1852, in Crittenden County, and died Oct. 20, 1893, with burial in Piney Fork Cemetery. She was married to Thomas Ezekial Porter on Nov. 23, 1876, in Crittenden County. He was born Dec. 10, 1850, in Kentucky and died Jan. 11, 1895, in the same county with burial in Piney Fork Cemetery.

F. PERMELIA, born May 21, 1823, in Livingston County, Kentucky, and died Nov. 7, 1909, in Crittenden County with burial in Shady Grove Cemetery of the same county. She was married on Oct. 21, 1840, in Livingston County to John M. McDowell, son of John and Elizabeth Boyd McDowell, who was born Apr. 22, 1816, in Kentucky, and died March 8, 1881, in Crittenden County, with burial in Shady Grove Cemetery. Their children were:

1. LINDLEY M., born Feb. 2, 1844, in Crittenden County, died Oct. 14, 1862, probably in the same county, with burial in Olive Branch Cemetery of that county.

2. DANIEL JASPER, born Nov. 18, 1847, in Caldwell County, died Oct. 31, 1929, in Crittenden County, with burial in Shady Grove Cemetery. He was married Oct. 15, 1874, in the same county to Elizabeth Ann Casner, who was born July 6, 1855, in the same county and died June 4, 1941, in Webster County, Kentucky, with burial in Shady Grove Cemetery of Crittenden County.

3. JAMES H., born circa 1850 in Kentucky, died March 10, 1929, with burial in Shady Grove Cemetery. He married R. I. C. (Unknown).

4. JOHN SHELTON, born Feb. 21,1852, in Kentucky.

5. SAMUEL D., born in Feb. 1854 in Caldwell County and died Aug. 21, 1917, in Crittenden County with burial in Shady Grove Cemetery. He first was married Oct. 26, 1873 in Caldwell County to Nannie Caroline Scott, who was born Nov. 6, 1857, and died March 9, 1895 in Crittenden County with burial in the same cemetery. He later was married on Dec. 12, 1897, in Crittenden County to Frances (Fannie) Mullen.

6. PERMELIA CAROLINE, born Feb. 10, 1856, in Kentucky, and died Sept. 10, 1923, in Caldwell County with burial in White Sulfur Springs Cemetery, Caldwell County, KY. She was married Feb. 19, 1873, in the same county to C. C./S. Williamson, who was born Sept. 18, 1851, in Kentucky and died Jan. 2, 1921, with burial in the same cemetery.

7. JOSEPH M. (JOE), born May 15, 1858, in Kentucky and-died June 4, 1913, in Caldwell County with burial in Shady Grove Cemetery, Crittenden County. He was married in 1884 to Sarah M. (Sallie) McDowell, born circa 1866 in Kentucky and died Jan. 26, 1914, in Caldwell County with burial in Shady Grove Cemetery.

8. SARAH ANN (SALLIE), born in Jan. 1861 in Crittenden County and died probably in the same county with burial in Shady Grove Cemetery. She was married July 24, 1881, in Caldwell County to Rufus M. Riley, born in July 1851 in Kentucky and died in 1927, probably in Crittenden County with burial in Shady Grove Cemetery.

G. SAMUEL FRANKLIN, born May 10, 1828, in Livingston County, Kentucky, died Sept. 10, 1856, in Crittenden County with burial in Piney Fork Cemetery, same county. He was married March 23, 1848, in Crittenden County to Mary Salena Crider, daughter of Samuel and Polly Foster Crider, who was born Jan. 25, 1830, in Livingston County, KY.

Their children were:

1. MARY J., born in 1849. She was married Aug. 11, 1867, in McDonald County, Missouri, to James M. Whitten.

2. ELIZABETH ANN, born in 1850.

3. SARAH L/S, born in 1852.

4. MATILDA FRANCES, born Jan. 8, 1853. She married Jackson Washington Corker.

5. GEORGIAN ANN (GEORGIE), born May 7, 1854. She was married Dec. 25, 1873, in Newton County, Missouri, to Isaac Newton Adkins.

6. PRESLEY DAVIS, born April 14, 1856, in Crittenden County, Kentucky, and died Nov. 19, 1857, in the same county, burial in Piney Fork Cemetery of that county.

III
Sarah (Sally) Debo Hughey

Sarah (Sally) Debo, daughter of Philip (2), was born in 1791 in Pittsylvania County, Virginia, and died Jan. 12, 1855, in Lyon County, Kentucky, the only one of his children born in Virginia. She was married December 26, 1811, in Pittsylvania County to Coleman Hughey by Joseph Hatchett. Abraham Debo was named as bondsman and her father was listed as Philip Debo Sr. Coleman died sometime before 1840 and possibly before 1830, because Sally probably came to Kentucky with her Debo siblings and others in 1830 and was listed as a widow by the time of the 1840 Census. Some of the Hugheys had migrated to Kentucky before Sally's brother Philip (3) came, possibly around 1810, at the same time that Samuel and Polly Crider, her brother-in-law and sister, came.

Coleman Hughey's father, Robert Hughey, came to America in 1776 as a drafted soldier under Sir Henry Clinton, and was in Colonel Tarleton's command at the battle of Cowpens, when he was captured by the American forces Jan. 17, 1781. Robert chose to remain in America after the war, and he and three of his sons defended their adopted country against the British in the War of 1812, from which they each held an honorable discharge. Robert was born in Glasgow, Scotland, in 1738 and was married to Lewraney Smith of Virginia in 1782, who was of Welsh descent. To them were born Allen, John, Sarah, Coleman, William, James, and Mornen.

After coming to Kentucky, supposedly in 1830, Sally and her four children would be found throughout the coming years in the area of Caldwell, Crittenden, Livingston, and Lyon counties of western Kentucky. As the last child of Philip Debo (2), she, her sister Mary (Polly), and brother Philip (3) would spend their remaining days in that state, while her remaining sibling all remained in Virginia, along with two of Philip's (3) sons, Benjamin and Joseph. Most of the Virginia group lived in Pittsylvania County, while Michael had moved over into adjoining Bedford County where he reared a large family and amassed quite an acreage for his plantation.

The children of Sally and Coleman Hughey are as follows:

A. MICHAEL, born circa 1812 in Bedford County, Virginia, and died sometime after 1873 in Lyon County, Kentucky. He was married seven times and had six children:

    1. Wife #1: Letitia Thompson, married Jan. 20, 1836, in Caldwell County, Kentucky, by Robert L. Cobb. No children.

    2. Wife #2: Muhuldah Thompson, Sept. 6, 1838, in the same county by W. Cash.

    3. Wife #3: Sarah Fralie, married July 6, 1840, in the same county by W. C. Love. Sarah was born circa 1825, died before 1848, and they had one daughter, Patricia Ann, who was born in April 1842 and died Feb. 28, 1868.

    4. Wife #4: Rebecca (last name unknown), married circa 1848, and they had three children: Rachel M., John D., and Elizabeth E.

    5. Wife #5: Jane Woodall, married Mar. 21, 1854; no children.

    6. Wife #6: Margaret Richards, married Jan. 30, 1855; two children, Mary K. and Margaret M.

    7. 7. Wife #7: Mary Russell, married Jan. 11, 1873.

B. ELIZABETH L., born circa 1814 and died Aug. 21, 1855, in Lyon County, KY of pneumonia. She married Stephen R. B. McElroy on March 26, 1838, in Caldwell County. He was born circa 1814. They had two children: Emily E. C. and Gilba.

C. WILLIAM ROBERT, born Mar. 9, 1818, and died Sept. 4, 1872. He was married to Ann Fraley Nov. 20, 1838, in Caldwell County. She was born Feb. 26, 1822, and died before Jan. 9, 1877. They had four children: Henry C., David E., Sarah L., and Daniel W.

D. COLEMAN A., born circa 1822 and died before 1860, who first married Elizabeth Moreland Dec. 26, 1842, in Caldwell County by J. W. Temple. She died before 1849, and they had two children: Thomas B. and Elizabeth A. He later was married on April 30, 1849, in Livingston County to Minerva Moreland (possibly Elizabeth's sister), who was born circa 1828. There were three children: Sarah E., William R., and Coleman A.

Sally Debo Hughey was married a second time to Robert Hughey on December 23, 1850, by James H. Owen in Caldwell County, Kentucky. He was born in Virginia circa 1811, died before 1860 in Kentucky, and was possibly a half-brother to her first husband, Coleman Hughey. Sally died Jan. 12, 1855, in Lyon County of what was noted as "fever pruperal." Robert later married a Mrs. Katherine Langsdon in Crittenden County on Feb. 4, 1857, and probably died before 1860 since he was not listed in the Census of that year; she is listed as a widow with four Langsdon children.

Chapter VII

"Other" Kentucky and Missouri Debo(e)s

[This chapter has delayed this book in time because of a lack of authentic information, the lack of knowledge as to how to organize what data I have gathered, and the need to use my own guesses and suppositions in presenting historical narrative (which I have always abhorred). Thus, in order to complete this work I have decided to go ahead and present the information I have in the best way I can with the hope that others in some future time may use what I have given and amplify the data to a greater degree. -The Author]

In Chapter III of this work I stated that the following branches of the family were possible descendants of John Conrad Debo, son of Philip(1), the immigrant. My considered thinking and opinion on the matter has not changed, even though I have no further authentic evidence to prove my contention and theory.

By 1775 (age 37) John Conrad was living in Dunmore County, Virginia, in the Shenandoah Valley (in 1778 Dunmore County was changed to Shenandoah County). In Capt. John Denton's census list of 1775, he was enumerated as having 5 white males and 3 white females in his family, and he was also on a list of men in the lower district of Dunmore County in a military unit under the command of Capt. Joseph Bowman. In the Virginia Census of 1790 he is reported living in Shenandoah County in 1785 with a family of 8 white souls, and possessing 1 dwelling and 2 other buildings. John C. Deboe and wife Esther (maiden name unknown) bought 200 acres of land in Berkford Parish from Christian Miller, but sold that same acreage in 1789 to Christian Stover.

My opinion is that Anne, Martin, Joseph, Henry, and possibly Ransom Debo were either children of John C. and Esther Deboe or grandchildren, and they later emigrated to Kentucky. In a letter dated Oct. 30, 1966, to Mr. Alex Rorer (a copy of which is in the possession of the author), Mrs. Alex M. Bower of Nicholasville (Jessamine County), Kentucky, gave the following account: "William Jameson married Ann

Deboe. He was supposed to have been a captain in the British army during the Revolution, and when quartered at the house of a French lady by the name of Deboe in Virginia, met and fell in love with her daughter Anne and married her. After the war they moved to Kentucky and settled in Jessamine Co. Joe Deboe, Sr., is supposed to be the brother of Anne. He had two sons, Joe and Tom." Mrs. Bower also reported that the 1850 Census for Jessamine County, Kentucky, named an 82-year-old man named Martin Deboe, who was born in Kentucky but whose parents were born in Virginia.

In 1972 a researcher whom I had used for some work, Mrs. Weldon Simpson of Nicholasville, Kentucky, found that the Deboes first bought land in Jessamine County in 1816 when Joseph purchased property in Nicholasville from James Carr. Joseph bought and sold much real estate in that county.

Anne Deboe

Anne Deboe was the daughter of a "French lady." Possibly the "French lady" was John Conrad's wife Esther; and since John Conrad was not mentioned, perhaps he was already dead or away in the Colonial army. Anne was born circa 1755 and died in 1818 (her husband, William James, was born circa 1755 and died in 1814). My assumption is that the Jamesons moved to Kentucky in the early 1780s. Anne and William's son William was born circa 1783 in Virginia, and son David in 1784, also in Virginia. Their son Bird was born in 1800 in Kentucky. Other Jameson children included John, Kitty, Jinny, and Archibald. William was born in 1783 and died May 16, 1877. He was married to Seluda Willis, born in 1785 and died before 1870.

David Jameson (another source says he was born in 1781) died Dec. 31, 1859, and was married twice: first, circa 1812 to (1) Mary (Polly) Jackson, born in 1794 and died in 1827; later, circa 1828 to Eliza Kersey, born Oct. 11, 1799, and died sometime after 1870. David and Polly had six children: Mary, born circa 1813 and died after 1854; (2) John Bluford, born circa 1814 and died after 1854; (3) Nancy Ann, born July 3, 1816, and died in 1902, who married Joseph Robb; (4) Rebecca J., born circa 1826 and died after 1854; (5) Tilford, born in 1820 and died after 1854; (6) Emily, born in 1826 and died after 1854. David and Eliza, his second wife, had seven children: (1) Henrietta, born circa 1829, who was married to Joseph Davis, born circa 1824; (2) David, born in 1830; (3) Cassandra, born in 1832, who was married to Louis H. Ferrill, born in 1829; (4) Eliza, born in 1833; (5) Ashford, born in 1835; (6) Meredith

K., born in 1837; (7) George, born in 1839.

There was another Anne Deboe and I'm not sure where she fits in. When Mrs. Bowers stated that Anne (who married William Jameson) was Joseph Deboe, Sr.'s, sister, I believe she got this second Anne Deboe mixed up with her because of the dates involved. This second Anne was born circa 1796 in Kentucky, about four years after Joseph Deboe, Sr.'s birth in 1792 and about two years before Martin Deboe was born in 1798. All three of these were married in Jessamine County, Kentucky. Anne married Pascal Broaddus (also spelled Paskil Broadas on the license) Dec. 21, 1815. He was born Dec. 1, 1796, and died in Kentucky in 1848. They had four known children: (1) Nancy Jane, 1817; (2) Joseph, 1818; (3) Beverly, 1820; and (4) Greenberry, 1823.

Joseph Deboe, Sr.

According to Joseph Deboe's will, dated Nov. 29, 1860, proven and presented on Dec. 17, 1860, he was about 68 years old when the will was made, indicating that he was born circa 1792 in Virginia. He was married June 29, 1824, in Jessamine County, Kentucky, to Milly Hudson, daughter of Joshua Hudson.

Joe and Milly Deboe had eleven children, including three triplet daughters. The children are as follows: (1) Frances (Fanny, born circa 1824; (2) Joseph T. (Joe), born circa 1825; (3) Western, born circa 1825/26, married a Nancy _____, and later lived in North Carolina for awhile; (4, 5, 6) the triplets, Mary, Martha, and Margaret, born in 1827; (7) Philadelphia, born in 1829 and married Richard T. Newland; (8) Sarah Elizabeth, born circa 1832, who was married March 13, 1855, to Thomas M. Mcilvain, who was born March 13, 1830; (9) Thomas (Tom), born in 1833; (10) Lucretia, born in 1836; and (11) Times (or Tines), born in 1839.

Martin Deboe

Martin Deboe was born in 1798, and was married September 19, 1835, to Lydia Walls, daughter of Eliza W. Walls. Lydia was born in 1806. One known child of this couple was a daughter, Martha E., born in 1837.

****

Henry Debo

The 1830 U.S. Census for Jefferson County (Louisville), Kentucky, lists a Henry Debo, born circa 1780-85, probably in Virginia. No female of near his age is listed, indicating possibly that his wife was deceased. A male, age 20~30; a male 15-20; a female 10-15; and two females 10-15 constituted his family. One son, Horatio D. Debo, born ca. 1807 in Virginia and a daughter, Elizabeth D. Debo, are known. It is my considered opinion because of the date of Henry's birth, the place of his son's birth, and an educated guess (which I hate to use in a historical presentation) that Henry was one of the sons of John Conrad Debo of Shenandoah County, Virginia - and I haven't been able to prove it. Henry died sometime prior to 1850. His daughter, Elizabeth, was married Dec. 3, 1835, to William Griffin, and that is the only data I have been able to ascertain about her.

Horatio Debo (listed as "Bibo" in the 1850 Census) was born in 1807 in Virginia and was married Dec. 8, 1831, in Kentucky to Elizabeth Porter, who was born in 1817 in Maryland. The 1840 Census lists two slaves, 1 male 10-24 and 1 female 10-24 along with 2 employed in agriculture. The known children of Horatio and Elizabeth Debo consisted of six sons, all of whom were born in Kentucky:

1. Richard - b. 1836
2. John - b. 1837
3. William Henry - b. 1840
4. Samuel- b. 1842
5. Francis (Frank) - b. 1846
6. Alonzo - b. 1848

The 1840 Census taken Aug. 29, 1850, reveals Horatio's worth as being $1,000 and his occupation was noted as a carpenter. The information I have been able together consists of only the line of William Henry, the third son.

William Henry Debo was born circa 1840 in Louisville, Jefferson County, Kentucky. At age 25 he was mustered into the 55th Mounted Kentucky Infantry (Union) with Gen. McLean Division commander, according to the Adjutant General's Report, State of KY, (Vol. 11, 1861-1866). After the conclusion of the war, he was mustered out on Sept. 19, 1865. He then came to Callaway County, Missouri, and was later married there November 26, 1874, to Nancy Jane (Nannie) Dunn. They had nine children, all of whom were born and reared in Missouri in Callaway and Audrain counties.

[Following is the obituary of William Henry Debo in the Mexico [Mo.] Evening Ledger of Nov. 1, 1915.]

W. H. DEBO DEAD - Dies at the hospital Sunday afternoon.

Burial in Callaway.

W. H. Debo, 75 years old, died Sunday afternoon of a complication of diseases. The funeral will be Tuesday [Nov. 2] at New Bloomfield. Mr. Debo was born in Louisville, Ky. He lived in Callaway county for a number of years and moved to this city [Mexico] later.

He leaves a wife and the following children: Sam, Springfield; Richard, Martinsburg; Mattie and Lonnie of this city. Mr. Debo was a fine man and well liked by all who knew him. The Ledger joins the many friends of the family in extending sympathy to the bereaved.

The nine children of William Henry and Nancy Jane (Nannie) Debo were: [taken from the family Bible in possession of Richard S. Debo of Wellsville, MO, 1955.]

1. Maggie Helen (Nellie) - b. Nov. 9, 1875; d. Oct. 31, 1915. She was married Jan. 9, 1895, to William Bull.
2. Samuel Wallace - b. Apr. 30, 1877; d. Mar. 17, 1932
3. Ora Elizabeth - b. Apr. 7, 1880; d. Oct 31, 1888
4. Richard Sanford - b. Mar. 16, 1882; d. Jan. 1966. He was married to Clara May Wallace Dec. 28, 1908. She died in 1969.
   Children of Richard S. and Clara W. Debo are:
   a. Floyd - b. Sept. 16, 1910; died Sept. 10, 1990.
   b. Richard L. -
   c. Ralph- b. Dec. 11, 1912; died. July 7,1992.
   d. Wallace -- d. 1961
   e. Harold
   f. Dorothy
   g. Thelma
5. Montie Churchel- b. Apr 2,1884; d. Aug. 2, 1884.
6. Albert Warner - b. Oct. 2, 1885
7. James Grover - b. Jan. 19, 1888. He was married Dec. 28, 1910, in Mexico, MO, to Martha Ann Mudd.
   Children of Grover James and Martha Ann Debo are:
   a. Agnes Marie - b. Oct 2, 1911. She was first married to Arthur Elmore in Feb. 1940 in Kansas City, MO .. They had a daughter, Patricia Annette Elmore, b. Nov. 7, 1942 Agnes Marie was later married to Clarence Kibodeaux on Dec. 18, 1944, and they had a daughter, Karen Marie, b. Nov. 23, 1946, who married Terry Lee.
   b. Charles Ivan- b. Aug. 11, 1912, Mexico, MO, who was mar-

ried Nov. 22, 1941, to Rijetta Alma Carlin. Charles Ivan enlisted in the U.S. Army Oct. 23, 1940, and was discharged June 21, 1943. Served as a police officer in Monrovia, CA since 1949.

1. Charles Wamer- h. Jan. 5,1944, Pasadena, CA.
2. James Anthony - b. Dec. 9, 1948, Pasadena, CA.
3. David Michael- b. Apr. 16, 1954, Pasadena, CA.

c. Hazel Lyda- b. Feb. 21, 1914. She first was married to Jack Park Feb. 17, 1932 in Kansas City, MO. Their children were:
1. Grover Freemont - b. Apr. 12, 1934 in British Columbia, Canada.
2. Gene Ronell- b. June 19, 1935.
3. Robert Donald - b. May 15, 1937.
4. David Brandor - b. Dec. 24, 1938.

She was later married to Robert Conley in Feb. 1953 in Kansas City.

8. Mattie Grace - b. Nov. 26, 1892; d. Mar. 6, 1926; She was married Dec. 15, 1919 to Stanley Devers.
9. William Alonzo (Lonnie) - b. June 27,1895; d. Oct. 31, 1915

Child of Lonnie and Georgia Ann Debo is:

a. William Bruce, b. Nov. 28, 1920; died Dec. 5,2002, who married Thelma Ann Elizabeth Leach, b. July 7, 1917; died May 17,2005. They were married Aug. 22, 1942. They lived in Devils Elbow, Missouri. Their children were:
1. Deborah Ann - b. Jan. 20, 1947
2. William Theodore (Bill) - b. Jan. 17, 1950. He was first married Sept. 8, 1973, to Sheila Kay Marsh, b. Aug. 19, 1953. They had a daughter, Jennifer Jean, b. Oct. 11, 1975. Bill was divorced in 1986, and later was married Apr. 9, 1993, to Carmen Lucas, b. Oct. 14, 1949.
   a. Jennifer Jean - b. Oct. 11, 1975 - was married Jan. 27, 2006, to Larry Dean Kelley, b. June 7, 1964. They had two children: Blayne William Edward - b. July 20, 1997; and Klara Paige - b. Oct. 28, 1998.

+++++

(There is another Debo family, the males of whom were born in Kentucky but later moved to Missouri, settling mostly in the Callaway and Audrain counties area. I have not been able to decipher to whom they belonged, but I am fairly confident that there is a connection with the rest of the Debos of

that area. I am including the data that I have in the hopes that some future researcher may settle the matter.)

John and Henry Debo, both of whom were born in Kentucky, John in 1818 and Henry in 1819, were evidently brothers, who married sisters. John married Ann Snell 23 September 1835. She was born in Indiana in 1815. Henry married Mary Snell 20 July 1841. She was born in 1821, also in Indiana. The marriages occurred in Callaway County, Missouri. Henry's wife, Mary, presumably died some time in the 1850s, for he later was married 24 January 1855 in Callaway County to Lucy Ann Setton.

The known children of John and Ann Snell Debo (all of whom were born in Missouri) were:

1. John H. - b. 1834, d. 19 December 1877. He was married to Mary E., who was born in 1833.
2. Samuel G. - b. 1836, d. 12 October 1867. He was married 1 September 1859 to Sarah Ann Austin, who was born in 1840.
3. Willis S. - b. 1842, d. 29 Aug. 1914. He was married 18 February 1868 to Ann Maria Carew, who was born in 1848.
4. Unknown-b. 18-
5. Millard Fillmore - b. 1852, d. 1916. He was married to Virginia E., who was born 2 February 1857 and died 17 May 1914.

Known children of Henry and Mary Snell Debo, all born in Missouri, were:

1. Nathan - b. 1842
2. William - b. 1844
3. John- b. 1845
4. Henry - b. 1849

(Following is some information gathered from various sources regarding the Debos in Callaway County that may be of use to future researchers.)

Deaths

Virginia E. Debo, wife ofM. F. - Feb. 2, 1857-May 17, 1914. Buried in Mt. Carmel Cemetery, 2 miles southwest of Fulton, MO, on Highway 54.

Nancy J. Debo, wife of Willis S. - d. June 17, 1896 - 52 years, 10 mos., 5 days. Buried in Prairie Chapel Cemetery, 8 miles northwest of Fulton.

John A. Debo, son of S. and S. A. - 1862-1884. Buried in Unity Baptist Cemetery, 7 miles south of Cal wood, MO.

Millard Debo, 1852-1916. Unity Baptist Cemetery. Elizabeth Debo, 1851-1890. Unity Baptist Cemetery.

Sam D. Debo, Dec. 1878 - Aug. 23, 1943. Buried in New Hope Cemetery, 1-1/2 miles South of Calwood, MO.

Martha J. Debo, May 26, 1849 - Feb. 19, 1926. New Hope Cemetery.

Henry Debo, Mar. 11, 1812 - June 24, 1901. New Hope Cemetery.

Marriages 1870-1922

1871 - August 13 - Annie Debo and Frederick Rigel

1872 - April 30 - Deborah A. Debo and Mark A. Craghead

1874 - February 5 - John S. Debo and Eliza J. Martin

1874 - March 18 - Henry C. Debo and Sarah E. Martin

1874 - November 26 - William H. Debo and Nancy J. Dunn

1875 - February 23 - Henry Debo and Martha Jane Bell

1877 - March 15 - Sallie A. Debo and Charles F. Boyer

1878 - January 16 - Mary F. Debo and Daniel N. Smith

1879 - December 25 - Catherine Jane Debo and William S. Owen

1882 - December 7 - Millard Fillmore Debo and Mrs. Bettie Williamson

1883 - January 15 - John S. Debo and Margarette Harvey

1885 - August 12 - Laura J. Debo and John H. Hill

1887 - January 12 - Willis S. Debo and Nancy J. Hill

1887 - March 21 - Julia V. Debo and Charles K. Gray

1891 - May 4 - Sarah A. Debo and Rev. Zachries Jones

1891- November 11- Dora Debo and Payton Foy

1893 - September 13 - Thomas J. Debo and Miss O. J. Wiggs

1895 - February 5 - Miss Elmer M. Debo and Alfred F. Kimball

1895 - August 1 - Miss Nellie Debo and William Bull

1897 - March 23 - W. S. Debo and Mrs. Oley Lawrence

1898 - April 4 - Nettie Debo and Charles A. Cuno

1898 - December 18 - Charles F. Debo and Lula Davis

1901 - December 18 - Minnie Debo and Thomas L. Lockridge

1902 - August 3 - Samuel M. Debo and Minnie E. Strickland

1908 - November 19 - Grace Debo and Vollie C. Robertson

1908 - December 28 - Richard S. Debo and Clara May Wallace

1913 - November 17 - Millard Fillmore Debo and Mrs. Virginia Baysinger

1915 - December 31 - John T. Debo and Lillie Branditz

1916 - November 29 - Esther Debo and W. D. McClellan

1917 - October 10- C. Frank: Debo and Mrs. Eva Ritter

1919 - December 14 - Mattie Debo and Stanley Owens

Audrain County

1910 - September 14 - Warner Debo and Miss Lydia Mudd

1910 - December 28 - Grover J. Debo and Miss Martha A. Mudd

Appendices

A. This snakebite recipe was found in the old Cornelius Debo family Bible, and I have deemed it worthy of inclusion in this family history.

Take pulverized alum and table salt and wet enough to make a poultice. Bind it on the bite and eat a piece the size of a buck shot.

B. Letters:
1. This letter (1863) is from an unknown Confederate soldier from Fauquier County, Virginia, to Sarah James (Sallie) Debo, whom he had seen in the hospital while she was in Richmond to see after her brother, Cornelius Debo, who was there with the measles.

    To Miss Sallie Debo

    You will I have no doubt be somewhat astonished to receive a letter of this discription from one with whom you are not at all acquainted. I am not the least acquainted with you only if I should again see your face I shold (k)now who you was by hearing others call your name. I have seen you regular in the past few days at Chimborazo Hospital near Richmond. I was anxious to become acquainted with you but was very unwell and low spirited. So I could not conveniently do what my heart promted me to do more than once. I am at a loss how to express the thousands of thoughts which now pass through my sickened heart. Oh if I only was acquainted with you I could better tell you what I now wish to do. But alas I am lost indeed in writing a letter to one who is a stranger to me.

    You started home unspected to me. I had understood you was not going home for several days. Therefore I was satisfied I would become acquainted with you before you started home. This grieves me. Shal I ever see you again? This is now the mystery which I cannot solve, shal I introduce to you my desire or shal I not. Oh I fear to do so for fear of giving offense. Let me say at the sight of you I was silenced and my heart throbed quick and fast and I could not for my life keep my eyes from you during the time of your pressence I believe you saw me gazing at you several times, which I hope you will pardon me for that which I could not help. Believe me when I first saw you I certainly came near starting to you thinking you was the sweet Sister which bid farewell to two years ago in yonder Fauquiere County. You are her identical picture believe me. But when I had gotten nearer to you I found that you was a stranger to me.

Let me tell you some truths although you are [un] acquainted with me. I am a resident of the County of Culpeper Virginia. I am a member of the 9th Va. Regiment now in the noble army of the Potomac and I never addressed but one young lady on the subject of matrimony and the happy moment never came to pass that I could call her mine own. (She was numbered with the blessed I hope) and I have never offered my heart to another since that time which has bin about three years but I am now resolved to offer it again. Was there ever a letter written to a lady in this manner before. I do not suppose there was. The writer is lost what to say and asshamed of an act of this sort which I may never be forgiven for indeed. Miss Sallie this is a bold step in me but how shal I ever make known to you my heart.

This may never reach you as I am not certain that I have your address properly.

Therefore I shal not sighn my name. I shal write to you again in a few days and shal assume the boldness to ask a few lines from you to know if my letters will be accepted by you. Your departure grieved me. .

A revival of religion is now going on here in the hospital church in my hearing which I am absent from. You will see I am a poor penman and am not posted in writing letters of this kind. I fear this will be the greatest insult to you, let it not Miss Sallie. I must now end this letter believe this as from one who is well pleased with you.

Chimborazo Ward 8
Richmond

May the 9th 1863

* * * * *

2.   A letter (1872) from Cornelius Debo to his brother Reed in Missouri, telling of his journey to Williamson County, Texas, from Missouri.

Mr. Reed P. Debo, Dear Brother

If you would like to know what I am doing and where I am just be patient and read this.

I could not begin to give you all the details of the trip. I can only tell you which way we came and that we had no axidents except such as one common to people traveling in that rout. We came by Baxter Springs [Kansas] and crossed the Arkansas river at Fort Gibson [Oklahoma] and camped Redriver at Colberts ferry and on to Sherman Texas. With three leading points and one who has ever went that rout can tell you any thing you want to know about the places we passed by.

Our teams all held out finely and we did not suffer on the road for any thing except water and not much for that. We stoped in Tarrant county [Texas] a week and all became dissatisfied before we had been there a week and such as were able hitched up and rolled down here where I believe all are pleased with the country and people.

Clay [Bowmer, Cornelius' brother-in-law] has rented a farm and is sowing wheat and seems to be well pleased with the prospect. Sallie [Cornelius' sister] is wonderfully pleased with her 1001 new aunts and cousins and uncles and so forth that she found in this county.

Thomas has hired to a farmer for $20 in gold a month. I went to Austin last Saturday to see how plastering is and I found plasterers enough there to put work out at 8 cts. I went to the old plasterers and they told me they had not had a job for four months because they would not work for less than 12 cts and the new comers would work at 8. I have been asking at all the towns away from the R.R. how plastering is and I know of several places where business is lively at 25 cts for good any town off from the R.R. its 25 cts for brown work.

I took my mules to Austin to see what I could do with them. I found big mules very dull sale because money is mighty scarce in Texas. I managed to sell them for $375 in gold cash. I sold my wagon for $80 in gold so now I have nothing left to trade except the saddle and it attracts more attention than anything else.

From the time I began to buy up my outfit counting all of

my expences up to the time I got here with the sales I have made after taking out the expences I have all my money back in gold and $80 over all in gold.

There is no Greenback in circulation here but when a man says dollars here he means gold or silver. They take greenback at 90 cts at stores but brokers must have it at 87-112 cts.

Reed I wish you would find out exactly where the Tinsley boys [who had served in the same Virginia regiment with the Debo boys] are and let me know as soon as possible so I can call on them when I pass that way. My address will be Bagdad [near present-day Leander] for the present but I don't know how long. But just direct to Bagdad Texas and I'll get it some time or other.

I have no more to write so I close.

As ever Cornelius Debo

To R. P. Debo

* * * * *

3. A letter (1891) from Cornelius Debo sometime after he had had a sunstroke to his brother, Reed Debo, in Missouri.

Burnet, Txs Dec 25 1891

Dear Brother

I guess I'll try and write you another letter. I recon you thought I was meddling where I had no business when you read my July letter which you did not answer, but if you rember [remember] I always did meddle in such cases.

We are all as well as common. I can go where I please in good weather and work some but when the weather is bad I have to keep close. I take cold just like some old woman and then it sets me back again.

I've raised a good crop of com, cotton, sorgham (for feed), potatoes, melons, peaches, and acorns. I had a good many big hogs and they all got fat on the mast. I have sold several they are worth 3-1/2 gross on 5 cts net.

I have five more big ones ready to kill for our own meat when the weather gets right.

I keep a hand hired all the time so that the children can all go to school. We built a splendid new school house just one mile from here and sold the old one. We have 65 scholars and room enough for as many more. Our teacher is a Methodist local preacher. Our children are all learning rapidly and all take a pride in trying to stand at the head of their classes just like father's children did some half century or so ago (more or less). I have good hopes of them taking an education if they get a chance. We are only sending five. Our Clay is just like his dady was at his age and Eppa is exactly like Thomas every motion and every expression makes me think of him (headache and all). I don't know who the others are like.

We are expecting Dabney and Clay' s [Bowmer] girls and his soninlaw to come and spend the Christmas with us but there is nothing sure about it since it rains so much.

When you go in a crowd here you can rarely hear any thing talked of except the Alliance the sub Treasury and the third party. There are plenty of men here that can not write their name nor pay for the bread and meat their family eats nor buy shoes for their wife and babies nor buy schoolbooks for their chaps nor pay the preacher one nickel, but they can tell you exactly how to payoff the U.S. debt and relieve the financial pressure and lift the burden from the shoulders of the laboring class of people. I have about as much use for such political dodges as father used to have and it takes me about as long to tell them so but maybe I have not got since enough to see into it as nearly all my neighbors do.

Our preacher this year is one of our own raising, licensed as a local at our church here. 8 years ago joined the itinerant ranks five years ago has been off ever since till last conference they sent him back here. Every body loves him.

I will close by asking you to read this if you can and then write to me as soon as you can afterward.

Respectfully as ever, Cornelius Debo

[The letter was written on pages from an old church register. D.D.] P.S. We bought a new one [church register] and I am using what is left of the old one. Our paper is all at the school house. C. D.

* * * * *

4. A letter (1894) from Reed Debo in Missouri to his brother Cornelius in Texas.

Bedford, Mo. Nov. 12th, 1894
7 0' clock at night

Dear Bro.

You wrote me in August and I ought to have answered it but I was waiting to find a suitable time to write a long letter but that time don't show up so I'll take 2 or 3 nights and write anyhow. So I'll begin on this piece till the girls come home from the singing school and tell me where the paper is at. We are all real well & have been OK for a long time 2 yrs or more. But we cain't boast of the rains you can. We had a good rain the last of June & no more until 2nd of Sept. but com is better than we expected to find it is worth 40 cts. A bushel here & $2 a barrel down at Boonville. I have 36 acres to gather yet 12 of that will be to sell. I think there is 35 bushels per acres. Wheat was very good but not so much raised here as down in the river country. I have some of that to sell yet its worth from 45 to 50 cts I have 50 acres sowed and it looks well. Luther helped me break 40 of it in July then left me & went back to Cooper [County] & put in 45 acres of wheat on Warren McFarland [Reed's father-in-law] & is now breaking com land on Byler's place all near Lee's where he lived. Then Grover & I finished breaking harrowed dragged & drilled the crop. I have a span of 17 hand mules that can pull a 3 horse plow anywhere we want them to & you ought to see that 10 year old kid [Grover] following them while I follow 3 horses. When that was done I put in a week or 10 days putting up prairie hay. Then you see I am road overseer & put in 12 strait days at that & since that I have plastered about 8 rooms & built some flues & put in 6 days painting on our church & now have Walter Hall's big 2 story house to paint all over. I am 62 years old & feel more like work this fall than I did 10 years ago but Lilburn Wright is a big boy goes to school from here & works out his board so that helps some.

Lee & his wife & Luther came up in Oct. Stayed 3 weeks. Made me a big cistern at the barn. Gathered my apples and straightened out things generally.

Well here is another piece [of paper] I found in the church

register & I fill it with something. We had a splendid meeting while the children was up. Had 16 accessions about a bushel of backsliders reclaimed & a general shaking up of all but several old hard cases like Frank Turner not yet reached. Our new preacher is name Renfro has preached 7 yrs in Mo. 7 in Texas (north west I believe) & 7 in Arkansas. Says he remembers your name but never met you. Luther was attending to his widow pretty closely till the preacher brought his daughter down from Chillicothe [Mo.]. then he hung to her as long as she stayed (as is his custom) then hung close to the widow till they went back to Boonville. I have the honor of being S.S. Supt., 1st or leader of 3 stewards, church conference secretary & one of the trustees of church property. We repaired our church this fall & now have the finest South Methodist church in the county, the station at Chillicothe included, for all of which I am proud & thankful.

Well I suppose the political landslide is a general thing even in Texas but I have not seen anything official from there but Missouri is sunk lower than she has been for 22 yrs. In 72 the Democrats came in power in the state & have held it continuously since until last Tuesday when the tidal wave came & swept her off & what will be the result the Master only knows & I shall trust it to him & let politics alone.

We have a new organ in our church too and our little widow (Blanche Alexander) & Julia Debo [his daughter] are the organists while Mamie Hall & May Culberson can play in the absence of the 1 or 2. We also have a women's missionary society here and are trying to start an Epworth League but I am afraid it will not be a success. I wrote to Sister Sallie last week & sent her a statement of our family record. Was going to send you one but the chaps say I sent you one a few years ago. If not I will any time.

(The last page or so must have been lost.)

* * * * *

5. A letter (1896) from Grover Evans Debo, son of Reed Debo, to one of his Texas cousins (not named) in Burnet County, a son of Cornelius Debo. Grover was 12 years old at the time, being born in 1884.

Bedford Mo.

March 8 1896

My dear cusin

I thought I would write you a letter. The sun shines bright. It snowed last night. It didn't look to me like snow yesterday.

We didn't put up any ice this winter. I have got me 5 rabbit traps. I haven't got them set now. I want to set them soon. I guess there are a good many rabbits now. I guess I ran around more when snow is on the ground then when it isn't on the ground. I like to take a slay ride in the snow. I thought we would get to ride on the sled to Sunday School but the snow is melting. I guess we will have to ride in the wagon or walk. A fine Sunday school is going on at Bedford. Ida is the secretary. Pa is superintendent. We have 2 horses to brake one is going on 4 the other is going on 3. I want pa to brake them to work. Pretty soon one of them is nearly broke to ride the other never had a bridle that I know of this very gentle. The oldest is a light bay the other is brown. I think he will be black. I want to ride the oldest. We have got 6 horses and mule. We had a team of mules one is 17 hands high the other was 16 hands and 2/4 high. But we sold the smallest for a $110.00. He was 6 years old. There are a good many wild ducks across the river in the bottom. Nearly all of the wild geese have gone. I never saw a wild goose very close to me. I saw some wild ducks about a 100 yards from me. I would like to see some clost to me. Geese and ducks too. I don't believe I will write any more on this letter. Write to your cousin Grover Evans Debo soon.

* * * * *

6.   A letter (1896) from Reed Debo in Missouri to his brother Cornelius In Texas, detailing conditions then present in Missouri.

Bedford, Mo. Nov. 16, 1896

Dear Bro.

I believe it would be impossible for me to fix up an excuse for not writing to you when I ought to have except I thought I would post myself on the subjects you wrote about but com has never had a fixed price until the last week or two and it's about settlin[g] down at 15 cents per bushel here and down at Boonville it's 15 cents a barrel. I have not found out exactly what it would cost to ship it though it would be from 35 to 40 dol's. a car from the south side of the river, say Boonville, Marshall or Lexington or Kansas City and they would allow you to put from 7 to 800 bushels on a car but even at 600 bus. On the car and the car at $40 to Austin would be only about 20 cents but it would be best to get it on the south side of the river as all our roads here run east and west. So it would have to go to Moberly or Kansas City to start to Texas. Com gathering has just commenced here and no one selling unless they have to. If you would like still to go into it you write to Jas. Z. Laughon or Lee at Boonville or Jas. M. Turner at Marshall. Jim L. always keeps posted & could tell you the price along the MK&T line through S.W. Mo. and into Kansas. I think Vernon, Bates, Henry are Cos. Are selling as low as up this way and a third more nearer to you. But if you conclude to come up you must come on up here too and come prepared to stay as long as the nature of the case will permit. Wheat is going up a little on account of the famine in India and it might have some effect on com after awhile or it may come up a little any way after McKinley sends his gold around any way. I think you could get to Austin at least so you could sell it for less than 40 cts or even to Burnett if your little RR has been changed to the standard (gage). Well I regard the result of the election as a sad calamity for 9/10 of the people of these U.S. but we shall see what we shall see and may the Lord protect and direct. Your Texas Pop [populists] must be a hard set or hard to manage. You see ours voted for Bryan like little men. You see he got 60,000 here while Stephens & the other State officers only got about 30 or 35,000 majority.

(Page 3 is missing.)

Society & organist at the church as well as teacher in S.S. Ida was secty of the League and S.S. but she went to Boonville and Howard [County] and spent the summer so she lost her hold on secty. I appointed a committee today to prepare a program & plans for a S.S. Christmas entertainment.

Well my youngest daughter is 15 yrs. Old and as tall as Ida and will be heavy like Mattie. Ida is just the size and make of Cass Debo and just as proud and frisky. Grover is 12 but a little small to his age but can help me a great deal when out of school. Did you know that I am getting a little old? Well I'll be 65 in Jan 19/97.

Well it's 10 o'clock & the girls have got back & are in the dining room eating and gabbing. Say & old Stray Preacher is going to start a meeting in town tomorrow night. Well I guess you will be at Waxahatchie at Conference (wherever that may be) when this letter gets to Burnet. I see our oldest Bishop is to preside there. Hope you will have a good time. I am going to get Old Green Saunders to help me gather com this week & we must put in 6 loads a day with side boards on. Our preacher & his wife & her sister stayed here last night but she is too young for me. She is a school marm & a chum of Julia.

I hardly ever hear from Va. nowadays on account of not writing myself. I love to get letters & would like to write them if I could get at it. I heard through Virge Turner that Milton Turner's oldest daughter died last week. She was the wife of one of Hike Fitzpatricks sons. I guess you knew Milton died 4 years ago or more maybe. I have not heard from Anise Rorer for a long time but its my fault if I could write she would.

I don't think of anything worth writing. Lee and Luther were well a few weeks ago. They farm together. They come up about once a year and some times drive through & sometimes on the R.R. its about 75 miles through down Grand River to Brunswick & then down the Mo. by Glasgow to Boonville. Luther started from here at about daylight one Sept. morn & got to Tom Ack Whittan at 10 that night with a pair of light horses to a buggy. Old Jule the pony I had when you left here is here yet. Was 26 last spring and looks pretty well yet has got pretty gray about the head & neck. Can still jump or work but we have not made a work horse of him for 8 years.

Love to all. As ever   R. P. Debo

* * * * *

7. A letter (1896) from Newt Simpson to Clay Debo, son of Cornelius Debo, in Burnet County, Texas. Newt was a kinsman of Andes Simpson, who would later become the husband of Sallie Esterline Debo, Clay's sister. Clay died at an early age.

Nov. 14, 1896
Lane P.O. Hunt Co., Tex
Mr. Clay Debo

Dear friend

I will seat my self to write you and Eppa a few lines to let you all no where I am as you once told me to write to you and I think I will. Well Clay I have seen a fine time since I have bin gone. I wish you could have bin with me. I am picking cotton now. I will be here about 15 days or more.

Tell Cousin Jinnie I was glad for her advice she sent to me tell her she can send all a letter can hold. I want you and Eppa to write as soon as you get this or I wont get it. I would like the best in world for both of you to be with me. I guess that I will be back in a year or 2. I think I will go over in the indine [Indian] nation in about 2 weeks.

Well I will close for this time. Write soon.

Yours truly, Lane P.O. Hunt Co., Tex.   Newt Simpson
Tell Eppa to write to.

* * * * *

8. (For this letter see above [#6] for an explanation. They are the same individuals.)

Mr. W. C. Debo

Dear friend

I received your Kind and welcom letter this eaving. Was glad to hear from you. It found me well hopeing when these few lines comes to hand they will find you the same. Well Clay I don't know who to writ only we are having some pretty cold weather now I think if it keeps on we will have some snow before many days. Well Clay you don't know how much fun I am having but wish you did. When you read this just think what good time we had them rainnie days when we would catch them old Buzzards. Think how that one hoped when we Cut his wings off. Well I beleave as supper is ready I will stop till morning.

Next time you write why sine my name in this way Newt Simpson for they is other Simpsons in here besides us and they will take my letters out if you don't. I am picking cotton at this time. I don't know how long it will last. When that gives out I don't know then what we will do unless it is Cutting Cord wood

Well Clay why didn't Eppa write to me when you wrote. Tell him to not keep so much good news way back in the back part of his head. Tell him I want him to write to me. Well Clay you no that pig you said you would give me I guess I will never get him. You keep him. Well as I have no more to write I will close. Write soon to your loveing friend excuse bad wrighting and bad spelling.

Newt Simpson   Lane P.O., Hunt Co., Tex

* * * * *

9.   A letter (1898) from a friend, Will Rountree, to Eppa and one to Clay Debo, sons of Cornelius Debo in Burnet County, Texas.

Brown Co., Texas
Feb. 18, 1898

Dear Eppa.

I thought I would write to you to tell you that I got home all right. It was four o'clock when I got to Uncle Will Hill's Monday night. Will and I slept till eight o'clock. It was dinner when I got home Tuesday. I didn't do nothing but sleep Tuesday evening and Wednesday all day. Eppa you all must not treat that old Swede to bad. When I come up there we will go a snipe hunting and get him to hold the sack.

I hope you all had a fine time at Mr. Sparks Monday night after Christmas. I wish I had a stayed and went to the party with you all. My horse give out with me be fore I got home that day. Well Eppa I cant think of any thing else to write so I will close. Good-by. Come to see me when you can.

Your friend,
Will.

Negro town, Texas
Feb. 18, 1898

Dear Clay

I thought I would answer your letter being as I have got some paper. Clay you ought to of been with me Tuesday after I came from up there. I went to a party at Uncle Plese Hill's. I sure had a nice time. They played till two o'clock. Two weeks after that on Friday night I went to a party at Mr. Potts and on Saturday night at Mrs. Cooks and went to a singing Sunday night at Mr.

Schoolys. Clay you ought to come down here and see these pretty negros that passes here They drive in a lope most of the time. I went hunting Thursday evening and killed seven mule-ear rabbits. The rabbits are so thick down here you can see them any time you look out of the house. I will close for this time. Write to your friend. Good-by.

Willie Rountree

* * * * *

10. A letter (1913) from Fannie Wilson Debo, wife of Thomas Benton Debo, in Texas to Martha (Mattie) Debo in Cooper County, Missouri. Thomas was a brother of Reed Debo, father of Mattie.

Killeen, Texas
Dec. 29 --13

Miss Mattie Debo
My Dier Neice
We received your card some days ago, glad to know we are not forgotten. We have enjoyed the holidays fine considering your Uncle Thomas has been almost laid up with Lagrippe for two weeks, not in bed but just able to sit around the fire. He has suffered a great diel with his head & neck. we had the Dr to come yesterday first time he had been for several days. He left some powders that eased his head some, so he had a very good nights rest. We had only one of the children with us during the last week. Bettie Lou is telephone operator, & you know they get no holidays at all, but she seemed to enjoy the time all right.

Myrtle spent last week in Burnet, said she had a good time with the folks. Left them all well.

Myrtle sets type at the printing office & she got one week off. She came in last night on the midnight train, so of course she feels a little stupid today, but she went to work this morning. Cornelius [son nicknamed "Pat"] is still working for the Santa Fe, so he didn't get any holiday to come home. Ollie lives west of Ft. Worth & she didn't get to come, but sent me a Xmas gift.

I haven't had a letter from your Aunt Sallie for quite awhile. They were doing very well when she wrote last. Emmets widow, Ethel Bowmer, is living about one block from us so we can see her most every day. She got a card from Prunie saying they had a new girl at her house, so Prune has one girl & one boy.

Your Aunt Mollie wrote just before Xmas, said Tot had spent a week at home but had gone back to her own home for the holidays. Mollie seems riel proud of her soninlaw. We have never seen him. I hope he is worthy of Tot, for I think she is such a sweet girl

Have you had plenty of rain up there This winters my if we haven't had plenty down here, but I guess you folks read it in the papers. The floods were not bad in Killeen, tho it took one bridge & several families moved from below the Railroad, but there was no one drowned here & no property destroyed by the water. But we sure have had the mud, yes plenty of mud. We are having nice cool weather now, which we are very thankful for. Do you ever hier from old Va.? My sister writes me sometimes. She & my oldest brother & youngest brother are all that are living of our family. My sister married about two months ago. She married Wm. N. Reece, he is a nice man & a good Christian. I don't suppose any of you folks remember him unless you heard your Papa speak of him. I knew him well, but I was a little surprised at my sister marrying after waiting so long, but it was her wish of course. I get letters from Cassie sometimes, & when I read her letters I imagine I can almost hear her Talking.

Mattie I wish you could make up your mind to visit down in Texas awhile. I believe it would do you good. Its true your Uncle & I are getting old, but I don't feel old. I can go all day & sit up half the night. I go to S.S. & church every Sunday & most every Sunday night, prayer meeting Tuesday & Wednesday nights, Ladies Aid every Monday, & visit the sick that are near enough.

Well I will make you tired as you will not want to read any more of my scribbling, so I will stop for this time & try to write again some day. We would be glad to have a letter from any of you folks. Wishing you a happy new year, I am your devoted Aunt Fannie. Much love to each one.

* * * * *

11. A letter (1916) from Mrs. Sallie Debo Bowmer of Comanche, Oklahoma, to her niece, Mattie Debo, in Boonville, Missouri.

Comanche, Okla.
Jan. 11th, 1916

Miss Mattie Debo
Boonville, Mo.

My Dear Niece

If you will excuse pencil, will try to write you, am too nervous to do much with pen & ink.

I received your Christmas greeting and was so glad to know that you thought of your old aunt some times.

We are all on foot but none of us real well. Your uncle has been housed up with lagrip for over two weeks and Earlie's wife was taken sick on the 22nd of Dec. and has not been up any till the last few days. She is able to be around some.

We are having the coldest weather that we have had for years. Everything that can freeze is hard frozen. Of course it is not as cold here as it is in Mo. Temperature two degrees above zero, but it seems cold to us. It has been cloudy for a week, and we had one thundershower during the time, but the rest was just cloudy & cold.

Saturday morning.

The weather is still disagreeable close cloudy & a cold S.E. wind. Am afraid it will cause more sickness, of which there seems to be plenty already. Lagrip and some pneumonia.

I had letters from my girls yesterday. They write to me every week. All were well in their last letters. I also had a card from Aunt Fannie. She said they were all well & that Thomas' health seemed better this winter than usual.

Sister Mollie wrote me since Xmas, said her health was not good, nor had been for several months.

Elsie's oldest son married the 24th of December. Now there are four of her children married, and she has five grandchildren. It makes me feel very old when I think of the bunch of great grandchildren, but in reality I am in my 70th year. The 20th of last Oct. I was 69.

I keep up very well for my age so far. I go to the post office whenever the weather is good, walk there & back, and it is half a mile.

I would be so much pleased if you would write to me some times. I would love to hear from you & the boys. Which one do you make your home with? Has Lee & Alice any children beside Thelma? I guess she is about grown.

Hoping to get a letter from you soon, I will close my remarks for the present. Your loving old aunt,

Sallie

* * * * *

12. The Lewis C. Debo family of Ottumwa, Iowa, had made a vacation trip to Texas in the summer of 1954. This letter is a reply to them from Mrs. Lilbon (Hattie) Debo of Burnet, Texas. The Iowa folks had visited the Burnet Debos during the trip and the boys had taken back home with them a Texas horned frog.

Burnet, Texas
Aug. 5 - 54

Mr. And Mrs. Lewis Debo

We received your nice letter some time ago [and] were happy to know you got back home safe and found everything O.K. We had read so much about the big rains, we were afraid the river had done a lot of damage. We enjoyed having you all come by and next time plan to make us a real visit. I've been trying to get Lilbon to answer your letter and he just wont so I'll try.

We enjoyed meeting you all and wish you could join us in the Debo reunion on Labor Day. Lib's sister from Houston has been here since July 4 and will stay till the reunion. Darrell said [he] sure wished [he] could have been at home. How are the boys? Did they get home with the frog? Bert has had an operation since you all were here, but is able to be at home now. The rest of the Debos were disappointed at not getting to see you all.

One of Aunt Sallie Bowmer's girls Elsie Cook is planning to be with us at the reunion.

We will be looking forward to you all making another visit to Texas next summer. Lib said you must plan to stay long enough for us to get to know each other better.

Maybe next time Lib will write. Lots of good luck.

Lilbon and Hattie

* * * * *

13. A letter (1958) from Lilbon Debo, Burnet, Texas, to his cousin, Luther Debo, of Boonville, Missouri. Luther had visited his Burnet, Texas, kinfolks about 1905, and was remembered by them.

Burnet Aug. 17/1958

Mr. L. C. Debo
Dear Cousin:

We were all glad to hear from you because we enjoyed your visit of so long ago so much.

Our family is scattered quite a bit. My oldest sister Jennie lives in Houston with her children. Sister Sallie lives in Winters, that is in Runnels Co. Nellie lives in Burnet Co. Julia lives in Austin. '

We boys all live in Burnet Co. Eppa, Frank, and Hardy all live on a farm. I live at Burnet. I have been working at the Buchanan Dam for about five years, had a good job. Was a guard, so you see I didn't have much work to do.

Well Luther, none of us are very old, but we have all been here a long time. We may [not] meet again, but we will never forget the nice visit you gave us. Would like to hear about your folk and [how] they are.

L. Debo

* * * * *

14. A letter (1958) from Mizpah Otto deBoe, wife of Dr. Michael Price deBoe, of Miami, Florida, to Lewis Debo, son of Luther Debo and grandson of Reed Debo, who lived in Ottuma, Iowa. Mrs. deBoe's memory must have been fading when she referred to old "Michael" Debo weeping upon remembering Valley Forge. It should have been Philip instead of Michael.

September 3rd 1958

Mr. Lewis C. Debo
717 Riverside Lane
Ottumwa, Iowa

Dear Mr. Debo,

Thank you for your letter about Debo (DeBoe, deBoe) family, of great interest to me. Although Doctor deBoe never interested himself in research lineage, and I can't be of much help. I think his great-grandfather, Doctor Michael DeBoe is a forebear of yours too, same neighborhood, Fancy Grove (once called Thurman). I still have his grandfather, Michael deBoe, Jr.' s Goose Creek Plantation in that vicinity where he was born.

Old Dr. Michael DeBoe was with Washington at Valley Forge. I have his medical scales and candle stand with 5 plates brought from Alsace-Lorraine to settle in Pennsylvania [where he] practiced medicine all his life.

When I can finish a piece of work here, I'll write [a] longer letter.

Sincerely,
Mizpah O. deBoe
(Mrs.) Michael Price deBoe

Family said old Dr. DeBoe telling about that winter at Valley Forge around his Virginia fireside never could keep the tears from streaming down his cheeks as he told how the ragged barefoot soldiers coming to abandoned camps where the horses had died would take their hoofs and roast them over camp fire, eat them to keep from starving to death.

M.O.deB.

* * * * *

C. The Rohrer (Rorer) — Towler genealogies were supplied me by the late Mrs. R. M. (Blanford T.) Anderson of Chatham, Virginia, more than 30 years ago. I deemed it wise to include it in the Appendices because of the close connection between the Debos and Rohrers through marriage: Betsy Debo Rohrer, daughter of Philip Debo (2); and two of the children of John David Rorer, who married two of the Hubbards (who were children of Taliaferro G. Hubbard and Mary Debo, daughter of Michael Debo of Bedford County, Virginia.

JOHN ROHRER married BARBARA WEIDMAN, daughter of Abraham Weidman, probably in Lebanon, Pennsylvania. They died circa 1810 in Pittsylvania County, Virginia. Their issue:

1. John Rohrer, Jr. Baptized Oct. 6, 1760, at Schwadara church, Lebanon, PA. He remained in Pennsylvania when his parents and two brothers moved to Virginia.
2. Dorothy Rohrer. Married Johannes Reid at Althoe, Berks Co., P A.

3. David Rohrer. Baptized 1766 at Tabor First Reformed Church. Married Betsy Debo, daughter of Philip (2). Born in 1769, Lebanon Co., PA; died circa 1851, Pittsylvania County, VA.
4. Abraham (Abram) Rohrer. Born in 1771; married Aug. 11, 1789, Pittsylvania Co., VA; died in 1830 in the same county. Married Nancy Cook, daughter of Harmon Cook (Koch), who was born Jan. 20, 1770, and died April 28, 1861.
5. Anna Barbara Rohrer. Baptized Mar. 15, 1772; died Feb. 26, 1773.
6. Jacob Rohrer. Baptized Feb. 25, 1776.
7. Heinrich Rohrer. Baptized Aug. 29, 1779 at Tabor First Reformed Church.
8. Catherine Rohrer.
9. Anna Maria Rohrer. Baptized May 3, 1788.
10. Polly Rohrer. Married a Mr. Cioof, Lebanon, PA.

(Only David and Betsy Debo Rohrer, and Abraham and Nancy Cook Rohrer genealogies were given, and therefore are the only ones submitted here.)

DAVID and BETSY ROHRER. Their issue:
1. David Alexander Rorrer, born Aug. 1, 1791; married to Nancy Ann W. Brown Mar. 3, 1814; died Aug. 25, 1880. Their children:
   a. John Rorrer, who married Jane Handy in 1836.
   b. Mike Rorrer, who married Elizabeth (Susan) Ingram in 1841.
   c. William Rorrer, who married Catherine Bowling in 1858.
   d. Thomas Dudley Rorrer, born June 12, 1822; married Arminda (Mindy) Davis in 1844; died Nov. 27, 1913.
   e. David C. Rorrer, who married Sarah Barbour, and died in 1871.
   f. Abraham Alexander Rorrer, who married Pernina Smith Shelton.
   g. Sally Rorrer, who married Tom Lawless.
   h. Mary Rorrer, who married John Morrison in 1842.
   i. Judy Rorrer, who married Booker Adkins.

2. MARY (POLLY) RORER, who married ELIJAH TOWLER, son of Joseph, Sept. 12, 1807, in Pittsylvania County, VA, and died June 30, 1833, in the same county. Their issue:
   a. Elizabeth Towler, born Sept. 19, 1808, who was married

Dec.18, 1828, to Shadrack Shockley, born Nov. 3, 1808.

b. Frances A. Towler, born June 7, 1811, who married Enos O. Robertson on Jan. 2, 1837, in Pittsylvania County, VA.

c. Benjamin Franklin Towler, born Mar. 1814, Callands, VA., died May 1893 the same place, and was married Dec. 30, 1846, in Pittsylvania County, VA to Mary Matilda (Tee) Harris, born Feb. 17, 1828, Strawberry, VA, and died Feb. 17, 1873, Callands, VA. Their issue:

(1) Anne Eliza Towler, born in 1849, Callands, VA, died May 20, 1886, in Mountain Valley, Henry Co., VA; married Oct. 28, 1867, to Jabez E. Graveley, born Nov. 28, 1836, Henry Co., VA and died in 1927 there. (2) Belle Boyd Towler, born May 28, 1857, died Nov. 22, 1804, married Jan. 12, 1882, to James Thomas Hines, born Jan. 12, 1855, Hinesville, VA.

(3) Lenorah Jimpse Towler, born Jan. 15, 1864, died June 17, 1944, Lynchburg, VA, married Robertson Linthicum, born Sept. 7, 1853, Climax, VA, died Aug. 1, 1932, Lynchburg, VA.

(4) William Benjamin Towler, born May 28, 1855, Pittsylvania Co., VA, died July 31, 1929, Callands, VA; married Mar. 6, 1879 Henry Co., VA to Mary Ann Elizabeth Towler, born July 21, 1859, Towler's Ferry, VA and died Dec. 17, 1934, Callands, VA. Their issue:

(a) Samuel Joseph Overton Towler, born Feb. 11, 1880, Callands, VA, died May 10, 1936; married Oct. 9, 1901, Rondo, VA, to Woodruth Nuckols, born June 6, 1880, Rondo, VA and died Jan. 11, 1975, Mineola, VA. Their issue:

1. Blanford Towler, born Sept. 28, 1902, Callands, VA, died after 1976; married Sept. 15, 1923, Chatham, VA to Richard Mortimer Anderson, born Oct. 23, 1902, Mineola, VA and died Mar. 13, 1969.

a. Richard M. Anderson, Jr., born Jan. 16, 1941, married Feb. 22, 1959, to Donna Shanaberger, born Feb. 4, 1941.

(I) Richard Mortimer Anderson III, born Sept. 13, 1959

(2) Sylvia Darlene Anderson, born Sept.d, 1961

(3) Donna Kathleen Anderson, born Sept. 16, 1962

(4) Diane Renee Anderson, born Feb. 11, 1965 (5) Sandra Kay Anderson, born May 4, 1968

    b. Carlisle Overton Anderson, born Jan. 30, 1945, Mebane, North Carolina

1. Samuel Byron Towler, born July 13, 1904, Callands, Married Oct. 15, 1930, to Edythe Bryant, born June 10

2. Moir Martin Towler, born Feb. 4, 1907, married April 5, 1930 to Doris Brumfield, born Feb. 25, 1906.

3. John William Parker Towler, born Dec. 28, 1909, marRied May 8, 1941, to Addie Yeatts, born Oct. 8, 1912

4. Woodruth Towler, born Aug. 22, 1912, married May 29, 1937, to Langhorne D. Motley, born Feb. 1914. Issue:

    a. Woodruth Motley, born May 1, 1946, married Jan. 30, 1965, Columbia, S.C., to Thomas Jackson Morgan, born Jan.25, 1945

    (1) Thomas Jackson Morgan, Jr., born Oct. 11, 1965, Portsmouth, VA

    (2) Langhorne Andrew Morgan, born Apr. 4, 1973, Lansing, Michigan

5. Floreine Elizabeth Towler, born Oct. 13, 1915, married Sept. 1, 1936, to Jesse Eppler Gilbert, born Mar. 12, 1912, died Aug. 6, 1955. Issue:

    a. Patricia Ann Gilbert, born Jan. 25, 1943, married Dec. 22, 1962, to Clarence Keen Hedrick, born June 19, 1940. Issue:

    (1) Anthony Keen Hedrick, born Mar. 24, 1964

    (2) Deborah Ann Hedrick, born Sept. 5, 1968

1. James Wilson Towler, born July 2, 1918, married May 19, 1951, to Bettie Graham Dixon, born Oct. 18, 1925.

2. Edwin Reid Towler, born Oct. 5, 1920.

(a) Pearl Towler, born Nov. 28, 1881, married Dec. 17, 1902, to BenjaminF. Tatum, born Nov. 18, 1871, Stuart, VA.

(3) James Justice Towler, born Oct. 15, 1869, married Sept. 15, 1897, Raleigh, N.C., to Minnie Barber. He died Jan. 16, 1945. Issue: J. Barber Towler.

3. JOHN DAVID RORER, born circa 1795, died in 1850, married in 1814 to FRANCES CUSTARD, born July 3, 1798, and died June 9, 1880. Their issue:

a. David J. Rorer, born in 1814; an M.D. in Georgia.
b. Elizabeth Rorer, born in 1818, married in 1840 to William G. Bailey.
c. Sarah W. Rorer, born in 1820, married in 1846 to James Keatts, Jr.
d. Anne Delilah Rorer, born in 1822, married George Edwards
e. Daniel B. Rorer, born in 1824.
f. John Quincy Rorer, born in 1826, died in 1899, married in 1854 to Sallie Baugh Hensley, born in 1837 and died in 1897. Their issue:

(1) James J. Rorer, born in 1855.

(2) Samuel D. Rorer, born in 1857.

(3) William Admire Rorer, born in 1859, died in 1921; married Lucy Rebecca Walker, born in 1866 and died in 1959. Their issue:

(a) John Alexander Rorer, born in 1894, died May 18, 1969, in Charlottesville, V A, a Professor of Education at the University of Virginia from 1929 until retirement July I, 1966; married Mabelle H. Clark. Their issue:

1. John A. Rorer, Jr., born in 1927, married Katherine Parker. Their issue:

a. Katherine Holland Rorer, born in 1950

b. John Alexander Rorer, born in 1954.

c. Richard Clark Rorer, born in 1955.

(b) William Asbury Rorer, born in 1898; married Genie Davis

(c) Henry Smith Rorer, born in 1900; married Virginia Arthur.

(4) Laura D. Rorer, born in 1861, married William T. Jefferson.

(5) Delaware Rorer, born in 1866, married J. T. A. Graves.

(6) Narcissa Zada Rorer, born in 1868, married William G. Lane

(7) Alonza H. Rorer, born 1870.

(8) Esca Owen Rorer, born in 1874.

(9) Florence Rorer, born in 1876, married Walter Graves.

a. Rebecca J. Rorer, born in 1826, died in 1899, married in 1850 to Charles Edwards.
b. Charles Henry Rorer, born Jan. 16, 1830, died Oct. 28, 1918,

married Nov. 15, 1857, to Annis Preston Hubbard, born May 14, 1839, died Mar. 16, 1926. (For their issue see the chapter on Taliaferro G. Hubbard and Mary Debo where their issue is given.)

   c. Mary C. (Polly) Rorer, born in 1832, married Terry Glenn

   d. Armistead D. A. Rorer, born Sept. 21, 1834, died Nov. 27, 1914.

   e. William A. Rorer, born in 1835.

   f. Samuel T. Rorer, born in 1840

   g. Virginia Frances Rorer, born in 1841, married Feb. 15, 1870 to Daniel Perry Hubbard, born July 14, 1849. (For their issue see the chapter on Taliaferro G. Hubbard and Mary Debo where their issue is given.)

   h. Lucie E. Rorer, born in 1842, married Alex Powell.

ABRAHAM (ABRAM) ROHRER, born in 1771, died in 1830, Pittsylvania County, VA, married Aug. 11, 1789, in the same county to NANCY COOK, daughter of Harmon Cook, born Jan. 20, 1770, and died Apr. 28, 1861. Their issue:

1. John Rorer, born Apr. 13, 1790, married Jan. 13, 1814, to Sally Bennett, daughter of Richard Bennett.

2. George Rorer, born Dec. 24, 1791, died Sept. 29, 1847, in Caldwell County, KY, married Mar. 28, 1811, to Nancy Nowlin, daughter of James Nowlin, born Apr. 28, 1795.

3. Charles Rorer

4. Abraham Rorer, Jr., born June 8, 1794, married Apr. 26, 1821, to Mary Wright.
Their issue:

   a. Ferdinand Rorer, born in 1827, married Julia Ann Hannah.

   b. Angeline Rorer, married Craighead James. Issue: a son Rorer A. James.

   c. Elvira Rorer, married a Mr. Harvey.

   d. Aquella Ann Rorer, married a Mr. Lipscomb.

   e. Malitta Rorer, married a Mr. Miller.

   f. Charles Rorer

5. Rudolph Rorer, married Mar. 6, 1823, to Millicent Lamb.

6. Henry Rorer, born Apr. 1, 1800, died Mar. 30, 1817.

7. Catherine J. Rorer, born Oct. 13, 1802, married July 31, 1817, to John Custard.

8. David Rorer, born May 12, 1805, married Martha Daniel; went

to Ohio where he became a distinguished jurist.
9. Samuel Rorer, born Mar. 27, 1810.

End Notes

INTRODUCTION

1 A. Stapleton, *Memorial of the Huguenots* in America, Baltimore, 1969, reprint, p. 97.

2. *Op. Cit.*, p. 159

3. *Op. Cit.*, p. 158.

4. A copy of the letter is in possession of the author.

5. Stapleton, p. 97.

6. *Ibid.*

7. Caswell County, North Carolina, Marriage Bonds.

8. Caswell County, North Carolina, Deed Records, Book 18, p. 20.

9. Genealogical data on this Debo family was copied by the author from a reel obtained from Latter Day Saints records, Salt Lake City, Utah.

10. Information received from correspondence between Lewis Debo of Ottuma, Iowa, and William Bruce Debo, Devil's Elbow, Missouri.

11. Israel Daniel Rupp, *A Collection of Upwards of 30,000 Names of German, Swiss, French and Other Immigrants to Pennsylvania from 1727-1776*, Philadelphia, 1927, p. 84.

CHAPTER I. BACKGROUND

1. G. Elmore Reaman, *The Trail of the Huguenots*, Baltimore, 1972 reprint, p. 28.

2. *Op. cit.*, p. 29.

3. *Op. cit.*, p. 44.

4. E. Bonjour, H. S. Offler, G. R. Potter, *A Short History of Switzerland*, Oxford, 1952, pp. 166-67.

5. Reaman, *op. cit.*, p. 45.

6. *Op. cit.*, p. 45.

7. Samuel Smiles, *The Huguenots*, Baltimore, pp. 18-19.

8. *Op. cit.* pp. 27-28.

9. *Ibid.*

10. *Ibid.*

11. *Op. cit.*, footnote, p. 38

12. Reaman, *op. cit.*, p. 44.

13. *Op. cit.*, p. 47.

14. *Op. cit.*, P. 48.

15. Smiles, *op. cit.*, P. 50.

16. Reaman, *op. cit.*, p. 49.

17. Smiles, *op. cit.*, p. 29.

18. Reaman, *op. cit.*, p. 50.

19. Smiles, *op. cit.*, p. 29.

20. Reaman, *op. cit.*, p. 50, 51.

21. *Op. cit.*, p. 52.

22. *Op. cit.*, p. 54.

23. *Op. cit.*, p. 60.

24. *Op. cit.*, p. 61.

25. Stapleton, *Memorial of the Huguenots in America*, Baltimore, 1989 reprint, p. 97.

26. Reaman, *op. cit.*, p. 62.

27. R. N. Bain, "Charles XII and the Great Northern War," in *Cambridge Modern History*, V, 600.

28. Public Record Office, State Papers, 84/2-32-, 248, cited as P. R. O., S. P.

CHAPTER II. COMING TO THE NEW WORLD

1. H. Frank Eshleman, *Swiss and German Pioneer Settlers of Southeastern Pennsylvania*, pp. 245-46.

2. From the minutes of the Provincial Council, printed in *Colonial Records*, Vol. III, p. 466.

3. Ralph Beaver Strassburger, *Pennsylvania German Pioneers*, edited by William John Hinke, Vol. I, pp. 101-105.

4. Michael Tepper, New World Immigrants, Vol. II, in an article, "Passengers from the Rhineland to Pennsylvania," p. 531.

5. G. Elmore Reaman, *The Trail of the Huguenots*, Baltimore, 1972, reprint, p. 61.

6. A. Stapleton, *Memorials of the Huguenots in America*, Baltimore, 1969, reprint, p. 37.

7. In the material preserved by Miss Era Deboe, a copy of which is in the possession of the author.

8. *Notes and Queries*, edited by William H. Egle, Annual Volume 1896, p. 82.

9. Tepper, *op. cit.*, p. 4.

10. Strassburger, *op. cit.*

11. *Pennsylvania Archives*, II Series, Vol. II, p. 82.

12. *Notes and Queries*, edited by William H. Egle, Annual Volume 1899, p. 187.

13. Register of Wills, Lancaster County, Pennsylvania.

14. Office of Records and Archives of Lancaster county, Pennsylvania, has this record in its indices, but the inventory document is in the possession of the Lancaster County Historical Society.

CHAPTER III. LEAVING PENNSYLVANIA

1. *Revolutionary War Records*, Vol. I, p. 596, 604.

2. Shenandoah County, Virginia, Deed Records, vol. D, pp. 162-63.

3. *Op. cit.*, Vol. G, pp. 282-284.

4. *Virginia Magazine of History*, Vol. 35, p. 206.

5. Jessamine County, Kentucky, Marriage Records, Box 25.

6. Virginia Taxpayers, 1782, p. 34.

7. U.S. Census, Kentucky, 1810.

8. *Colonial Men and Times*, by Harper.

9. Stapleton, *op. cit.*, p. 97.

10. *Pennsylvania Archives*, II Series, Vol. IX, p. 138.

11. *William and Mary Quarterly*, 2nd Series, Jan. 1934. Vol. 14, pp. 38-39.

12. *Pennsylvania Archives*, Series V, Vol. VII, p. 1105, 1108.

13. Letter from Mrs. Michael Price (Mizpah Otto) deBoe to Lewis C. Debo Sept. 3, 1958; copy in possession of author.

14. Stapleton, *op. cit.*, p. 134.

15. *Op. cit.*, p. 133.

16. Maud Carter Clement, *The History of Pittsylvania County, Virginia*, Baltimore, 1973, pp. 46-47.

17. Pittsylvania County, Virginia, Deed Records, Vol.8, p. 314.

18. PCDR, Vol. 13, pp. 406-407.

19. PCDR, Vol. 13, pp. 407-409.

20. U.S. Census 1850 shows Betsy as 81 years of age; therefore born in 1769, and born in Pennsylvania.

21. Marriage Records of Pittsylvania County, Virginia (hereafter MRPC), p. 18.

22. Rohrer (Rorer) research, a copy of which was supplied by the late Mrs. R. M. Anderson of Chatham, Virginia.

23. Interview by John Alexander Rorer in 1966 with Frank Jackson

and supplied by Rorer's son, John A. Rorer, Jr. of Charlottesville, Virginia.

24. John Debo family Bible record.
25. MRPC, p. 20.
26. John Debo Bible, *op. cit.*
27. *Ibid.*
28. *Ibid.*
29. MRPC, p. 22.
30. *History of Crittenden County, Kentucky*, Marion, Kentucky, 1991, p. 87.
31. *Ibid.*
32. U.S. Census 1850, *op. cit.*
33. MRPC, p. 23.
34. U.S. Census 1850, *op. cit.*
35. Deed Records of Pittsylvania County, Va., Book 18, p. 239.
36. MRPC, p. 26.
37. Caldwell County, Kentucky, Court Order Book 1, p. 390.
38. *History of Crittenden County, Kentucky, op. cit.*, p. 87.
39. MRPC, p. 42.
40. *History of Crittenden County, Kentucky, op. cit.*, p. 87.
41. *Ibid.*
42. MRPC, p. 50.
43. U.S. Census, 1850, *op. cit.*

CHAPTER IV. MICHAEL DEBO AND BEDFORD COUNTY, VIRGINIA

1. John Debo family Bible record, a copy of which is in the possession of the author.
2. U.S. Census for 1850, Pittsylvania County, VA. She was 81 at that time and born in Pennsylvania.
3. Marriage Bonds for Pittsylvania County, VA. (Hereinafter called MBPC.)
4. John Debo Bible, *op. cit.*
5. Deed Records of Bedford County, VA. (Hereinafter called DRBC), Book 11, p. 122.
6. DRBC, Book 12, p. 168.
7. DRBC, Book 12, p. 275.
8. DRBC, Book 15, p. 222.
9. DRBC, Book 17, p. 98.
10. DRBC, Book 17, p. 99.

11. DRBC, Book 19, p. 58.
12. DRBC, Book 21, p. 505.
13. John Debo Bible, op. cit.
14. DRBC, Book 30, p. 456.
15. DRBC, Book 33, p. 144.
16. Will book of Bedford County, VA (WBBC), Book 11, p. 434.
17. DRBC, Book 31, p. 317.
18. WBBC, Book 13, p. 318.
19. DRBC, Book 92, pp. 193-94.
20. DRBC, Book 130, p. 183.
21. DRBC, Book 164, p. 11.
22. DRBC, Book 170, p. 288
23. Obituary in possession of author.
24. DRBC, Book 342, p. 583.
25. DRBC, Book ?.
26. *John Hubbard Descendants from Body Camp Creek, Bedford County, Va.* By William David Hubbard and Oliver Shelton Carter, p. 3; copy in possession of author.
27. Supplement to *The Smith Mountain Eagle*, May 22, 1991, p. 22.
28. Ibid.
29. Court Order Books of Bedford County, VA (COBC), BOOK 18, P. 327.
30. COBC, Book 21, p. 127.
31. COBC, Book 24, p. 139.
32. DRBC, Book 11, p. 396.
33. WBBC, Book 11, p. 504.
34. Marriage Records of Bedford County, VA (MRBC).
35. MRBC.
36. Henry Debo's administrator qualified, and appraisers of estate appointment (Oct. 1837), COBC, Book 26, pp. 61, 71.
37. John Debo Bible, *op. cit.*
38. MRBC.
39. *Op. cit.*
40. *Ibid.*
41. *Ibid.*
42. MRBC.
43. Blankenship research supplied by Irvin W. (Sonny) Blankenship, Lynchburg, VA.
44. MRBC.
45. *Ibid.*

46. Saunders research supplied by Mr. And Mrs. Donald Saunders, South Point, Ohio.

47. *Ibid.*

48. *Ibid.*

49. MRBC.

50. *Hubbard Descendants, op. cit.*

51. *Ibid.*

52. MRBC.

53. *Hubbard Descendants, op. cit.*

54. *Ibid.*

55. *Ibid.*

56. *Leftwich-Turner Families of Virginia* by Hopkins.

57. MRBC.

58. Death Records of Bedford County, VA (DRBC)

59. *Leftwich-Turner, op. cit.*

60. DRBC.

61. MRBC.

62. Will of Samual Debo, Wills of Franklin County, VA.

63. U.S. Census, 1850, for Franklin County, VA.

A. HENRY DEBO

1. Bedford County Marriage Records (hereinafter BCMR).

2. Bedford County Deed Records (BCDR), BOOK 31, P. 317.

3. BCMR.

4. Bedford County Court Order book 26, p. 72.

5. BCMR.

6. Bedford County Will Book 9, p. 362.

7. BCMR.

8. Bedford County Birth Records.

9. *Ibid.*

10. Tombstone at Parrish Chapel Cemetery, Bedford County, VA; Death Records of Bedford County.

11. *Ibid.*

12. Confederate War Record in possession of author; also "28th Virginia Infantry," by Frank E. Fields, Jr., Lynchburg, 1985, p. 56.

13. Tombstone at Parrish Chapel Cemetery, Chamblissburg, VA.

14. *Ibid.*

15. *Bedford Bulletin*, Feb. 2, 1994; also a brochure in possession of the author which was given me by the owners, Carl and Christine Brodt;

also personal knowledge handed down by family members.

16. *Green Stone*, by Rachel Parsons Flynn Bishop, p. 112.

17. The dates of birth, marriage, and death of this entire branch of the family were supplied by various members of the family from Bible records and authentic sources. Some other pertinent information is from obituaries in possession of the author.

B. JOHN DEBO

1. John Debo family Bible.
2. Bedford County Marriage Records (BCMR).
3. Debo Bible, *op. cit.*
4. *Ibid.*
5. *Ibid.*
6. *Ibid.*
7. *Ibid.*
8. Confederate service records in possession of author.
9. Debo Bible, *op. cit.*
10. *Ibid.*
11. Reed Debo family records provided by Missouri relatives.
12. Debo Bible, *op. cit.*
13. *Ibid.*
14. *Ibid.*
15. Copy of letter in possession of author, dated Sept. 8, 1878.
16. Original letter in possession of author.

1. REED PERRY DEBO

1. John Debo family bible.
2. Bedford County Marriage Records (BCMR).
3. Tombstone in Heptinstalll family cemetery, Bedford County, VA.
4. Reed Debo obituary in a Boonville newspaper.
5. Penned at the top of a clipping from *The Bedford Democrat* of June 5, 1958, by Mrs. Michael P. (Mizpah) deBoe. The clipping advertised the auction sale of the Providence Methodist Church building on June 14, 1958.
6. Reed Debo family records, supplied by Lewis C. Debo and updated to 1981.
7. *Ibid.*
8. Confederate service records in possession of author.
9. *Ibid.*

10. In a letter of July 26, 1986, from Lewis C. Debo to this author.
11. Letter from Cornelius Debo to brother Reed dated November 5, 1872, a copy of which is in the possession of the author.
12. Debo Bible, *op. cit.*
13. *Ibid.*
14. Letter from Reed Debo to his children, written the day of Mary Jane's death (copy in possession of author).
15. *Ibid.*
16. Letter from Reed Debo to brother Cornelius dated November 6, 1896 (original and copy in possession of author).
17. Letter of July 26, 1986, from Lewis Debo, *op. cit.*
18. Reed Debo family records, *op. cit.*
19. *Ibid.*
20. Reed Debo obituary from an unknown Booonvile (Mo.) paper.
21. Reed Debo family records, *op. cit.*
22. Lewis C. Debo obituary, *Ottumwa Courier.*
23. Reed Debo family records, *op. cit.*

2. ALLEN BURTON DEBO
1. John Debo family Bible record.
2. Confederate army records.
3. Pittsylvania County (VA) Marriage Records (hereinafter PCMR).
4. Debo family, op. cit.
5. U.S. Census for 1900, Yavapai County, Arizona.
6. PCMR.
7. Cornelius Debo letter in possession of author.
8. Cornelius Debo letter in possession of author.
9. U.S. Census for 1900, op. cit.

3. DABNEY CLAYBOURN DEBO
1. John Debo family Bible record.
2. A copy of the essay was supplied the author by Lewis C. Debo, Ottumwa, Iowa, no deceased.
3. Confederate record in possession of author.
4. Debo Bible, *op. cit.*
5. Confederate records, *op. cit.*

4. THOMAS BENTON DEBO
1. John Debo family Bible.

2. Confederate service records.

3. *Ibid.*

4. Williamson County (TX) Marriage Records (I have the original marriage license).

5. Debo Bible, *op. cit.*

6. A copy of the letter is in the possession of the author.

7. The clipping from an unknown paper is in the possession of the author.

8. The dates and information on the Thomas Debo family were provided by the late Sallie Debo Simpson and by various members of the family.

5. CORNELIUS (PATRICK) DEBO

1. Debo family Bible.

2. Article by Cornelius Debo, "A War Experience for the Boys," *Burnet Bulletin*, July 17, 1898.

3. Debo Bible, *op. cit.*

4. Confederate army record in possession of the author (IPOA).

5. Obituary from an unknown Methodist paper, a copy IPOA.

6. D. Claytor Brooks, *Cause and Effect*, New York, p. 135.

7. Clipping from *The Bedford Democrat* of June 5, 1958, advertising an auction sale of the Providence Methodist Church building on June 14, 1958, IPOA.

8. Confederate records, *op. cit.*

9. Article by Cornelius Debo, see n. 2. *Op. cit.*

10. Obituary, *Burnet Bulletin*, Oct. 20, 1898.

11. Confederate records, *op. cit.*

12. Copy of a letter written to Sarah James (Sallie) Debo by an unnamed Confederate soldier IPOA.

13. Confederate records, *op. cit.*

14. Kathleen R. George and John W. Busey, *Nothing But Glory: Pickett's Division at Gettysburg*, Hightown, N.J., p. 5.

15. Letter from J.H. Holt, mailed May 21 (year unreadable, but probably 1896); original IPOA.

16. *Burnet Bulletin*, date unknown, but letter notarized May 14, 1896; copy IPOA.

17. George and Busey, *op. cit.*, p. 502.

18. Frank E. Fields, Jr., *28th Virginia Infantry*, Lynchburg, ip. 32.

19. *Burnet Bulletin*, May 14, 1896.

20. Confederate Records, *op cit.*
21. *28ᵗʰ Virginia Infantry, op. cit.* p. 37.
22. *Idid.*
23. *Burnet Bulletin,* July 17, 1898.
24. Told to me by Cornelius Debo's daughter, Sallie Debo Simpson, as told to her by her father.
25. *Burnet Bulletin,* Oct. 20, 1898.
26. Letter to brother, Reed Debo, Nov. 5, 1872; copy IPOA.
27. Obituary of Henry Clay Bowmen; copy IPOA.
28. H.C. and Sallie Debo Bowmer family records.
29. Letter to brother, Reed Debo, Nov. 15, 1872, *op. cit.*
30. Interview with Jennie Debo fisher, oldest daughter of Cornelius Debo.
31. Burnet County (TX) Deed Records (BCDR).
32. Jennie Fisher interview, *op. cit.*
33. BCDR, Book J. p 823.
34. BCDR, Book X, p. 176.
35. Letter to brother, reed Debo, dated Dec. 25, 1891; copy IPOA.
36. Darrell Debo, *Burnet County History*, Burnet, TX. p. 219.
37. The original license IPOA.
38. The original document IPOA.
39. Researched by Darrell Debo in Burnet County Marriage Records.
40. Letter to Reed Debo, dec. 25, 1891, *op. cit.*
41. Debo family Bible; obituary in *Burnet Bulletin, op. cit.*
42. *Burnet Bulletin,* Oct. 20, 1898.
43. Obituary from an unknown Methodist paper, a copy IPOA.
44. Debo Bible, *op. cit.; Burnet Bulletin,* Jan. 13, 1944.
45. Death dates are from Debo Bible and various family records.
46. BCDR.
47. *Burnet Bulletin,* Jan. 13, 1944, *op cit.*

a. JENNIE PRUDENCE DEBO FISHER
1. Debo Family Bible.
2. Tombstone in Odd Fellows Cemetary, Burnet, Texas.
3. Darrell Debo, *Burnet County History*, Vol.II, p. 93
4. Lindsey Fisher obituary, *Burnet County History, op. cit.* p. 94.
5. *Burnet County History, ibid.*
6. Tombstone, *op. cit.*
7. *Burnet Bulletin*, June 26, 1930.

8. *Burnet Bulletin,* July 29, 1976.
9. *Ibid.*
10. Dates in lives of Jennie and Lindsey Fisher's children were supplied by family members.
11. Obituary from a Houston newspaper.

B. MARY THOMAS (MOLLIE) DEBO MCFARLAND
1. Debo Family Bible.
2. Burnet County Marriage Records.
3. Family Records
4. *Ibid.*
5. *Burnet Bulletin,* no date.
6. Some dates supplied by the J.D. McFarlands.

c. LILBON DEBO
1. The dates and much of the information is from personal knowledge and dates from personal records.
2. *Burnet Bulletin,* Jan. 1891.

d. EPPA DEBO
1. Dates and data are from personal records of the author.

e. FRANK DEBO
1. Dates and data are from personal records of the author.
2. Postcard in possession of the author given to him by the late Neil Debo Johnston.

6. SARAH JAMES (SALLIE) DEBO BOWMER
1. Most of the data on this family was assembled and supplied by the late Mrs. Sallie Debo Simpson of Winters, Texas.
2. The obituaries and other information was supplied by Mildred Moreland of San Angelo, Texas.

7. MARIE ELIZA (MOLLIE) DEBO MCCLURE
1. Data supplied by Sallie Debo Simpson and Cloyce McClure Strickland.

8. MARTHA PRUDENCE; BETTIE JANE; AND JOHN BRUCE DEBO
1. Dates taken from the Debo Family Bible records.

C. ELIZABETH (BETSY) DEBO BLANKENSHIP
1. I am indebted to Sonny Blankenship, 107 Roberts Ave., Lynchburg, VA 24501, for most of the data on the Blankenships.
2. Marriage Records of Bedford County, VA.

D. SALLY DEBO BLANKENSHIP
1. I am also indebted to Sonny Blankenship of Lynchburg, VA for the above data.

E. MARGARET DEBO SAUNDERS
1. The data on the John R. and Margaret Debo Saunders family was supplied by Mr. and Mrs. Donald Saunders, 7163 County Road 1, South Point, Ohio 45680. The author is most grateful for their contribution.
2. Marriage Records of Bedford County, Virginia.

F. VALENTINE DEBO
1. Marriage Records of Bedford County, Virginia.

G. DANIEL PERRY DEBO
1. John Hubbard Descendants from Body Camp Creek, Bedford County, Virginia, by William David Hubbard and Oliver Shelton Carter, p. 3.
2. *Ibid.*
3. Bedford County, Virginia, Will Book 13, p. 318.

H. MARY DEBO HUBBARD
1. Many of the dates and some of the data as well as the descendants of Mary Debo and T. G. Hubbard were taken from *John Hubbard Descendants from Brody Camp Creek, Bedford County, Virginia,* by William David Hubbard and Oliver shelton Carter. The author is indebted to and grateful to Mr. Carter for the use of this material.
2. Marriage Bonds of Befotrd County, VA.
3. Will Book 16, pp 536ff.
4. Original letter in possession of author.
5. Copy of letter supplied by the late Lewis Debo, grandson of Reed P. Debo.

1. MICHAEL DEBO , JR.
1. Where not footnoted and specified otherwise, the dates for this family are from family Bibles and private sources in possession of the author.
2. Marriage Records of Bedford County, VA.
3. Will Book No. 26, pg 96, Bedford County.
4. Birth and death date, Death Certificate, Missouri Bureau of Vital Statistics.
5. Supplied by Nancy Maude Stevens in a letter to the author dated July 25, 1973.
6. Birth and death dates, Death Certificate, Commonwealth of Virginia, Bureau of Vital Statistics.
7. Original letter in possession of the author.
8. Confederate war record in possession of author.
9. Dates supplied from records in Ruby Price DeBoe Bible, a copy of which is in possession of author.
10. Family Bible and obituary.
11. Marriage Records of Monroe County, Florida.
12. Dates of Death Certificate, Commonwealth of Virginia Bureau of Vital Statistics.
13. Marriage Records of Roanoke County, VA.
14. Dates on Death Certificate, Commonwealth of Virginia, Bureau of Vital Statistics.

CHAPTER VI: KENTUCKY DEBOES
I
PHILIP DEBOE
1. Pittsylvania County, VA, Marriager Records.
2. Listed in the "Dalton Register."